"Despite the ominous title, Mi
than leaving Canada, God is l
a century ago. Amidst the loss of church buildings and other places of worship because dwindling faith communities are no longer able to support them, this book may be ushering in a new, more diverse movement across Canada of dynamic spiritual life for the twenty-first century."

—BRIAN GRIM
President, Religious Freedom & Business Foundation

"In this innovative and timely book, Wood Daly correctly observes that for many, the church as we know it has simply lost its relevance.... Historically, institutional religion faced many crises and managed to rebound. Our generationally needed rebound is yet unclear. While the focus is on Canada, every student of religion in all Western countries should be assigned this book."

—RAM A. CNAAN
University of Pennsylvania

"Brave, credible, necessary, and urgent. Every congregation, adjudicatory, municipality, activist, or fund looking at the future of Canada's places of faith must read this carefully. Wood Daly's skill, experience, and love for the Canadian church all combine for this essential diagnosis and prescription."

—GRAHAM SINGH
CEO, Trinity Centres Foundation

"Michael Wood Daly weaves together his personal experience of church life and mission in Canada with an integrated and engaging discussion of Canadian church history and the latest research on the health and life of the church. In addition, he makes an important contribution by critically engaging the dark history of the mission of Christian churches in Canada in relation to indigenous people on Turtle Island."

—CHARLES FENSHAM
Knox College, University of Toronto

"A stimulating, richly documented, and well-written contribution to an understanding of the origins of the Christian church and its rise and fall in Europe and Canada. Wood Daly sees the current situation as a place from which resurrection is possible—a place from which the church in Canada can start again and God can live again. This provocative book warrants a wide reading and a significant response."

—REGINALD W. BIBBY
University of Lethbridge

"Wood Daly offers realistic, courageous insight into the decline and transformation of the church in Canada without descending into pessimism or despair. The historical account he offers is especially rich. Above all, this book's hopefulness about the goodness of God and the enduring importance of God's purposes, beyond the emptying buildings and the dying forms of Christianity, challenges the complacency of today's churches and inspires a new future."

—ROB FENNELL
Atlantic School of Theology

"There are few researchers like Michael Wood Daly with their finger on both the pulse and the survey data of Canadian church life. For both the sober reality and a thoughtful contemporary examination of the way ahead for people of faith, this is the book to read."

—PETER NOTEBOOM
General Secretary, The Canadian Council of Churches

God Doesn't Live Here Anymore

God Doesn't Live Here Anymore

Decline and Resilience in the Canadian Church

Michael Wood Daly

Foreword by Joel Thiessen

CASCADE *Books* • Eugene, Oregon

GOD DOESN'T LIVE HERE ANYMORE
Decline and Resilience in the Canadian Church

Cascade Books
An Imprint of Wipf and Stock Publishers
199 W. 8th Ave., Suite 3
Eugene, OR 97401

www.wipfandstock.com

PAPERBACK ISBN: 978-1-6667-3205-4
HARDCOVER ISBN: 978-1-6667-2531-5
EBOOK ISBN: 978-1-6667-2532-2

Cataloguing-in-Publication data:

Names: Wood Daly, Michael [author]. | Thiessen, Joel [foreword writer]

Title: God doesn't live here any more : decline and resilience in the Canadian church / Michael Wood Daly.

Description: Eugene, OR: Cascade Books, 2023 | Includes bibliographical references and index.

Identifiers: ISBN 978-1-6667-3205-4 (paperback) | ISBN 978-1-6667-2531-5 (hardcover) | ISBN 978-1-6667-2532-2 (ebook)

Subjects: LCSH: Canada—Church history | Church history

Classification: BR570 W66 2023 (print) | BR570 (ebook)

01/12/23

To Jan and Bethany

In honor of the Indigenous People
of Turtle Island

"There are better things ahead than any we leave behind."

—C.S. LEWIS, THE COLLECTED LETTERS OF C.S. LEWIS, VOLUME 3

Contents

List of Tables and Illustrations

Tables

Figures

Foreword

For the past fifteen+ years, I have devoted my career to studying religious and cultural trends in Canada. In books such as *The Meaning of Sunday: The Practice of Belief in a Secular Age* (2015) and *None of the Above: Nonreligious Identity in the United States and Canada* (2020, with Sarah Wilkins-Laflamme), I consistently advanced that, on the whole, Canadians are less religious today than in previous generations. There are many complex and nuanced reasons for this shift, but as you might imagine, this social change has implications for local churches across Canada.

Against this backdrop, a number of years ago I collaborated with several scholars to launch the Flourishing Congregations Institute at Ambrose University, in Calgary, Alberta. Our central task is to draw on social scientific tools to look for, understand, and explain the varied signs of life and vitality in Canadian churches, across Catholic, mainline, and conservative Protestant contexts. Our team and network includes theologians and local church practitioners, which has enabled us to grapple with congregational flourishing in theological and practical terms too.

One thing that I never could have anticipated when I started my career was how often church and denominational leaders would reach out to me to assist them in describing and explaining Canadian religious and cultural trends. In turn, they have asked me to help them make sense of what these trends might mean for local churches . . . their church. I applaud churches with this disposition to understand the data—to see the empirical realities for what they *are* versus what people *think or wish* they were.

As I have worked with congregations over the years, I have increasingly argued that scholars and church practitioners could best serve the

Church in Canada with a more robust engagement with solid empirical data, theological reflection, *and* practical considerations. Mike Wood Daly's *God Doesn't Live Here Anymore* helps church leaders toward these ends. He brings readers up close with difficult but necessary realities that, if properly understood, could help local churches to thrive in the years and decades ahead. To the best of my knowledge, Mike Wood Daly is among the first to provide a comprehensive picture of exactly how many churches are closing and starting anew in Canada since 2009. In doing so, he offers a nuanced analysis into the denominations, regions, polity structures, and urban/rural contexts where these trends are occurring, along with a range of reasons for why churches are closing (including one-fifth due to a failure to file financial reports or who received failed audits).

Empirical realities such as these position those in congregations to reflect carefully upon three questions that appear at the mid-point of *God Doesn't Live Here Anymore*: "Who have we been? Who have we become? And who do we want to be?" The pages to follow provide a historical, biblical, and theological exposition of Christian corporate worship in Christianity's formative years. On their own, these materials are instructive for Christians navigating the COVID-19 pandemic. Wood Daly also sketches out widespread Christian expansion, growth, and power in Canada in the early to mid-twentieth century. Churches arose in suburbs to keep up with immigration growth; congregations helped immigrants assimilate to be both Canadian and Christian; and Christianity benefitted from large social influence through institutions like education, healthcare, and law. Since then, Christian communities in Canada have confronted steep numeric declines, ongoing mistreatment of Canada's Indigenous communities, growing religious and social diversity, a perceived (and in some respects real) loss of social power, and a global pandemic. Wood Daly is among a growing number who are pressing the Canadian church to take seriously the Truth and Reconciliation Commission of Canada's Calls to Action, and more generally to consider its understanding of, approach to, and practice of power.

As Canadian churches consider next steps, Wood Daly reminds us that, "Power is not about controlling other people. Power is about controlling oneself." Historically, there is no denying that Canadian Christians have, in many respects, failed miserably at this, notably relative to Indigenous communities. The rest of the story is yet to be written; the closing pages of this book might inform that story. Wood Daly interacts with the letters to the seven churches in Revelation. He invites those in congregations to take seriously their theological and practical orientations toward topics of focus, suffering, worshipping false idols, compromise, life and death, church size and faithfulness, and commitment. As a sociologist of religion with a deep commitment to and love for the local church, I cannot envision readers concluding this book without asking—and hopefully answering—this timely question: *What is unique about Christian church communities, and what difference does the answer to this question make to Canada?* This question, and subsequent answer, demands that those in Canadian churches interact with social scientific data, deep theological reflection, and imaginative adaptations. Mike Wood Daly opens the door to this possibility as many Canadian congregations seek to find their bearings into the unknown future.

Dr. Joel Thiessen
Professor of Sociology and Director of the
Flourishing Congregations Institute
Ambrose University

Preface

IN 1968, THE AMERICAN author Stanton Coblenz released a science fiction novel entitled *The Day the World Stopped.*[1] Set in the year 2020 CE, Coblenz prophetically wove a tale in which not only world peace but the continued existence of the planet's inhabitants lay in the hands of two world leaders: Carl Armitage, President of the United States, and Yu Luwai, Chairman of the People's Republic of China.

Astonishingly, in 2020, almost forty years after Coblenz's death, the world did stop! A novel virus, commonly known as COVID-19, brought the world to its knees early in that year. On December 31, 2019, Chinese officials first reported an outbreak of pneumonia in Wuhan province due to an unknown source. By early January of 2020, researchers had identified the source and given it a name: SARS-CoV-2. By the end of the month, Chinese officials had imposed a stay-at-home order on the residents of Wuhan to prevent its spread, and American President Donald Trump had banned travel from China into the United States. Just as Coblenz had imagined, the world had stopped, and the continued existence of the entire earth lay eerily in the hands of two of its most prominent leaders.

More than a year and a half later, Canada is only just beginning to re-emerge from a series of prolonged restrictions. These restrictions included the closure of all non-essential businesses, including schools, theaters, libraries, childcare, retail, recreation, and restaurants (except for takeout and food delivery). In Toronto, where I live, restaurants were closed to in-person, indoor dining for more than 400 days—one of the

1. Coblenz, *The Day the World Stopped.*

longest lockdowns in the world. Compare this to Paris at more than 260 days, London (259 days), and Hong Kong (just two days).[2]

Since that time, Canada has reported close to 1.6 million cases of COVID and approximately 27,500 deaths.[3] Most indoor work and retail settings still require individuals to wear masks in common spaces to prevent the spread of the virus. Vaccine passports have become the standard in most provinces. The Canadian Border Services Agency has re-opened the border to U.S. citizens for non-essential travel, but the United States has not yet reciprocated. Canada leads the G7 countries in vaccination rates. Almost 80 percent of the population has received their second dose, alleviating fears for some and steeling others against a fourth Delta-variant wave.[4]

For religious Canadians, this lockdown has been particularly hard. Not only has it confined them to their houses, condominiums, townhomes, and apartments, they have also been locked out of their religious homes. Since the pandemic began, church buildings, mosques, synagogues, and temples have mostly been closed to in-person worship. Buildings have been shuttered. Their sanctuaries have remained dark. Programs and supports, especially those meant for some of society's most vulnerable, have been suspended or dramatically limited in their ability to serve. And while the vast majority of these closures are temporary, the locked doors and darkened windows have foreshadowed what many Canadian Christians have feared for decades: the demise of the Canadian church.

Since the 1960s, when Pierre Berton challenged Canadian religious institutions with his controversial book, *The Comfortable Pew,* Canada's largest mainline traditions have experienced significant declines. Millennials are becoming less religiously affiliated than ever before. While two-thirds of Canadians still identify as Catholic or Protestant, both groups have seen their place and significance in Canadian life erode. Over the last four decades, the number of Canadians who identify as Catholic has dropped from 47 percent to 39 percent. The number of Protestants has fallen even more steeply, from 41 percent to 27 percent. Even fewer Canadians are going to worship. The Pew Research Center reports that in 1986, more than four in ten Canadian adults aged fifteen and older (43%)

2. Levinson-King, "Toronto lockdown."

3. Worldometer.

4. Canada, "Covid-19 Vaccination."

were attending religious services at least once a month. By 2010, that figure for Canadian adults had fallen 16 percentage points, to 27 percent.[5]

With these kinds of numbers, it is little wonder that churches are closing. One estimate from the National Trust for Canada suggests that as many as one-third of Canada's churches are expected to close over the next ten years.[6] In 2013, Canada's largest Protestant denomination, the United Church of Canada, reported closing one congregation a week.[7] The Anglican Church of Canada anticipates closing its last worshipping congregation by the year 2040.[8] And Canada's most prominent religious denomination, the Roman Catholics, report having closed 450, or nearly one-fifth, of the tradition's 2,500 congregations.[9]

Against this bleak backdrop, many Canadians appear to be relying on organizations outside the church to find belonging, meaning, and accountability. Increasingly, Canadians are looking for their "religion" outside the church. For some, the church has simply lost its relevance. They see it as an institution that has struggled on far beyond its "best before" date. For others, the church has grown dangerous—even toxic. The discoveries of more than a thousand unmarked graves at Canada's former Indian Residential Schools through the spring and summer of 2021 have sparked a wave of anger and mistrust. They have reignited an inferno of debate around the church's abuse of power and mistreatment of Indigenous Canadians, women, and the LGBTQ2S communities and prompted a social backlash that has seen dozens of Christian churches across the country burned or vandalized.[10] Statues of Canada's founding Prime Minister, John A. Macdonald, have been toppled in protest.[11] Media reports have highlighted the millions of dollars raised by Catholics to repair and build new churches while failing to meet its commitments to compensate residential school victims.[12]

Canadian churches are not alone in their decline or their turmoil. Callum Brown in *The Death of Christian Britain*[13] and Frances Meslet's

5. Pew Research. "Canada's Changing Religious Landscape."
6. Allen, "From Sacred to Secular."
7. United Church Observer, "National Survey."
8. Anglican Samizdat, "Latest Anglican Attendance Statistics."
9. Faris, "The Catholic Church Is Worried."
10 Vikander, "'Quit Burning Down Churches'"
11. Draaisma and Ng, "Sir John A. Macdonald Statue Toppled."
12. Warick, "Catholic Church Dedicated."
13. Brown, *Death of Christian Britain.*

striking visual portrayal of *Abandoned Churches*[14] remind us of the church's plight throughout most of the western world. In his book, *The American Church in Crisis,*[15] David Olson paints a similar picture of the church in the United States, including the strained relationship between the Christian Right and the Black Lives Matter movement. Catholic parishes have experienced a decline so dramatic that, in November 2018, the Vatican's Pontifical Council for Culture, the Italian Bishop's Conference, and the Gregorian University of Rome met to consider the question: "Does God not live here anymore?"

In writing directly to conference participants, Pope Francis stated:

> The observation that many churches, which until a few years ago were necessary, are now no longer thus, due to a lack of faithful and clergy, or a different distribution of the population between cities and rural areas, should be welcomed in the Church not with anxiety, but as a sign of the times that invites us to reflection and requires us to adapt.[16]

These are the times for which this book is written.

I grew up in a small but vibrant Baptist congregation in Toronto. As a child and then teenager, I was profoundly influenced by the investment of Sunday School teachers and youth leaders. My strongest and most endearing friendships continue to be with those I met growing up in the church. I worked summers at a Christian camp and met my wife at a weekend denominational retreat. In 1983, I felt called to ordained ministry, entered seminary, and was ordained in 1988. Since then, I have pastored in suburban and downtown churches, worked in community-based ministry with vulnerable and employment-disadvantaged youth, taught Doctor of Ministry students, and, more recently, have engaged in helping congregations and faith leaders through the Halo Canada Project to explore the socioeconomic relationship between congregations, their neighboring communities and Canadian society in general. The church is central to who I am.

But I am also concerned with where the church is heading. I am concerned with questions like, "Who are we serving?" "How are we leading?" And, "Where is God in all of this?" So, while congregations continue to close across the country, it has become increasingly important for me to

14. Meslet, *Abandoned Churches.*

15. Olson, *American Church in Crisis.*

16. Pope Francis, "Message of the Holy Father."

share words of both challenge and hope for the Canadian church. Any faith that relies on buildings more than its spiritual source is bound for failure. Christians who depend on the preservation of worship structures, at the expense of exercising their faith unfettered by walls of brick and stone, are sure to discover that God doesn't live there anymore.

I want to be clear, though. Saying, "God doesn't live here anymore" is not the same as saying, "God is dead." I believe that God is very much alive. I am just not convinced that God's existence is dependent upon buildings. God's presence does not rely on our God-worship.

At a time when the world has stopped due to COVID-19 and is only just now beginning to re-emerge, religious congregations are discovering what it means to minister to and care for one another without buildings. It presents unique opportunities for the church to reimagine community, uncover purpose, foster personal and social transformation, inspire creativity, and nurture accountability. It calls us to reflect, renew, and refocus in ways that are less dependent upon buildings and more reliant on the exercise of God-within-us. As our planet "starts up again" and our world society endeavors to imagine a new normal, Christians in Canada and around the world have been gifted the chance to be proactive in setting social agenda, rather than simply adopting or adapting to it.

The assumption that God dwells only in our places of worship, or that God is somehow confined to physical spaces defined by walls and roofs built by us, only demonstrates how small our capacity is to believe, how limited our understanding of the Holy is, and how restricted our imagination of what the Divine intends to accomplish for and through the people of this world must be.

This book is about church decline, but it is also about resilience. While it acknowledges the heartfelt loss of many decades of witness and worship in specific places and the circumstances that have brought us here, it is also about the innate capacity of the church to be bigger than these buildings we call churches. Religion in Canada is changing. Recovery and renewal will not be easy work. Difficult choices await. My hope for the church, and other religious institutions, is that they can mature into the kind of communities where all people can find a home. As they evolve, I hope they can be clear about the need for change and what they are changing towards. And finally, my prayer is that members and leaders alike will be able to recognize the size and stake of what lies ahead.

It is difficult to say what is impossible; for the dream of yesterday is the hope of today and the reality of tomorrow.

—ROBERT H. GODDARD

Acknowledgments

WHILE MOST BOOKS HAVE one or two voices that ultimately put pen to paper, many more often stand in the wings. I want to begin by thanking the many friends, congregations, communities, and ministry leaders I have met, worked with, and learned from over the years. Because of the faith and witness of people like you, there still exists a church in Canada to write about.

To Ralph and Dorothy, Wendy and Dave, thank you for the example that faith is as much about character as it is belief. To Murray, Andrew, and Charles, thank you for your confidence in me and for challenging the power of pedestals. To Ram, Milton, Mitchell, and Peter, thank you for your dedication and commitment to the value of research and critical inquiry.

To my families, of birth and choice, I will be forever grateful for your grace, persistence, encouragement, and support along the way. And above all, to Jan and Bethany, thank you for being the hands and face of God.

1

The House of God

Biblical Perspectives on Places of Faith

"It's still going to be used as a house of God: Century-old Windsor Protestant church will become a mosque."

—*WINDSOR STAR*

FOR 100 YEARS, LINCOLN Road United Church stood at the corner of Lincoln Road and Wyandotte Street as a mark of Christian witness in the Canadian border city of Windsor. In 2015, the church building was sold. Constructed in 1915 as a Methodist church, this century-old House of God had been on the market for almost three years. "It was very sad when we closed," lamented Ross Mitton, chair of the Finance and Property Committee of the United Church's Essex Presbytery. But with dwindling resources and an aging congregation, Mitton added, "Unfortunately, there just wasn't enough of the next generation. It had to close."[1]

Was this a "Sign of the Times," as the *Windsor Star* reported?[2] Perhaps. According to Statistics Canada, in 1991, there were approximately 167,000 Christians in Windsor. The city's Muslim population at the time

1. Post Media, "Still House of God."
2. Pearson, "Sign of the Times?"

was listed as 3,400, and the number of people who listed no religious affiliation was 15,000. By 2011, the National Household Survey indicated that Windsor's Christian population had dropped to 144,000, despite an overall increase in the general population of more than 10 percent. The Muslim population had increased to 14,000, and those who listed no religious affiliation were 42,000. In 2014, Windsor's Church of the Assumption's dwindling congregation had closed its doors due to maintenance and safety concerns.[3] And in 2008, Our Lady of the Rosary was deconsecrated by the London Diocese, only to re-emerge in 2015 as an event center.[4]

With the National Trust for Canada estimating that one-third of Canada's churches might close by the year 2030,[5] Windsor's story of church closings is not unique. It is a tale rapidly playing out in urban and rural communities across the country. Despite the concern expressed by many faithful Canadians, not all is lost. While the congregation of Lincoln Road United Church had disbanded three years before the sale of its property, its members (or at least those who wanted to) would find homes in other religious congregations. And as for the building itself? After 100 years of Christian ministry, the building would now be owned and occupied by the Masjid Noor-Ul-Islam Madressa and Cultural Centre of Windsor. "Their religion is different than ours," offered Mitton, "but it's still going to be used as a house of God. So, we're okay with that."

While many church buildings, like the one formerly owned by Lincoln Road United, find their way into the hands of other worshiping congregations, others do not. Memorial University's *After Church Atlas*[6] documents the stories of more than fifty Canadian churches that have closed and transformed into everything from brewhouses to event spaces, retail, yoga studios, antique shops, libraries, restaurants, housing, and rock-climbing centers. For example, in the confines of what used to be St. Stephen's United Church in Alma, New Brunswick, there now sits the Holy Whale Brewing Company. According to the property's new owners, the business takes its name from its unique location in a church and because the Fundy coast is well known for its whale sighting. Rebuilt in 1932, after a fire destroyed the original structure, the building still bears the names of those who donated money to resurrect the building from

3. CBC News, "Windsor's Assumption Church."
4. Hill, "Revival."
5. Fry and Friesen, "No Space."
6. Stephenson and Lynch, "After Church Atlas."

the ashes etched in its stained-glass windows. Instead of signaling the start of worship, the old church bell now marks the beginning and end of happy hour from 4 p.m. to 6 p.m.

Where the Gods Dwell

Anthropologists and theologians tell us that no culture in recorded human history has been without some form of religion. In English, the word "religion" first appeared in the fourteenth century, and is derived from the Latin *religare,* meaning "to bind fast" or *religionem,* meaning "to show respect for what is sacred."[7]

In ancient times, religion was essentially indistinguishable from what we might call "mythology." When we use the word "myth" in conversation, we are usually referring to something we do not believe to be true. But when historians of religion use "myth," they are generally referring to words and stories that point to something sacred. These ancient stories were often associated with rituals based on a belief in supernatural entities who had created and maintained a presence in the world and the surrounding cosmos. These deities were most often anthropomorphic in nature, sometimes behaving in ways that mirrored the values of culture (as in Egypt) and sometimes in ways that seemed contrary to those values (as with the gods of Greece). From the earliest recorded times until now, religion has engaged the spiritual side of human existence with god(s) and goddess(es), the creation of the world, humanity's place in the world, life after death, eternity, and how to escape suffering in this world and the next.

Not surprisingly, these gods often appeared to take on images resembling the form and appearance of those who worshipped them. In about the fifth century BCE, the Greek philosopher Xenophanes poignantly describes this tendency:

> Mortals suppose that the gods are born and have clothes and voices and shapes like their own. But if oxen, horses and lions had hands or could paint with their hands and fashion works as men do, horses would paint horse-like images of gods and oxen oxen-like ones, and each would fashion bodies like their own. The Ethiopians consider the gods flat-nosed and black; the Thracians blue-eyed and red-haired.[8]

7. Harper, "religion (n.)."
8. Mark, "Religion in the Ancient World."

In this ancient polytheistic environment, Xenophanes believed that there was "one god, among gods and men the greatest, not at all like mortals in body and mind."[9] But he was in the minority. Apart from the visionaries and prophets of Judaism, monotheism did not make sense to most of the ancients.

From their perspective, everyday life suggested that no one person could meet everyone's needs; wholeness in life involved interacting with many different kinds of people and in various ways. In the same way that we interact with parents, siblings, spouses, partners, teachers, friends, colleagues, and neighbors to support, care for and encourage us—so it was with the ancients and their gods.

As Joshua Mark writes in his encyclopedic description of the ancient world:

> Ancient people felt that no single god could possibly take care of all the needs of an individual. Just as one would not go to a plumber with one's sick dog, one would not go to the god of war with a problem concerning love. If one were suffering a heartbreak, one went to the goddess of love; if one wanted to win at combat, only then would one consult the god of war.[10]

Many ancient religions claimed that these gods lived in high or unattainable places. For the Greeks, it was Mount Olympus. Created during the epic battle between the Olympians and the Titans, its peaks shrouded by clouds from human view, Mount Olympus became home in Greek culture to all twelve Olympian gods.[11] Meeting daily in the Pantheon, they would gather to discuss the fate of the mortals, dining on nectar and ambrosia to preserve their mortality.[12] For the Hindus, Mount Kailash, embedded in the Himalayas, was home to Shiva, the god of untamed passion, and his wife, Parvati, whose name means "daughter of the Himalayas."[13] The Norse gods lived either in Asgard or Vanaheimd,[14] the most powerful deities in Japanese mythology on a vast plain called Takamagahara. In China,

9. Mark, "Religion in the Ancient World."

10. Mark, "Religion in the Ancient World."

11. The most famous description of Olympus and its Pantheon is recorded in Homer's *Odyssey*. The story follows the Greek hero Odysseus, King of Ithaca, and his journey home after the Trojan war.

12. Thornton, *People in Homer's Odyssey.*

13. Daniélou, *Gods of Love and Ecstasy.*

14. O'Donoghue, *From Asgard to Valhalla.*

the Jade Emperor, the supreme ruler of heaven, ruled from there with fairness, benevolence, and mercy.[15] The Incas of South and Central America built their towns in the Andes, believing the mountain peaks to be portals for the gods,[16] while in New Zealand, the Taranaki regarded the mountain streams as gifts from the gods, intended to quench their thirst.[17]

While the gods had their heavens, they also needed places on earth to dwell. In order to consult, commune with, worship and offer sacrifices to these gods, monuments and temples were constructed. These structures, often complex in shape and size, were considered the literal homes of the gods. Here, statues fashioned in honor of the gods were fed with sacrifices, bathed and even clothed daily, with the priests and priestesses caring for them as they would kings and queens. In the case of the Babylonian god Marduk, the statue was carried out of his temple during the Akitu (barley-cutting) Festival and carried through the city of Babylon so that he could appreciate its beauty while enjoying the fresh air and sunshine.[18]

Historians tell a similar story of the goddess Nerthus, who was worshipped in Scandinavia and throughout the Germanic territories. Writing in the first century CE, the Roman historian Tacitus refers to her as *Terra Mater* or "Earth Mother" and as "the bringer of peace." Linked to Nord, the Norse god of the sea, perhaps as his consort or even as the sea-god's feminine alter-ego, Nerthus was believed to reside on an unknown *insula Oceani* or "island in the Ocean."[19] Tacitus describes a ritual procession in which an image of Nerthus stands concealed in a cart within a sacred grove.[20] Only her priests are permitted to approach or touch the sacred image. Tacitus writes that the priests would wheel the cart through the Germanic villages, causing the inhabitants to put aside their arms and embrace each other in celebration. After the procession, the statue and its accoutrements would be cared for and washed in a special lake by slaves,

15. Giddens and Giddens, *Chinese Mythology*.

16. Roza, *Incan Mythology*.

17. Andrews, *Nature Myths*.

18. Tenney, "Elevation of Marduk."

19. Reaves, "Njord and Nerthus."

20. According to Reaves, a divinity wagon is well-known in Germanic lore. According to Snorri Sturluson's *Edda* from about the thirteenth century CE, Thor is depicted as driving a wagon drawn by goats, Freyr arrives at Baldur's funeral in a cart led by a boar, and Freyja rides in a cart pulled by cats. Odin is known as the "mover of wagons" and the sky itself, home of the gods, is known as the land of wagons, indicating that the constellations were imagined as the gods circling the heavens in their carts. See Faulkes, "Snorri Sturluson—Edda."

who were then thrown into the lake and drowned as a sacrifice.[21] Some even suggest that a glimpse of this ritual is found in the Anglo-Saxon "Charming of the Plough" that emerged in the eleventh century. In this observance, *Eordan Modor,* or "Earth Mother," is invoked in the early months of the year to bless the fields for plowing and planting.[22]

This idea that houses could be built for gods to dwell in first appears in Judeo-Christian thought in the book of Genesis:

> Jacob left Beersheba and set out for Haran. When he reached a certain place, he stopped for the night because the sun had set. Taking one of the stones there, he put it under his head and lay down to sleep. He had a dream in which he saw a stairway resting on the earth, with its top reaching to heaven, and the angels of God were ascending and descending on it. There above it stood the LORD, and he said: "I am the LORD, the God of your father Abraham and the God of Isaac. I will give you and your descendants the land on which you are lying. Your descendants will be like the dust of the earth, and you will spread out to the west and to the east, to the north and to the south. All peoples on earth will be blessed through you and your offspring. I am with you and will watch over you wherever you go, and I will bring you back to this land. I will not leave you until I have done what I have promised you."
>
> When Jacob awoke from his sleep, he thought, "Surely the LORD is in this place, and I was not aware of it." He was afraid and said, "How awesome is this place! This is none other than the house of God; this is the gate of heaven."
>
> Early the next morning, Jacob took the stone he had placed under his head and set it up as a pillar and poured oil on top of it. And he called the place Bethel.[23]

The Old Testament town of Bethel was one of the first places in scripture where the Hebrew people witnessed God's presence. So vivid was Jacob's encounter with God that he renamed the town Bethel (*bet-'el*), which in Hebrew means, "house of God." To mark the place, Jacob "took the stone he had placed under his head and set it up as a pillar and poured oil on top of it."

Jacob's association with Bethel as the House of God mirrors the ancients' experience and conveys the early Judaic belief that the House of

21. Lindow, *Norse Mythology,* 33.

22. Krasskova, "Nerthus, Mother of Vanahelm."

23. Gen 28:1–9a.

God was an earthly, physical place. Later in Genesis 35, God says to Jacob, "Go up to Bethel and settle there, and build an altar there to God, who appeared to you when you were fleeing from your brother Esau."[24] When Jacob and his household returned to Bethel, he stopped everything until he had built another altar to God. There he bowed and called the altar El-Bethel (*'el bet-el*), which in Hebrew means "the God of the House of God."

Sinai and The Ark of the Covenant

According to the Hebrews, God's "high and unattainable place" was found on Sinai. While modern scholars differ widely as to the mountain's exact location,[25] the Jewish historian Josephus describes it as being "between Egypt and Arabia" in a region known as *Arabia Petraea,* a Roman province encompassing modern Jordan, the southern-most part of modern Syria, the Sinai Peninsula and northern Arabia. It was, he writes, "the highest of all the mountains that were in that country, and is not only very difficult to be ascended by men, on account of its vast altitude, but because of the sharpness of its precipices."[26]

It is here that Moses first encountered God in the burning bush of Exodus chapter 3, where he received the Ten Commandments,[27] and most significantly for our present discussion, where Moses received God's instructions for the building of the Tabernacle:

> The Lord said to Moses, "Tell the Israelites to bring me an offering. You are to receive the offering for me from everyone whose heart prompts them to give. These are the offerings you are to receive from them: gold, silver and bronze; blue, purple and scarlet yarn and fine linen; goat hair; ram skins dyed red and another type of durable leather; acacia wood; olive oil for the light; spices for the anointing oil and for the fragrant incense; and onyx stones and other gems to be mounted on the ephod and breastpiece. Then have them make a sanctuary for me, and I will dwell among them. Make this Tabernacle and all its furnishings exactly like the pattern I will show you.[28]

24. Gen 35:1.

25 Mount Horeb, referenced in the Deuteronomic tradition as the site where Moses received the ten commandments, is seen by most scholars as being synonymous with Mount Sinai. (See Davies, "Significance of Deuteronomy 1:2.")

26. Josephus, *Antiquities II*, xii, 1; III, v, 1.

27. Exod 20:11–17.

28. Exod 25:1–9.

Having lost and fled their home, the Israelites fashioned a gold-covered box known as the tabernacle to house the ark of the covenant, God's commandments to Moses at Sinai.[29] In Hebrew, the word for tabernacle, *mishkān,* means "residence" or "dwelling place."[30] Having lost and fled their home, the Israelites fashioned a gold-covered box known as the ark of the covenant. The ark was intended to house the tablets containing the commandments God gave to Moses at Sinai,[31] and be carried within the tabernacle.

From Tabernacle to Temple

Israel wandered in the wilderness for forty years, carrying the tabernacle and God's presence with them. Finally, the Jewish scriptures tell us that they came to the plains of Moab, on the east side of the Jordan River, opposite Jericho and the promised land. Their conquest of Canaan is told in the book of Joshua, and in a series of battles that stretched over a period of six or seven years, Israel finally took hold of what they believed to be God's promised land:

> So the LORD gave Israel all the land he had sworn to give their ancestors, and they took possession of it and settled there. The LORD gave them rest on every side, just as he had sworn to their ancestors. Not one of their enemies withstood them; the LORD gave all their enemies into their hands. Not one of all the LORD's good promises to Israel failed; every one was fulfilled.[32]

With their transition from wandering to settling and a growing belief that God's presence was now tied to the promised land, so too grew the people's desire to build bigger and more extravagant monuments to celebrate, invoke, and accommodate God's presence. Deuteronomy records that the First Temple was built in Jerusalem by King Solomon in 957 BCE. The tabernacle they had carried for 400 years, from the year after they had crossed the Red Sea until then, was no longer needed.[33] God had taken up a new residence.

29. Exod 25:22.

30. Tent of meeting or tent of congregation.

31 Exod 25:22.

32. Josh 21:43–45.

33. "The Temple" in *Oxford Dictionary of the Christian Church.*

With the transition from tabernacle to temple, the ark of the covenant took up its new place in the holy of holies, a windowless, interior room considered the most sacred space within the temple. It was here that God's presence rested. Only the high priest was allowed to enter the room once a year on the Day of Atonement. The Day of Atonement, or Yom Kippur, represents one of the highest holy days on the Jewish calendar. On this day, the high priest would offer an atoning sacrifice for the people's sins, bringing about a restored relationship between God and God's people. After sacrificing a lamb upon the altar, a goat was released into the wilderness, symbolically carrying away the people's sins. This "scapegoat" was meant never to return.[34]

For almost another 400 years, the temple remained the center of Jewish life and their experience of God. But with the destruction of the First Temple in 586 BCE and the fall of Jerusalem to the Babylonians, the Hebrew's perception of God and place began to shift. With the temple gone, where would God reside on earth? The Jews believed that eventually, they could—and would—rebuild the temple. But until it could be, at least in brick and stone, it could be rebuilt in a spiritual sense. Even though the temple had been destroyed, the Jews began to see that God could find a place in their synagogues, in their houses of study, and most importantly, in their behavior and in their hearts.

New Kids on the Block

With the emergence of the Christian faith in the New Testament, our understanding of the House of God shifts from temple to church. Christians commonly hold that the church came into being on the Day of Pentecost, as described in the second chapter of Acts:

> When the day of Pentecost came, they were all together in one place. Suddenly a sound like the blowing of a violent wind came from heaven and filled the whole house where they were sitting. They saw what seemed to be tongues of fire that separated and came to rest on each of them. All of them were filled with the Holy Spirit and began to speak in other tongues as the Spirit enabled them.[35]

And in the days that followed:

34. Lev 16:8–34.

35. Acts 2:1–4.

> They devoted themselves to teaching and to fellowship, to the breaking of bread and to prayer. Everyone was filled with awe at the many wonders and signs performed by the apostles. All the believers were together and had everything in common. They sold property and possession to give to anyone who had need. Every day they continued to meet together in the Temple courts. They broke bread in their homes and ate together with glad and sincere hearts, praising God and enjoying the favor of all people. And the Lord added to their number daily those who were being saved.[36]

While the norm for many Christians in modern western society is to meet together in buildings called churches, this was not the case for Jesus' earliest followers. Outside of a few references to meeting in the temple courts,[37] the church's birth story offers no mention of buildings built specifically for Christian worship. Instead, the New Testament speaks of groups of believers meeting in people's homes. Writing to the Christians in Corinth, Paul references one of these churches: "The churches in the province of Asia send you greetings. Aquilla and Priscilla greet you warmly in the Lord, and so does the church that meets in their house. All the brothers and sisters here send you greetings."[38] Similarly, in Colossians 4:15, Paul writes, "Give my greetings to the brothers at Laodicea, and to Nympha and the church that meets in her house."

The transition, of course, was a gradual one. The earliest Christians were still Jews. Jesus himself went to the temple to observe the religious festivals.[39] Scripture even records the apostle Paul as taking part in the purification rights of the temple.[40] While their religious beliefs were evolving, the temple would still have played an important role in their lives. The transition, of course, was a gradual one. The earliest Christians were still Jews. Jesus himself went to the temple to observe the religious festivals.[41] Scripture even records the apostle Paul taking part in the purification rights of the temple.[42] While their religious beliefs were evolving, the temple would still have played an important role in their lives. However, even in

36. Acts 2:42–47.
37. Acts 5:42.
38. 1 Cor 16:19.
39. John 2:13; 5:1.
40. Acts 21:26.
41. John 2:13; 5:1.
42. Acts 21:26.

wider Judaism the temple was not the focus of daily religious life. Over the preceding centuries, with Jewish communities spread across the ancient world, geographic distance had made it difficult to attend, and so the local synagogues gained increasing importance in Jewish life. In fact, when the temple was eventually destroyed in 70 CE, its loss was much less traumatic than might otherwise have been expected, since the temple had already been superseded in daily Jewish life for most people by the synagogues.[43]

Homes, too, already played an important role in Jewish religious life. This dynamic was true in many ancient cultures, especially where the veneration of ancestors represented an important part of spiritual life. Many pagan families even worshipped their own family deities who, it was believed, would protect and watch over their homes.[44] While these practices would have been abhorrent to the Jews, their homes were still important as religious spaces. In fact, it was in their homes that they celebrated their tradition's most important religious festivals, including the feast of the Passover.[45] Everyday meals and even the Sabbath's arrival was seen in the context of faith and offered opportunities to celebrate life and give thanks to God.

It is not surprising, then, that Jesus' earliest followers would continue this practice of meeting in their homes. There was no reason to abandon this practice, especially as they became increasingly unwelcome in their synagogues and the temple. While he was alive, Jesus had gone regularly to the synagogues and to the temple to share his "new teaching." After his death, so did the disciples, where they were met with the same kind of opposition Jesus had encountered. So, they stopped, found different ways to communicate their message, and continued to meet in their own homes or those of other followers. And while some buildings, like the lecture hall at Tyrannus, could be rented out or loaned to them,[46] for the most part, homes served as their regular meeting places until about the third century, when larger meeting places started to be built.[47]

The earliest surviving example of a house-church is in the town of Dura-Europas on the Euphrates River. The house, built around 232 CE, was converted into a Christian meeting place sometime prior to the

43. Marshall, "Church and Temple."

44. Albertz and Schmitt, *Family and household religion*.

45. Mark 14:14f.

46. Acts 19:9.

47. Snyder, *Ante Pacem*, 128.

capture of the town by the Persians in 256. The two most significant features of the house are a meeting hall and a baptistry. The hall, created by removing a wall between two smaller rooms, and placing a low platform at the eastern end of the room, would likely have held about sixty people.[48]

Another of the earliest worship sites includes a large residential building discovered near Megiddo in Israel in 1995. Dating from about the third century CE, artifacts recovered from this building suggest that at one point it was used by Roman soldiers and that one of its wings was used as a prayer hall by the local Christians. Representing a period shortly before the official recognition of Christianity by Constantine in 313, the room contains mosaic panels, a podium, and references to a table *(trapéza)*, clearly pointing to the presence of a Christian community.

People or Place? The House Church Phenomenon

Communal meetings such as those described in the New Testament were not unique to the Jews or the early Christians. During the Hellenistic age, clubs and associations had become commonplace. As the city-states of Greece lost their importance, voluntary associations emerged throughout the Graeco-Roman world. There were associations for honoring certain gods, workers' guilds for trades such as carpenters and blacksmiths, music associations, and philosophy clubs. Almost all of these groups were local, consisting of people living in the same community, usually with an average membership of less than fifty. In these groups, people sought the kind of connections, equality, and sense of community (*koinōnía, communitas*) that society as a whole could not offer.[49]

Many of the clubs and associations would mark their communal meetings with a meal. Scheduled regularly, they often observed special events, such as the feast-day of the god associated with the guild or the anniversary of when the group was established. Sometimes, they would meet once a month for a meal, depending on the group's intent or purpose. Usually, the meetings consisted of a supper (*déipnon*) followed by some kind of meeting or lecture (*sympósion*).

At the time, nearly every meal of this kind included some form of prayer or tribute to a deity. The tribute usually involved some type of libation in which a special cup of wine, generally as part of the meal's first

48. Alikin, *Christian Gathering*, 55.

49. Alikin, *Christian Gathering*, 18.

course, was dedicated to a specific deity. During the ritual, an individual or the group would offer the words "To the Good Deity" while a small amount of wine was poured out of the cup onto the ground. Almost all of these groups would be connected to a particular god or deity, whether the group had any religious aims or not.[50]

Typically, these meals followed a set pattern. First, members would bathe before arriving at their host's house. They would take their seat, and then servants would wash their feet. Afterward, they would recline on the couches, leaning on their left elbows, leaving their right arms free to take food from the table or servers who would attend to them. This practice, adopted from wealthy circles in the Middle East, became popular amongst the aristocracy as a sign of privilege and prestige. As part of their communal meals, though, lower social classes would often imitate the practice as a sign of marking the significance of their gathering.

The meetings, known as symposiums, often involved more wine, desserts, and discussions on current events, politics, or literature. The guests would either sing, or play instruments, or both. Sometimes they would have games and almost always music. In his book on the history of early Christian gatherings, V. A. Alikan describes three kinds of singing that would occur: choruses that the guests would sing together; songs where the group would be divided to carry a different part of the song; and finally, solos for those with training and ability. Depending on the occasion, performers might also have been hired to take part.

Early on, participation in these meals was restricted mostly to men. In the Greek world, women's attendance was usually limited to serving the food or offering sexual favors. However, by the first century CE, especially in Roman culture, the role of women at these meetings was changing. Often, they would attend these special events with the men. For example, the Gospel of Thomas describes a trend-setting Salome,[51] reclining together with Jesus on a dining couch and eating from the same table.[52]

These clubs and associations, and the meals associated with them, often became the social setting for both the ordinary and extraordinary events in people's lives.[53] It is no surprise, then, that many religious groups during this period adopted similar models. Josephus, for example,

50. Alikin, *Christian Gathering*, 19.

51. Salome is one of the Galilean women and disciples that accompanied Jesus to Jerusalem (see Mark 15:40; 16:1).

52 Lambdin, *Gospel of Thomas*.

53. Alikin, *Christian Gathering*, 23.

describes how the members of an Isis community in Rome would often be invited to share a meal at the temple of Isis.[54] In the first century BCE (probably between 695–98 BCE), members of the Guild of Zeus Hypsistos are recorded to have held monthly banquets in the sanctuary of Zeus. And the worshippers of Diana and Antinous at Lanuvium, located about 70 km southeast of Rome, appear to have held communal suppers about six times a year.

In summary, the meetings of these religious sects, cults, and associations were comprised of meals, conversation, worship, ritual, and instruction. These groups had leaders who were responsible for planning and officiating at the meetings. Rules were established to keep order amongst the members, while each person was expected to contribute financially.[55]

Sound familiar? Modern-day churchgoers will have little trouble in recognizing many of these same elements in today's churches. Historians Philo, Josephus, and the writer of 3 Maccabees offer numerous examples of how these patterns were present in Jewish life and culture. One prominent Jewish example appears in the Community Rule of Qumran, where it is written, "They shall eat in common and pray in common, and they shall deliberate in common."[56] These daily meals began with blessings offered for the bread and wine, while the latter part of their time together was marked by discussion and teaching of the law.[57]

In Jerusalem, the Pharisees formed an association. Jews living outside of Judea who had returned to Jerusalem had their own society. First-century records from Egypt describe Jewish burial associations and even contributions made by the members of a Jewish dining club in Apollinopolis Magna. Today's celebrity chefs would have been proud.

Jews, at the instruction of Moses, had met regularly for centuries. Philo writes:

> Moses required [the Jews] to assemble in the same place on these seventh days, and sitting together in a respectful and orderly manner hear the laws read so that none should be ignorant of them and indeed they do always assemble and sit together, most of them in silence except when it is the practice to add something to signify the approval of what is read. But some priest who is present or one of the elders reads the holy laws to them

54. Josephus, *Antiquities of the Jews*, 18:65–80.
55. Alikin, *Christian Gathering*, 25–26.
56. Metso, *The Community Rule*.
57. Metso, *The Community Rule*.

> and expounds them point by point till about the later afternoon, when they depart having gained both expert knowledge of the holy laws and considerable advance in piety.[58]

The only difference for Christians was that homes, rather than synagogues, were becoming the meeting place of choice. Early on, this would have occurred in the homes of wealthy Christians. Later on, groups of Christians would likely have acquired a house and remodeled it as a church building. The word that New Testament writers used to describe these "houses" was *oikos*. But while modern-day theologues describe these early Christian meeting places as "house-churches," the emphasis at the time was not so much on these homes as a physical structure, but rather as a way to describe the group of people who met regularly in that particular place. By using the word *oikos*, the writers wanted to communicate that these homes were more than just a place to meet; they were describing a specific sociological unit in much the same way that guilds, clubs, and associations of the Graeco-Roman world did.[59]

Acts 2:46 tells us that the believers met in these houses to break bread. It is not clear whether this "breaking of bread" was meant strictly in a eucharistic sense or in the sharing of communal meals. Both were probably the case. Either way, a careful investigation of the wording suggests that the phrase meant that they broke bread "according to" or "by the house" (*kat' oikon*). When they met for mutual support, teaching, or worship, they also did so "according to" or "by the house." When the writer of Acts uses the phrase *kat' oikon*, he is saying not only *where* these people were, but also *who* they were.

The case for seeing the house-churches not merely as physical structures but as identifiable social units organized around a particular purpose or intent can also be made linguistically. The Greek words *oikos* and *oikia* were largely used interchangeably in the New Testament to describe this house-church phenomenon. These two words have a range of meaning that includes "house" in both a literal and metaphorical sense, referring to family, households, clans, and even bigger tribal units such as the "House of Judah."[60] In this context, when the words *oikos* and *oikia* are combined with God's name, the Hebrew scripture's idea of the temple as God's dwelling place is transformed into a phrase that means, "the

58. Colson, *Praeparatio Evangelica* 8.7.12–13.

59. Donkor, "New Testament House Churches."

60. 2 Sam 2:11.

congregation who worships God there."[61] Regardless of whether a roof or walls surrounded these congregations, the church was *the people*, not the house in which they met.

The New Testament word that we translate as "church," *ekklēsia* (pronounced *ek-lay-**see**-a*), actually appears only three times in the Gospels (all of them in the Gospel of Matthew) and 111 times in the remainder of the New Testament. *Ekklēsia* means "a calling out"—a meeting or gathering of people. It is the Greek equivalent of the Hebrew *qāhāl*, which means an assembly or congregation of people. We also find remnants of the Greek *ekklēsia,* or the Latin *ecclesia,* in many of the later Romance and Celtic languages, as with the French *église,* which emerged around the eleventh century.

In the New Testament context, *ekklēsia* is used in at least four ways:

1. A group of God's people assembled for worship (1 Cor 14:43–45)
2. A group of God's people in a given region (Acts 9:31)
3. A local congregation of Christians (1 Cor 1:2 and Rev 1:11)
4. The universal body of believers, over which Christ acts as the head (Matt 16:18; Eph 1:22)

It is of particular note that scripture does not use the related word *ekklēsiastērion.* In ancient Greece, an *ekklēsiastērion* was a building specifically built to hold meetings of the *ekklēsia,* or assembly of the people. As we saw earlier with the word *oikos* and the phrase *kat oikon,* the emphasis for the New Testament writers was never on the *ekklēsiastērion* when speaking of God's people, but the *ekklēsia*—the gathering of God's people, not the building in which they met.

The picture emerges as a network of Christian groups operating simultaneously in homes in cities throughout the Mediterranean, including Jerusalem. Acts 8:1 speaks of the church in Jerusalem as a single entity, but Acts chapters 1 and 12 describe at least two distinct "house-churches" meeting in Jerusalem at the time.[62] These homes were churches. These churches were "the church." And "the church" was made up of all those who followed Christ.

For this reason, as a matter of principle, the early Quakers refused to call the buildings they met in "churches" since their understanding of the

61. Brown, *Dictionary New Testament Theology,* 247.

62. Acts 1:21–25; 4:31 and 12:10–17.

biblical word "church" was that it referred to God's people, not a building. Instead, they adopted the term "Meeting Place" or "Meeting House" along with many Anabaptist, Congregationalist, and Mormon traditions. As historian Peter Williams explains, these reforming traditions argued, contrary to the traditional Catholic and Anglican view, that "the physical setting for worship was no different from any other secular space and had only to provide an appropriate setting for the preached Word." The very term "Meeting House" implied a neutral public space that could be used for both religious and secular activities. For these groups, there was nothing wrong with using these meeting spaces for worship as well as for political functions, such as town meetings, elections, and other public gatherings. This is also why these buildings were typically simple, modest, and functional. The goal in building them was not to set them apart for "religious" use only, but rather to make them as inclusive of as many community functions as possible.[63]

We see this same approach amongst today's Jehovah's Witnesses, who refer to their meeting places as "Kingdom Halls." Addressing this terminology on their website, the Jehovah's Witnesses explain:

> When the apostle Paul wrote to the Christians in Rome, he sent greetings to a couple named Aquilla and Priscilla and added: "Greet the church that meets in their home." (Romans 16:5, Contemporary English Version). Paul didn't intend for his greetings to be conveyed to a building. Rather, he was sending his greetings to people—the congregation that met in that home. . . . So instead of calling our place of worship a church, we use the term "Kingdom Hall."[64]

The Mystery of Circles

So, where does our word "church" come from? And how is it used in the modern sense? Etymologists suggest that the word "church" appears to derive from an Old English word, *cirice* or *circe*, meaning "a place of assembly set aside for Christian worship; the collective body of Christian believers; or an ecclesiastical authority or power."[65] In these definitions, we begin to see the tension we have described between people and place.

63. Loveland and Wheeler, *Meeting House to Megachurch.*
64. Jehovah's Witnesses, *Why Don't Jehovah's Witnesses?"*
65. Harper, *Online Etymology.*

We also begin to see several variants of *circe* emerging throughout the languages of central and northern Europe at the time, from the Proto-Germanic and Old Saxon *kirika* to the Old Norse *kirkja,* the Old Friesen *zerke,* the Dutch *kerke,* and the German *kirche.* Later variants also appear in the Slavic languages, including the Russian *cerkov,* the Finnish *kirkko,* and Estonian *kirrik.*[66]

Most ecclesiastical sources trace the origins of *circe* (and its variants) back to the Greek *kyriakon,* which has its roots in the words, *kyrios* or "lord" and *oikos* or "house," as referenced earlier, to literally mean "the Lord's house." While less common than *ekklēsia* or even *basilikḗ,* we see *kyriakon* in common use from about the year 300 CE, especially in the East, to refer to houses of Christian worship.

An intriguing alternative put forward by some researchers addresses the idea that the Greek *kyriakon* focuses our attention more towards a specific building or "place" than it does towards the "people who use that place," pulling us away from what appears to be the focus of the New Testament writers. To address this tension, these researchers suggest that our answer lies in seeing the Anglo-Saxon word *circe*[67] as a literary remnant of the Greek combination of *kirkos/kyklos* meaning *circle,* which in turn is derived from the earlier Greek κρίκος *(krikos),* meaning "hoop" or "ring."[68] Similar variants of *circe* occur in Scotland *(kirk),* Germany *(kirche),* and in England *(cirche),* but with the "c" having a hard sound like a "k."[69] This idea that the church is a circle or gathering of people brings us closer to the idea of God's people conveyed by the Greek *ekklēsia* and Hebrew *qāhāl,* neither of which implies the idea of a building.

It is perhaps not surprising, then, that some of the earliest known Celtic and German worship sites were, in fact, circular. The most well-known of these is the ancient prehistoric monument known as Stonehenge, located near the town of Wiltshire in England. Archeologists believe that the ring of standing stones that makes up the site, each measuring about thirteen feet in height and weighing about twenty-five tons, was constructed between 3000 BCE and 2000 BCE. The site, presumed to have been a burial site for the community's stone-age elite, is marked by a surrounding circular earth bank and ditch that pre-dates the placement

66. Harper, *Online Etymology.*

67. Naas, *Etymology of Church,* 1–11.

68. Liddle and Scott, "Greek English Lexicon."

69. Naas, *Etymology of Church,* 1–11.

and construction of the stones. Radiocarbon dating of these mounds, which contain more than 50,000 cremated bone fragments from at least sixty-three individuals, suggests they were constructed about 3100 BCE.[70]

In 2020, archeologists using remote sensing technology and sampling also uncovered a wide circle of pits near Stonehenge that is significantly larger than any other prehistoric monument in Britain. Located about 3 km from Stonehenge, this discovery marks a two-kilometer-wide circle consisting of at least twenty shafts surrounding an ancient settlement at Durrington Walls, which also includes a henge, or circular structure, originally made of timber posts. Each shaft is about five meters deep and ten meters wide. Evidence suggests that these pits date back to the same period, around 4,500 years ago.[71]

As the place where the builders of Stonehenge lived, this discovery at Durrington Walls offers important insights into the lives and beliefs of these Neolithic ancestors. Archeologists suggest that the precise and sophisticated way the pits were positioned indicates that Britain's earliest inhabitants used a complex counting system to track their paces across long distances. Vince Gaffney, a professor of archeology at the University of Bradford and one of the senior researchers on the project, suggests that the discovery highlights the importance to this Neolithic community of celebrating and recording "their cosmological belief systems in ways, and at a scale, that we had never previously anticipated."[72]

Circles are valued in both modern and ancient cultures as a sign of unity—an unbroken line with no beginning, no end, and no direction. Because of these attributes, many regard circles as representing a completeness that encompasses all of space and time. As Heraclitus writes, "The beginning and the end are one."[73] Symbolically, circles depict for us something unending, unknowable, unmeasurable, and indefinable. They stand as markers of perfection, completeness, and unity. We might even suggest that, in this way, circles offer humanity a glimpse of the Divine, or what the German theologian and philosopher Rudolf Otto refers to as the "Holy Other."[74]

70. Kennedy, "Stonehenge Burial Site."

71. Thomson Reuters, "Circle Pits Near Stonehenge."

72. Thomson Reuters, "Circle Pits Near Stonehenge."

73. Schindler, "The Community of One and Many," 413–48.

74. Otto, *The Idea of the Holy*.

Some will argue that a circle is just a circle. But mathematicians in the audience will remind us that the only way we can attempt to describe a circle mathematically is to measure its area as being equal to the circle's radius squared, times a value called π (*Pi*). Simple enough, until we acknowledge that π, a factor that is equal to 22 ÷ 7, is an irrational, unending number. An irrational number is any number whose final decimal place can never be resolved. Regardless of how many decimal places we carry the equation to, we can never resolve or finalize its ultimate decimal place. Although we can get closer and closer to measuring the circle, the answer is always slightly beyond our grasp. Π can never be resolved. It, and the circle it describes, is and always will be, a mystery.

And so it is with the Divine. While our rational minds may bring us closer and closer to understanding Divinity, in the end, there is always something left unresolved, always something un-measurable, un-knowable, un-speakable, and in-definable. For this reason, *circe* or the word we translate it as "church" may well be the perfect word to describe the places Christians gather to meet *as well as* the people who gather there. For I would suggest, it is in our "circling" together that we are best able to catch glimpses of meaning in the midst of the un-measurable, un-knowable, and un-speakable. In the company of God's people, we are best able to witness the mystery of God. In each other's presence, the relationship between humans and the Divine becomes at least partially measurable, partially knowable, and partially speakable. It is in the midst of God's people that God comes closest. And wherever that is, be it in nature, in someone's home, or a congregational structure designed for worship, that is where we find the House of God.

2

Expanding Markets

Growth of the Mediterranean Church

The area that stretches around the western end of Lake Ontario has long been known as the "Golden Horseshoe." Surrounded by rich agricultural lands with Metropolitan Toronto at its center, this area represents Canada's most densely populated and industrialized area. With a core population of more than 7.6 million and another 2.4 million in the area immediately surrounding it,[1] the Golden Horseshoe accounts for more than 27 percent of Canada's entire population and about 66 percent of the provincial population.[2,3]

1. Hemson Consulting, "Greater Golden Horseshoe." Note: Population figures as reported by Hemson Consulting for the Province of Ontario's Ministry of Municipal Affairs are—Greater Toronto Area Hamilton (GTAH): 7,557,000 and total for the Outer Ring (OR): 9,977,000.

2. Statistics Canada. "Canada's Population Estimates."

3. Hemson Consulting, "Greater Golden Horseshoe."

Figure 1: Greater Golden Horseshoe

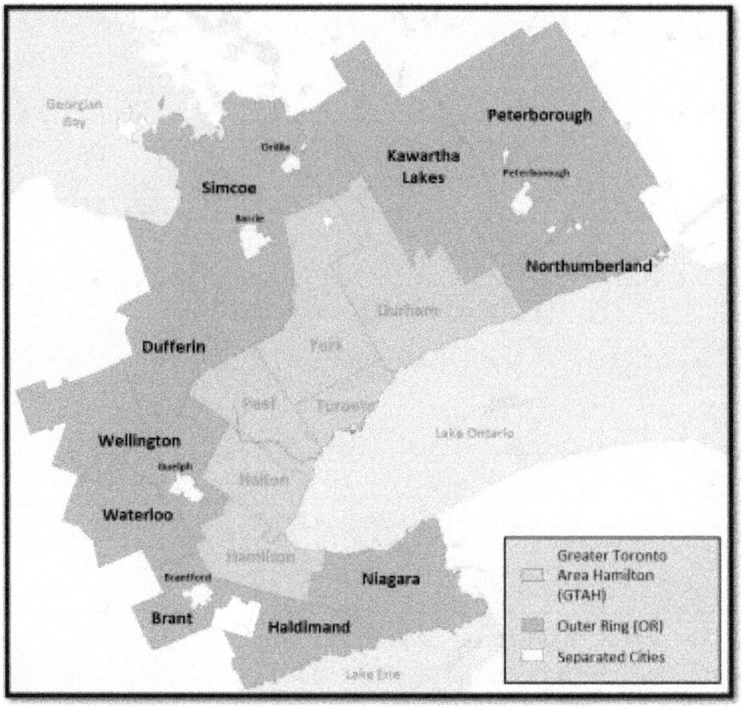

Source: Hemson Consulting, 2020.

In the summer of 2020, Toronto's Ryerson University released a study revealing that in 2019, the Toronto region had surpassed the Dallas/Fort Worth/Arlington area of Texas as North America's fastest-growing city. To add to the City's accolades, in 2015, London-based magazine *The Economist* rated Toronto as the best city in the world to live in.[4]

As a born-and-bred Torontonian, this comes as no surprise. I love living in Toronto. But for readers who do not live in, or aren't familiar with, Toronto (apart from the C.N. Tower), this ranking begs the question: "What makes Toronto (or any city for that matter) one of the fastest growing and best cities in the world to live?" Groups like *The Economist* consider various qualitative and quantitative factors when determining these rankings. These factors include things like green space, access to nature, cost of living, safety, cultural assets, diversity, connectivity, the

4. Economist Intelligence Unit, "Safe Cities Index."

environment, political stability, health care, education, and infrastructure.[5] Cities do not attract new residents, businesses, and investment by accident; there are reasons why they grow. There are reasons why people choose to live and work there.

Christianity would have been at the top of the list if *The Economist* had been around in the fourth century CE and been inclined to rank the world's fastest-growing religions. In 40 CE, there might have been 1,000 Christians. By 200 CE, religious sociologist Rodney Stark estimates that roughly 211,000 Christians lived in the Roman Empire, representing less than 1 percent of the population. By 250, that number had risen to about 1.1 million or 2 percent of the population. By 300, there were about 6 million (10% of the population), and by 350, Christians living in the Roman Empire numbered close to 32 million, more than half the population.[6]

By the end of the fourth century, nearly everyone had been converted, and Christianity had been adopted as the state religion of the entire Roman world. From a first-century fledgling sect, Christianity had grown to dominate the religious landscape of the Mediterranean world. If world faiths, like cities, do not grow by accident, what was it that caused the Christian faith to take root and grow so quickly?

Historically, Christian scholars have tended to describe this emergence of Christianity as a relatively clearly defined "parting of the ways."[7] This narrative is rooted in what Jacobs calls a "theologically conditioned, supersessionist reading of the New Testament"[8] in which the Christian church succeeds the nation of Israel as the definitive people of God. This point of view teaches that relations between Jews and Christians were rare and usually competitive in nature. By focusing on what set Christians apart from Jews, too often the overlapping identities have been ignored.[9]

This line of thinking also assumes that, "the Jews were an undifferentiated community living amicably in the part of the world that we now call the 'Holy Land.'"[10] But, as R. T. France writes, in his commentary on the Gospel of Matthew, this was a "gross distortion" of the historical

5. The Economist Intelligence Unit, "Safe Cities Index."

6. Stark, *The Triumph of Christianity*, ebook, ch. 9, p. 10.

7. Jacobs, "Jews and Christians," 169.

8. Jacobs, "Jews and Christians," 169.

9. Harland, *Dynamics of Identity in the World of the Early Christians*, 2.

10. France, *Gospel of Matthew*, 73.

and cultural reality of the time.[11] During the first half of the first century, Judaism was comprised of about two dozen different groups, each expressing their core beliefs in different ways. These groups included the Sadducees, Pharisees, Essenes, Zealots, followers of John the Baptist, and the followers of Jesus of Nazareth, along with several other charismatic leaders. In today's real estate terms, the religious landscape into which Jesus emerged was a "buyer's market.[12]"

A Prophet Has No Home

Jesus of Nazareth, also known by his followers as Jesus Christ, was a first-century teacher and Jewish religious leader, described by some as an end-time preacher and apocalyptic prophet who came declaring that the kingdom of God was near. According to the Gospels, Jesus appears to have had a relatively short public ministry, most of it in the obscure northern province of Galilee.

During this short time, people often went to great lengths to hear or catch a glimpse of him. The Gospel of Luke tells the story of a man from Jericho, a wealthy tax collector named Zacchaeus, who climbed a tree to see Jesus as he moved through the city.[13] In Capernaum, there was a paralytic man whose friends carried him to a house where Jesus was staying so that he could listen and be blessed by Jesus. But the area outside the house was too crowded with followers, so they made an opening in the roof and lowered the man to the floor near Jesus.

Crowds seemed to follow Jesus wherever he went. Some were curious. Some desperate. Others, hopeful and amazed. They came to hear his teaching and to bring their sick, their demon-possessed, their lame, their injured, and their blind. They came to be fed. And they were astonished when he told them the kingdom of God belonged to them.[14]

But as the crowds and his attractiveness for many grew, so did the fear and contempt of others. The northern province of Galilee, in which Jesus' hometown of Nazareth was situated, was significantly different from the southern province of Judea, where Jerusalem and the temple were located. Jerusalem marked both the cultural and religious center of

11 France, *Gospel of Matthew*, 73.

12 France, *Gospel of Matthew*, 73.

13. Luke 19:1–10.

14. Luke 6:20.

the Jewish faith; Galilee had its own distinct history, politics, and culture. Since its capture by the Assyrians in the eighth century, the population of Israel's former northern kingdom had been more racially diverse than in Judea. Conservative towns like Nazareth and Capernaum stood next to largely pagan cities like Tiberias and Sepphoris, heightening cultural tensions. Geographically, Galilee was also separated from Judea by the largely non-Jewish territory of Samaria and from Perea in the southeast by large Greek settlements like Decapolis.

Politically, Galilee had operated separately from Judea up until the tenth century BCE. In Jesus' time, however, Galilee was administered by Herod Antipas, who had succeeded his father, Herod the Great, around 4 BCE. Judea and Samaria, in contrast, had been under the direct rule of a Roman prefect since about 6 CE.

In terms of economics, Galilee offered far better agricultural and fishing resources than the dry mountainous terrain of Judea, making the wealth of some Galileans the envy of their Judean neighbors. This dynamic, along with the Galileans' lack of Jewish sophistication and greater openness to the influence of Hellenistic culture, served as a constant insult to Judeans in the south.

Linguistically, Galileans also spoke what R. T. France describes as a "slovenly" form of Aramaic, where the consonants were typically "dropped" in everyday conversation. As a result, Galileans often became the butt of Judean humor, taking on a regional derogatory association, similar to the one many Canadians ascribe to our country's Newfoundlanders.[15,16]

But it wasn't only the Galileans' relaxed speech that offended the Judeans. So too did their lax and lazy observance of Jewish rituals, which had been exacerbated by the province's distance from the temple and theological leadership based in Jerusalem.

The result was that even an impeccably Jewish Galilean in first-century Jerusalem would have felt like a fish out of water. They would not have felt at home. Their accent, and all the cultural prejudice attached to that, would have immediately set them apart as "not one of us." In retrospect, it is hard to imagine that this obscure Jewish sect with a Galilean leader, however engaging, could have grown so fast, let alone become the

15. King and Clarke, "Newfie Politics" 537–58.

16. Newfie is a colloquial term used by Canadians for someone who is from Newfoundland, often in a derogatory sense to portray them as lazy or foolish.

largest religion in the world. As far as Judea was concerned, nothing good could come from Nazareth. And certainly not the Messiah.

One Jesus, Many Christs

Despite his popularity, or more likely because of it, Jesus was eventually charged by Jerusalem's religious authorities with sedition. What today's courts would have probably regarded as "aggravated assault," they viewed as "crimes against the state."[17] And under Roman law, the penalty for this was death.

Four decades later, in 70 CE, the Roman Army attacked Jerusalem, destroying the central focus of Jewish life—the temple. God's house had been destroyed again, creating an entirely new watershed of opportunity for the Christian faith to emerge more fully. It is hard for us to imagine what might have happened to the Christian faith had the Roman armies not invaded Jerusalem, if the Second Temple had survived, and Jewish life had continued in the way it had for centuries. But it didn't. And out of the disaster arose two dominant movements: Rabbinical Judaism, centered not in the temple but in local synagogues, and the new and emerging Jesus movement.

In the years following Jesus' death, the Christian movement showed remarkable resilience and even greater diversity. As Gregory Riley describes it, there was one Jesus but many Christs. Some of Jesus' followers settled in Jerusalem, while others spread across the Mediterranean world. And while they all claimed to follow Jesus, they often shared very different views of who this Jesus was and what he represented.[18]

It has become common practice amongst early Christian scholars to categorize these divergent groups as "sects," defining them in terms drawn from modern sociological studies.[19] Scholars who espouse a definitive "parting of the ways" between Christians and Jews have also tended to parse early Christians into one of three primary groups: the Jewish Christians, Pauline Christian's and the gnostics. However, as Philip Harland recognizes, "The emphasis in such sectarian categorizations is often

17. Matt 21:12–13; Mark 11:15–18; Luke 19:45–46; and John 2:13–17.

18. Riley, *One Jesus, Many Christs*, 4.

19. For a further discussion of the concept of sects, their development and their relation to society, see Wilson, *Religious Sects* and Wilson, *Religion in Sociological Perspective*.

placed on the negative or ambivalent social relations that existed between the sect and surrounding society. Discourse of separation and distinction predominate".[20]

In her article on "Lived Religion among Second-Century 'Gnostic Hieratic Specialists,'" Nicola Denzey Lewis further highlights the problem of distinguishing Christianity from Judaism, and even between different expressions of Christianity itself. She argues that even as late as the second century, Christianity was not sufficiently developed to receive a "monolithic designation."[21] Referencing Irenaeus' discussion of the gnostics, she writes:

> If Irenaeus' claims in *Adv. Haer.* about these hieratic specialists are true, then each of them pushed beyond the limits of licit Christian behaviours. Some of these ritual innovators explored the interface between baptism, death, and exorcism. Others worked in the fringes of Christian practice, drawing on traditional practices of oracular utterance and dream-interpretation. Most were accused of dealing in magic. Whether or not Irenaeus and his continuators were accurate or truthful in their sketches of these specialists remains a matter of debate; nevertheless, the second century found nascent Christianity at perhaps its most audaciously experimental, and historically at its closest point to Roman, Greek, and Egyptian hieratic behaviours. Without established limits to confine them, one might argue that all these figures operated "beyond duty," creating moments of religious meaning in the intersections of life, sex and death.[22]

To this end, Lewis suggests "sorting behaviours, not groups."[23] She describes six activities or "lines of praxis" that were demonstrated to varying degrees across this diverse collection of believers:

1. Texts, exegesis, allegorical readings and explanation of Scripture.
2. Cultic practice and ritual innovation, particularly in the area of baptism and the eucharist.
3. Prophecy and oracular utterances.
4. Miracles, healing, and exorcisms.

20. Harland, *Dynamics of Identity in the World of the Early Christians*, 25.
21. Lewis, "Lived Religion," 82.
22. Lewis, "Lived Religion," 82.
23. Lewis, "Lived Religion," 83.

5. Sharing of knowledge and beliefs to groups or individuals.
6. Social innovation, change and growth particularly relating to disadvantaged groups or individuals.[24]

How these behaviors or practices were exercised amongst Christians in their earliest years are less important to our discussion than simply acknowledging the diversity that existed.[25] Modern-day orthodoxy points to the "One True Church" of the early believers, suggesting at times that it is more important to return to something rather than discover a new path and way of being in society as it is now. In this way, we are confronted with the question of whether the "One True Church" has ever existed at all. The New Testament itself attests to the entrepreneurial spirit of its believers to find meaning. Acknowledging this reality pushes us, of course, towards the slippery slope of relativism. As John Ladd writes, "This is the skeleton in the closet for every philosophical oralist since the time of Plato and the Sophists."[26]

There is a significant difference, however, between relativism and relevance. Relativism is the claim that knowledge, truth and morality exist in relation to culture and society without any universal truth. Relevance is the degree to which something is related to, useful to or brings meaning to the present moment. Relativism, at its most extreme, says: "Everyone for themselves." Relevance seeks to keep a shared sense of truth and morality as part of the equation, and engage as many participants as possible in the conversation. Relativism seeks to collapse the truth; relevance, to expand it. The significance of this to our discussion will become more readily apparent in our final chapters as we seek to chart a way forward for today's church.

Periods of Persecution

Up until the time of Constantine, Christians of all types had lived under a constant state of threat. History tells us that this was mostly at the hands of Rome. But before 35 CE, the persecution that Christians experienced

24. Lewis, "Lived Religion," 84.

25. .For a thorough discussion of these various praxis, see Lewis, "Lived Religion," 79-102 and Lewis, *Introduction to "Gnosticism."*

26. Ladd, "The Issue of Relativism," 585.

was perpetrated mostly by the Jews, as witnessed in the dramatic judgment and stoning of Stephen in Acts 7.

Early in the book of Acts, we read:

> All the believers were one in heart and mind. No one claimed that any of their possessions was their own, but they shared everything they had. With great power the apostles continued to testify to the resurrection of the Lord Jesus. And God's grace was so powerfully at work in them all that there were no needy persons among them. For from time to time those who owned land or houses sold them, brought the money from the sale and put it at the apostles' feet, and it was distributed to anyone who had need.[27]

Not everything in the early church, though, was peaches and cream. In Acts 6, we find the Hellenistic Jews complaining to the Hebraic Jews that their widows were being overlooked in the daily distribution of food. So, the apostles gathered together and appointed seven deacons to oversee the sharing of food and other matters pertaining to the community. Stephen was among the seven.

Stephen was already known as a fearless and charismatic leader who had "worked great signs and wonders among the people." As with Jesus, this angered Stephen's enemies. Because they couldn't outdo him on the merit of his arguments, they opted for a more sinister plan. They went to the religious leaders, accusing Stephen of publicly blaspheming against both God and Moses, a crime punishable by death. As a result, Stephen was arrested and brought to appear before the Sanhedrin.[28]

As was customary in Jewish law, Stephen was given the opportunity to defend himself. Taking advantage of the opportunity, he delivered one of the most famous speeches in the New Testament. In it, Stephen carefully summarized Jewish history, up to and including the building of the First Temple in Jerusalem. He connected the laws of Moses to the teachings and person of Jesus, arguing that a new way of worshipping God had been made possible through his death and resurrection.

Nor did Stephen hold back any of his criticism for the Jewish authorities:

27. Acts 4:32–35.

28. The Sanhedrin was a council of elders appointed to serve as the highest court of justice in ancient Jerusalem.

> You stiff-necked people! Your hearts and ears are still uncircumcised. You are just like your ancestors: You always resist the Holy Spirit! Was there ever a prophet your ancestors did not persecute? They even killed those who predicted the coming of the Righteous One. And now you have betrayed and murdered him—you who have received the law that was given through angels but have not obeyed it.[29]

As far as we know, Stephen's death marks the first time a person was murdered for their belief in Christ. While it was the Jewish authorities who stoned him, increasingly, the persecution of Christ's followers shifted to Roman hands.

As Christianity spread across the Mediterranean, many Romans felt threatened by this strange new religion.[30] Because Christians didn't participate in Rome's pagan rituals and instead kept to themselves, most Romans considered them to be anti-social. When the imperial guard took an interest in them, they became even more withdrawn, adding fuel to the belief that Christians belonged to secret societies intent on treason.[31] Secondly, because Christians wouldn't participate in activities that were believed to appease the gods, they were seen as threats to the very well-being of the community. Writing around 196 CE, Tertullian[32] said:

> The Christians are to blame for every public disaster and every misfortune that befalls the people. If the Tiber rises to the walls, if the Nile fails to rise and flood the fields, if the sky withholds its rain, if there is earthquake or famine or plague, straightaway the cry arises: "The Christians to the lions!"[33]

In 64 CE, a fire began in the merchant shops near Rome's chariot stadium. The fire burned for nine days, destroying two-thirds of the city. Christian tradition records that Emperor Nero, acting out of this common belief, blamed the devastation on Christians living in the city, prompting a new reign of terror against them. The apostles Paul and Peter were reported to be among the victims.

29. Luke 7:51–52.

30. Bruce, *The Spreading Flame,* 165.

31. Bruce, *The Spreading Flame,* 169.

32. Tertullian was an early Christian theologian and polemicist who is widely regarded as the founder of Latin Christianity.

33. Bruce, *The Spreading Flame,* 180.

For the next 250 years, Christians continued to reject Rome's pagan rituals and, as a result, suffered sporadic, localized, and sometimes intense periods of persecution. Among those killed during this time were some of Christianity's most influential early leaders: Ignatius of Loyola, Polycarp, Justin Martyr, Origen, and Cyprian.[34] Despite the hostility and the penalties it provoked, Christianity continued to grow. By the beginning of the fourth century, it had become an empire-wide phenomenon. Some estimate that approximately 10 percent of the Roman world at the time was Christian. Church buildings could now be found throughout the Roman world; a hierarchy of bishops, presbyters, and deacons was evolving, and a diverse group of people—from slaves and the poor right up through the upper classes—had become converts to the Christian faith.

Still, the persecution continued. In 303 CE, Emperor Diocletian became convinced that Christianity's growing numbers posed an increasing threat to the empire, prompting him to issue an edict ordering churches to be destroyed, scriptures to be burnt, community leaders stripped of their offices, and others forced into slavery.

As the noted historian Eusebius writes:

> It was in the nineteenth year of the reign of Diocletian [A.D. 303] . . . when the feast of the Saviour's passion was near at hand, that royal edicts were published everywhere, commanding that the churches be leveled to the ground and the Scriptures be destroyed by fire, and ordering that those who held places of honor be degraded, and that the household servants, if they persisted in the profession of Christianity, be deprived of freedom.[35]

In 308 CE, the emperor, Galerius, issued a further edict, ordering all men, women, children, and servants to offer sacrifices to the gods, "and that all provisions in the markets should be sprinkled with sacrificial wine."[36] Christians had to comply or starve. As the noted church historian Philip Schaff writes, "all the pains, which iron and steel, fire and sword, rack and cross, wild beasts and beastly men could inflict, were employed."[37]

A significant turning point, however, occurred five years later with the conversion of Constantine in 312 CE. In the late third and early

34. For an excellent discussion of the early church fathers, see Papandrea, *Reading Early Church Fathers.*

35. Eusebius, *Ecclesiastical History*, 8:2

36. Schaff, *History of the Christian Church II*, 68.

37 Schaff, *History of the Christian Church II*, 68.

fourth centuries, battles between rival emperors and usurpers were common. The emperor Diocletian had instituted a tetrarchy, a consortium of four emperors meant to deal with the empire's expanded borders. As Raymond Van Dam writes, "Multiple emperors, large armies, and insecure frontiers were a recipe for repeated wars."[38] In this litany of wars, the Battle of Milvian Bridge was, in one sense, unremarkable. This was a conflict between the sons of two former emperors, both of whom had been vying for legitimacy since their father's death. There is one feature about this battle, however, that sets it apart from all others in its time—Constantine's vision and subsequent dream.

After conquests in Gaul and northern Europe, history records that Constantine was preparing to invade Italy in hopes of defeating the emperor Maxentius. Like Paul, Constantine claimed to have had a vision prior to the battle, leading to his acceptance of the Christian God.

There are two primary accounts of Constantine's conversion. The first is by Lactantius, a tutor of Constantine's son and later an advisor to Constantine, who helped guide his religious policy in its early stages. Lactantius writes that while still in Gaul, before setting out for Rome, Constantine and his army saw a great cross in the sky, above the sun, shining brightly with the inscription *In Hoc Signo Vinces* or "by this sign, you will conquer."[39]

Similarly, Eusebius, in his Life of Constantine, writes:

> Since the victorious emperor himself long afterwards declared it to the writer of this history, when he was honored with acquaintance and society, and confirmed his statement by an oath, who could hesitate to believe it, especially since other testimonies have established its truth? He said that about noon, when the day was already beginning to decline, he saw with his own eyes the sign of a cross of light in the heavens, above the sun, and bearing the inscription, "By this symbol you will conquer." He was struck with amazement by the sight, and his whole army witnessed the miracle.[40]

38. Van Dam, *Remembering Constantine*, 2–3.

39. Vanderspoel, "Lactantius."

40. Eusebius, *Life of Constantine*, para 28.

Figure 2: Chi Rho

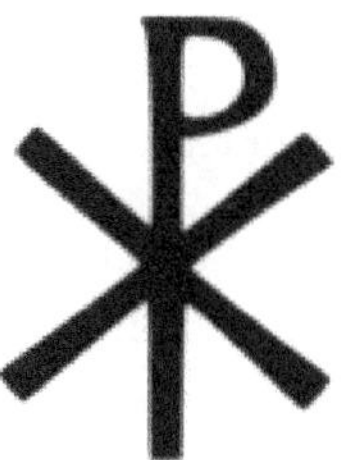

The monogram that looks like a combination of an X and P in English represents the first two letters of the Greek word for Christ—Chi (X) and Rho (P).

"Unsure of what this apparition could mean," Eusebius tells us that while Constantine "continued to ponder, night suddenly came on. In his sleep, the Christ of God appeared to him with the same sign which he had seen in the heavens and commanded him to make a likeness of that sign which he had seen in the heavens and to use it as a safeguard in all engagements with his enemies."[41]

Lactantius, in his account, expands on Constantine's dream this way:

> Constantine was directed in a dream to cause the heavenly sign to be delineated on the shields of his soldiers, and so to proceed to battle. He did as he had been commanded, and he marked on their shields the letter X, with a perpendicular line drawn through it and turned round thus at the top, being the cipher of CHRIST. Having this sign, his troops stood to arms.[42]

On October 28, 312, Constantine's forces, despite being outnumbered four to one, defeated Maxentius's army on the plains near Milvian Bridge. Lactantius reports that part of the bridge collapsed in their opponent's attempt to retreat across the Tiber River, leaving Maxentius and many of his men to be trampled or drowned. Victorious, Constantine rode into Rome, and at the age of twenty-four, was hailed as emperor of the Roman empire's western half.

To mark the event, and to honor the God who had ensured his victory, Constantine issued in the following year the Edict of Milan, thereby granting:

41. Eusebius, *Life of Constantine*, para 29.
42. Vanderspoel, "Lactantius," ch. 34.

> both to Christians and to all others full authority to follow whatever worship each person has desired. . . . Every one of those who have a common wish to follow the religion of the Christians may from this moment freely and unconditionally proceed to observe the same without any annoyance or disquiet.

Modern historians have often interpreted Constantine's vision and subsequent victory as a pivotal moment in the trajectories of both the Roman empire and early Christianity. The Battle of Milvian bridge represents not only a contest for control of the coveted Roman empire but ultimately the triumph of Christianity over paganism. It ended the persecution of Christians, accelerated the conversion of Roman society throughout the empire, and initiated an era in which politics and Christianity were intimately intertwined.

From Movement to Institution

There's no denying it. There's something about a royal decree that has its benefits. For a faith that had grown despite persecution, largely on the merits of its willingness to care for the sick, widows, and orphans, its rejection of adultery and abortion, its acknowledgment and acceptance of women, its capacity to understand culture and develop social networks, its persistence in the face of persecution, and above all, its tireless insistence that the Christian God was a God whose judgement was rooted in love, the profound impact of Constantine's conversion cannot be denied.[43] With no more persecution, freedom to worship openly, public funds to build churches, and political influence, fourth-century Christians must have felt as though they had just won the lottery.

But while Constantine's "conversion" brought immediate relief and lasting benefit for the newly established faith, there is little evidence that the man who was at least partially responsible for this religious revolution was himself an exemplary Christian. Nor did it mark a significant shift towards a uniquely Christian style of rule.

On the one hand, Constantine made great strides in ending centuries of persecution and securing political and social rights for Christians. He established Sunday as a unified day of rest and ordered that the feasts held in memory of the Christian martyrs be recognized and granted the same legal rights as pagan feasts. Constantine outlawed gladiatorial

43. Stark, *The Rise of Christianity*, ebook, ch. 10, pp. 2,18–19.

events and made it illegal for Jews to stone other Jews who had converted to Christianity. He ended the practice of infanticide and the abuse of peasants and the poor. He committed vast resources to build churches and support Christianity publicly, and his leadership at the Council of Nicaea helped clarify some of Christianity's central doctrines.

On the other hand, Constantine continued many pagan practices, including his veneration of the sun. Beginning in 324, Constantine began reconstructing the city of Byzantium as his new imperial city. And while Christian writers played up the idea of the newly named Constantinople as the "new Rome," they also had to find ways to explain the embarrassing fact that this new, supposedly Christian city, had been ornately adorned with pagan temples and statues. His association of Christian worship with the pagan sun-god blatantly disregarded the Judeo-Christian belief in the "one true God."[44] In 314, the cross began to appear on Constantine's coins, but so did the figures of Sol Invictus and Mars Converator.[45,46] Figure 3 portrays a rare silver medallion issued from Ticinium in 315, depicting Constantine with images of the chi-rho in the upper portion of the coin and a cross on the right side of the coin.

Figure 3: Silver medallion of Constantine from Tycinium 315

Source: constantinethegreatcoins.com.

44. Deut 4:35; John 1:14.
45. Stanley, "History of the Eastern Church." Lecture vi, par. 14.
46. Clark, "Christian Symbols on Coins."

Constantine raised his children as Christians and had Christian clergy as advisors, but he also retained the title of *pontifex maximus* as chief priest of the state religion until his death. And while the persecution of Christians had ended, his new laws also permitted Christians to essentially "do unto others as Rome had done unto them," as evidenced by their subsequent persecution of the gnostics.

Julian the Apostate, who during his brief reign as emperor (361 to 363) tried to re-establish paganism, denounced Constantine as an insincere and self-indulgent tyrant. In the nineteenth century, historian Jacob Burckhardt (1818–97) characterized Constantine as "a calculating politician who shrewdly employed all available physical resources and spiritual powers to the end of maintaining himself and his rule."[47]

Constantine was a man of great contradictions: a brave soldier, a brilliant general, and an astute politician. But was he also a man of genuine faith? A sincere convert to the Christian God? Or was Constantine merely a self-interested opportunist who saw the rise of Christianity as a means to further the empire and secure his own place in human history? While these questions may best be left for modern historians to debate, one thing is clear: The House of God had moved up a notch in the world—if not in God's eyes, at least in the world's.

Elements of Change

What sparks the kind of seismic social change seen during the reign of Constantine? Social structures, attitudes, and laws can, for a time, seem unchangeable. And then, in the historical blink of an eye, society is transformed.

Change theorists suggest that every societal change exhibits a series of key elements that are each demonstrated to a greater or lesser degree. What these key elements are, of course, remain a matter of significant debate. Hegel's theory of social evolution suggests that change is based on the interaction of opposing forces. Change occurs when opposing ideas or beliefs clash and eventually reach a resolution, either through synthesis or the rejection of one idea or another. With respect to the history of human ideas and events, these concepts shift and change through conflict over time, ideally arriving at a set of ideas, or even a single idea,

47. Burckhardt, *The Age of Constantine*, 281.

that meets the needs of everyone involved.[48] To Hegel's dialectic, Marx added the concept of materialism, seeing human history as a fundamental "struggle between the social classes."[49] In the *Structure of Scientific Revolutions,* Thomas Kuhn argued that people are most likely to continue using apparently unworkable paradigms until a better one comes along.[50] Centuries before, the Greek philosopher Heraclitus compared change to a river. "On those stepping into rivers," he wrote, "staying the same, other and other waters flow." Or as Plato explains, "Heraclitus, I believe, says that all things go and nothing stays . . . you cannot step twice into the same river." In other words, for a river to remain a river, it must constantly be changing.[51]

We started this chapter by asking, "What caused the Christian faith to take root and grow so quickly?" While it is not our intent (or desire) to systematically apply these theories to the entirety of the Judeo-Christian experience, still, some key insights can be distilled from our previous experience.

Opportunity and Danger

Perhaps you have read or heard of motivational speakers who suggest that the word *crisis,* when written in Chinese, is represented by two characters. One of these characters, they argue, when taken alone, means *danger.* The other by itself means *opportunity.* This theory has now largely been debunked by linguists.[52] But a key insight remains: crisis almost always leads to change. In times of social crisis, there is always a danger that change will worsen the situation. But there is also the possibility it may change for the better—reforming it—improving it. The early church lived in crisis. From its earliest days following the death of Christ, right up until the time of Constantine, danger *and* opportunity were the church's constant companions.

48. Blunden, *Hegel for Social Movements,* 6.

49. Alcock et al., eds., *Student's Companion to Social Policy,* 152.

50. Kuhn, *Structure of Scientific Analysis,* 10.

51. Stern, "Heraclitus' and Wittgenstein," 579–604.

52. Mair, "Danger + Opportunity ≠ Opportunity."

Leaders and Vision

In his book *The Tipping Point,* Malcolm Gladwell writes, "The success of any kind of social epidemic is heavily dependent on the involvement of people with a particular and rare set of social gifts."[53] Regardless of which side of the Jesus divinity debate one takes up, there can be little doubt that Jesus was someone with a "particular and rare set of gifts." Scripture and tradition both depict a dynamic leader—someone with a singular purpose, a visionary who could inspire and motivate and yet still be relatable enough to connect, identify, and create a "tipping point" amongst his followers.

We see further examples of these rare and particular gifts in the disciples, Paul, New Testament characters like Priscilla and Aquilla, and the persecuted martyrs. Even with Constantine, we find a rare determined capacity to assess the present and move towards the future. And yet, while change might receive its spark from inspired leaders, its success often depends on the rank and file. As Margaret Mead writes, "Never doubt that a small group of thoughtful, committed citizens can change the world. Indeed, it is the only thing that ever has."[54]

Patience and Persistence

Change rarely happens in an instant—especially change that holds any significant meaning. The historical blink of an eye can sometimes seem interminable, but for change to be sustainable, most people need to experience it in order to embrace it. This also means that many will become frustrated along the way. There will be some for whom the change can never come fast enough, and they will tend to push others further away from the vision rather than towards it. Societies and organizations that achieve change do so because they are able to engage people even during hard times. Part of this engagement means not being afraid to ask hard questions. I once had a professor who remarked, "Easy questions, easy answers." Our willingness to ask hard questions helps people in the midst of struggle. It encourages them by demonstrating that we are willing to listen and not dismiss their anger, fears, grief, or despair.

53. Gladwell, *The Tipping Point,* 31.

54. Meade, *Earth at Omega,* ch. 6.

Context and Culture

Context typically refers to the circumstances surrounding a particular statement, idea, or event. Culture usually refers to the customs, arts, institutions, and achievements of a particular country, people, or social group. Jesus excelled at understanding both. He recognized how context and culture shape people's views, values, hopes, loyalties, and fears. He understood that people see the world differently; he never pretended that culture and differences do not matter. But Jesus also knew how to build on common experience in ways that could bring people together rather than drive them apart.

What caused the Christian church to take root and proliferate? In his book *The Rise of Christianity*, sociologist Rodney Stark describes how these factors played out:

> Christianity did not grow because of miracle working in the marketplaces (although there may have been much of that going on), or because Constantine said it should, or even because the martyrs gave it such credibility. It grew because Christians constituted an intense community, able to generate the "invincible obstinacy" [against paganism] that so offended the younger Pliny but yielded immense religious rewards. And the primary means of its growth was through the united and motivated efforts of the growing numbers of Christian believers, who invited their friends, relatives, and neighbors to share the "good news."

Stark's offering registers as profound, especially when we discover that when he wrote these words, he identified as agnostic (although he now identifies as an "independent Christian"). "Christianity," he writes, "radically and attractively redefined" the way humanity relates to the divine. The Judeo-Christian notion that God loves those who love God was alien to the pagan world. What mattered to the pagans, where the gods were concerned, was not love, but rather whatever service or benefit the gods could provide. Equally foreign to the pagans was the notion that because God loves humanity, Christians cannot please God unless they love one another.[55]

And so, Christianity began to provide social services that the government did not. At a time long before employment insurance and family benefits, the church provided aid. And not only to their own, but to those outside their community as well. They tended to the sick and the dying.

55. Stark, *The Rise of Christianity*, 86.

They accepted people of all ethnicities. And they treated women better than other faiths did. Stark writes that this was no mere "pie in the sky" sort of faith. It was not something "out of this world," but rather very much in it. He continues, "Christianity often puts pie on the table! It makes life better here and now. Not merely in psychological ways, as faith in an attractive afterlife can do, but in terms of concrete, worldly benefits."[56]

Why did the early Christian church take root and grow so quickly? In part, because those who belonged to the House of God were beginning to learn, as one thirteenth-century poet and philosopher writes:

"Love is the house of God
And you are living in that house.
—RUMI

56. Stark, *The Triumph of Christianity*, ebook, ch. 6, p. 1.

3

Moving Heaven and Earth

Dominance in Europe

Those who know that the consensus of many centuries has sanctioned the conception that the earth remains at rest in the middle of the heavens as its center, would, I reflected, regard it as an insane pronouncement if I made the opposite assertion that the earth moves.[1]

—NICOLAUS COPERNICUS

Copernicus Meets Luther

IN THE SIXTEENTH CENTURY, a mathematician, astronomer, and Catholic cleric named Copernicus (1473–1543) unraveled the world's popular belief that the earth stood at the center of the universe. Until that time, most believed the Ptolemaic view that placed the earth and not the sun at the center of the universe. While many, and most significantly the early church scholars, came to interpret this astronomical positioning as a reflection of humanity's importance to God, their emphasis did not actually hold true to the Ptolemaic view of the universe. For Ptolemy, the spheres increase in importance the higher one ascends. While he physically

1. Copernicus, *On the Revolutions*, 41.

situated the earth at the center of the universe, he actually regarded it as less important than all the other spheres in the heavens. Rather than promoting the earth's importance, Ptolemy deflates it.

Copernicus's assertion that the sun stood at the center of the universe turned both of the previous interpretations on end, causing humans not only to see the universe differently but their own place within it. As his discovery began to take hold, it became increasingly apparent to humanity that they occupied only a small and very remote part of the cosmos.

While Copernicus may not have intended or even imagined the radical cultural and intellectual consequences that his scientific discoveries would prompt, in retrospect, they reveal some dramatic parallels between the scientific and religious worlds of his day. Around the same time that Copernicus was developing his theories and delivering preliminary lectures on the subject, another historical figure was preparing for his own cosmic change.

Martin Luther (1483–1546) was a German priest, professor of theology, and contemporary of Nicolaus Copernicus. Ordained to the priesthood in 1507, Luther came to reject many of the Roman Catholic Church's teachings and practices. Key to Luther's objections was the Catholic Church's practice of offering indulgences. The Catechism of the Catholic Church describes an indulgence as:

> a remission before God of the temporal punishment due to sins whose guilt has already been forgiven, which the faithful Christian who is duly disposed gains under certain prescribed conditions through the action of the Church which, as the minister of redemption, dispenses and applied with authority the treasury of satisfactions of Christ and the saints. An indulgence is partial or plenary according as it removes either part or all of the temporal punishment due to sin. Indulgences may be applied to the living or the dead.[2]

For Luther, these "prescribed conditions" amounted to nothing more than a "sale of favors" by the church. The yield from these indulgences was enormous, especially because trained and commissioned "salesmen" would travel throughout Europe advertising their "benefits." As one contemporary sales pitch put it, "The moment the money tinkles in the collecting box, another soul flies out of purgatory."[3]

2. The Vatican, "Indulgences," 2:4.

3. Chadwick, *The Reformation*, 43.

In 1517, a prominent indulgence salesman named Johannes Tetzel arrived in Wittenberg to organize a campaign that would see the proceeds of indulgences go towards rebuilding St. Peter's Basilica in Rome. Religious and social historian Rodney Stark cites excerpts from some of Tetzel's sermons where he writes: "Do you not hear the voices of your dead parents and other people, screaming and saying, 'Have pity on me, have pity on me. . . . We are suffering severe punishments and pain, from which you could rescue me with a few alms if you would."[4]

Incensed by this, Luther, like Copernicus, concluded that somehow his "universe" had fallen off its axis and that the church's perspective on life and faith had gone awry. Instead of religion revolving around God, Luther saw it revolving around the church. And so, on October 31, 1517, tradition tells us that Martin Luther nailed his famous Ninety-Five Theses to the Wittenberg Church door, formally challenging church leaders to a debate on the practice of selling indulgences and the biblical doctrine of justification by grace.

By the following year, Luther's ideas had reached Rome, prompting Leo X to order the head of the Augustinian order, of which Luther was a part, to silence him. When this failed, the pope appealed to Frederick of Saxony, but to no avail. On June 15, 1520, Leo issued Exsurge Domini, a papal bull condemning Luther for his actions and ordering him to recant within sixty days or be excommunicated. "By the authority of the Almighty God, the blessed Apostles Peter and Paul, and our own authority," wrote Leo, "we condemn, reprobate, and reject completely each of these theses or errors." "Moreover," Leo continued, "because the preceding errors and many others are contained in the writings of Martin Luther, we likewise condemn, reprobate, and reject completely all the writings of the said Martin."[5] Everything Luther had written was to be gathered and burned.

Leo's order only spurred Luther on further, and having gained the support of several influential figures in Germany, including Frederick of Saxony, he defied the pope. While Luther's early writings had focused on theological objections, his writings soon became more openly critical of Rome itself, identifying the papacy's treatment of the church with the Babylonian captivity of the Jews and the papacy itself with the Antichrist. Luther left the Pope with no alternative, and so on January 3, 1521, Leo issued Luther's excommunication from the church.

4. Stark, *The Triumph of Christianity*, ebook, ch. 18, p. 7.

5. Leo X, *Exurge Domine.*

In April of 1521, Luther was summoned to the Diet of Worms, an imperial council held in the City of Worms, where he would be given the opportunity to recant. Called before the court, Luther apologized for the tone his writings had taken but refused to recant, saying:

> Unless I am convinced by the testimony of the Scriptures or by clear reason (for I do not trust either in the pope or in councils alone, since it is well known that they have often erred and contradicted themselves), I am bound by the Scriptures I have quoted and my conscience is captive to the Word of God. I cannot and will not recant anything, since it is neither safe nor right to go against conscience. May God help me. Amen.[6]

Realizing that his defiance had put him in mortal danger, Luther headed back to Wittenberg by coach. On the way, Luther was overtaken in a staged attack by Prince Frederick's guards, disguised as highwaymen. Fearing for his safety, they escorted Luther to Wartburg Castle, where Luther would remain hidden for the next ten months.

Did Luther anticipate the radical shift that would soon come about? He could well have imagined the opposition he would receive at the hand of the religious authorities, since he was not the first to pitch the idea of Catholic reform. In 1374, a professor and cleric from Yorkshire in England named John Wycliffe (1320–84) had forecast many of Luther's objections. Commissioned by the English government to resolve a series of disputes between the King of England and Pope Gregory XI, Wycliffe became so disgusted with the arguments put forward by the church that he publicly began to protest the practice of selling offices and indulgences. He argued that the English monarchy should divest itself of all church property to distance itself from this practice.

Also anticipating the Reformation was Jan Hus (1372–1415), a Bohemian theologian and philosopher who opposed many of the Catholic Church's views and practices. Beginning in 1401, Hus became dean of Faculty of Philosophy at the University of Prague. A keen student of Wycliffe's work, Hus started to observe how church control was feeding social discontent. In Bohemia,[7] the church owned about one-half of all the land. In addition to this monopoly on real estate, the Bohemian lower

6. Brecht, *Martin Luther*, 460.

7. From 1918–39 and from 1945–92, the historical country of Bohemia was part of Czechoslovakia. Since 1993 it has formed much of what is currently the Czech Republic.

and middle-classes resented the church's wealth and simoniacal[8] practices of well-to-do priests purchasing status and office within the church. Beginning in 1402, Hus also assumed responsibility for the Bethlehem Chapel in Prague. Almost immediately, he began to attract attention with his sermons, which were delivered in Czech instead of the more traditional Latin. In 1403, he vigorously defended several extracts from the religious writings of Wycliffe, calling for church reform. In 1410, he was excommunicated by the city's archbishop, but refused to appear before the papal court and continued to preach. Two years later, he was excommunicated again for protesting against the church's sale of indulgences. While Hus agreed to leave Prague, he continued to preach in smaller towns and villages throughout the country until he was arrested on November 28, 1414. On July 6, 1415, he was burned at the stake, having been convicted by the church of heresy.

Knowing full well what had happened to Hus, Luther would have been well prepared for the potential consequences. It is hard to imagine, though, that Luther could ever have envisioned the full-scale religious separation that would eventually come about. Like James, the brother of Jesus, along with the early Jewish Christians, who expected their movement to spark a reformed Judaism, it is far more likely that Luther envisioned a reformed Catholic Church, rather than a break-off movement that would eventually bear his name. Luther's goal wasn't to die a martyr, but rather restore the church to its rightful place—not at the center of the religious universe, but set in orbit around a gracious, loving, and forgiving God.

Power and Politics

The world in which Copernicus and Luther lived represented a complex relationship between church and state. In chapter 2, we explored the beginnings of this embattled marriage with Constantine's conversion, his embrace of the Christian church, and later Theodosius's Edict of Thessalonica, making Christianity the official faith of the Roman Empire. What had emerged in the third century as an official state religion had seemingly evolved into something closer to a religiously controlled state.

8. Simony is the act of selling church offices and roles. It is so named after Simon Magnus who, in the Acts 8:12–14, is described as having offered two of Jesus' disciples a payment in exchange for their empowering of him to impart the power of the Holy Spirit to anyone upon whom he would place his hands.

When the western half of the Roman Empire collapsed near the end of the fifth century, the most obvious reason was a string of military losses to the Barbarian tribes from the north. The term Barbarian originates from the Greek *barbaros*. In Ancient Greece, the term was typically used to describe someone who did not speak Greek or follow Greek traditions and customs. Amongst Romans, its use had devolved into something much closer to meaning anyone more primitive and less civilized than they were. This included mostly tribal non-Romans, such as the Goths, Celts, Vandals, Gauls, Saxons, and the Huns.

Rome had battled against these Barbarian groups for centuries, but by the fourth century, their threat had deepened as they began to gather along the Empire's borders. The Romans weathered an attack by the Gauls in the late fourth century, but in 410, the Visigoths, under King Alaric, successfully sacked the city of Rome. The Empire and its "Holy City" spent the next several decades under constant threat until it was raided again by the Vandals in 455. Finally, in 476, the Germanic leader Odoacer (433–93) attacked the city, successfully deposing Romulus Augustus, the last of the western Roman emperors.

Raiding Barbarians, however, were not the only reason for Rome's collapse. The western Roman Empire's fate had been partially sealed decades before when the Emperor Diocletian had divided the Empire into two halves.[9] While this division made the Empire more easily governable in the short term, dramatic tensions arose over time. Increasingly, the interests of East and West appeared divergent as they failed to unite against outside threats, often disagreeing over the deployment of resources and military aid. The largely Greek-speaking Eastern Empire grew in wealth as the gap widened, while the Latin-speaking Western Empire descended into economic crisis.

At its height, the Roman Empire stretched from the Atlantic Ocean to the Euphrates River that runs through modern-day Turkey, Syria, and Iraq. But its grandeur may have also been one of its downfalls. With such a vast territory to govern, the Empire faced an administrative and logistical nightmare.[10] Constant wars and overspending had drained the Western Empire's reserves, while oppressive taxation and inflation had widened the gap between rich and poor. In the hopes of avoiding taxation, many of the wealthier classes had fled to the countryside, setting up

9. Mango, "Constantinople," 5081–82.

10. History Channel, "Eight Reasons."

their own fiefdoms. At the same time, the Empire was suffering from a deficit of workers. Rome's economy depended heavily on slaves to farm its fields and work as craftsmen. Traditionally, its military conquests had provided the Empire with conquered people to fill these roles. But when the Empire's expansion slowed in the second century, their supply of slaves and spoils of war dried up. In the fifth century, a further blow came when the Vandals claimed North Africa and began to disrupt the Empire's trade routes.[11]

While Rome's size made it difficult to govern, inconsistent and ineffective leadership only served to magnify the problem. Being the Roman Emperor had always come with risks, but it was almost tantamount to a death sentence during the turbulent second and third centuries. Civil war plunged the Empire into chaos, and over a span of more than seventy-five years, more than twenty men assumed the throne—usually after the murder of their predecessor. The Praetorian Guard—the emperor's bodyguards—assassinated and installed new sovereigns seemingly at will. After only three months in power, the Praetorian Guard murdered Pertinax, the emperor, in the spring of 193 CE, brazenly auctioning off the imperial position to the highest bidder. This political rot also extended to the Roman Senate, its own corruption and incompetence preventing it from keeping the emperor's excesses in check. With the Empire divided, its economy faltering, and its people in a constant state of unrest, the Empire's authority in Europe began to diminish.[12]

Stepping into this emerging vacuum was the Roman Catholic Church. Having maintained its seat of ecclesial authority in Rome, the church prevailed as the only social institution that the countries of Western Europe held in common. If anything, the barbarian invasions strengthened the church's influence and authority as people looked to its bishops for protection. Bishops, who by this time were often drawn from the local aristocracies, had both the religious and economic authority to negotiate with the barbarian leaders and mitigate the worst effects of the raids. In the absence of imperial officials, the bishops soon emerged as the leading political figures in the towns and cities of the former Empire.

Under Constantine, Christian bishops had already begun to assume the role of imperial officials tasked with administering the Empire's

11. The Vandals were a Germanic tribe who had first inhabited what is now southern Poland. During the fifth century, they established kingdoms in the Iberian Peninsula, several Mediterranean Islands, and North Africa.

12. Brown, *Eye of a Needle*.

laws. These "imperial bishops" answered directly to the emperor, thereby strengthening his imperial dominance over the church. In the post-Roman period, the bishops came to represent the greatest source of continuity between the Empire and the Germanic kingdoms.[13] The Germanic kings used the bishops to connect with the Roman citizens living in their domains. Recognizing the benefit of their influence, these rulers also appointed bishops to positions of political power.

However, this arrangement also had its downside. "One of the sad ironies of life," writes Rodney Stark, "is that sincere efforts to do good can so often have unfortunate results."[14] Such was the case with Constantine's evolving relationship with the church. One of his first acts as emperor was to grant Christian clergy special privileges, exempting them from taxation, military service, and forced labor, inadvertently creating a "stampede into the priesthood."[15] The result was that, in addition to the many deeply committed Christians who sought to provide leadership, a great many intolerant, insincere, and immoral men gained influential positions in the church. In addition to those who meant to inspire, encourage, and empower, there were also those who were intent on controlling, manipulating, and deterring in order to achieve their own goals and aspirations.

The priests were notoriously corrupt and, in many cases, only held their position due to family influence and favor. Scholar G. G. Coulton cites one letter of 1281 in which the writer warns how "the ignorance of the priests precipitates the people into the ditch of error."[16] Later, he records the correspondence of Bishop Guillaume le Marie de Angers, who writes:

> The priesthood includes innumerable contemptible persons of abject life, utterly unworthy in learning and morals, from whose execrable lives and pernicious ignorance infinite scandals arise, the Church sacraments are despised by the laity, and in very many districts the lay folk hold the priests as [vile].[17]

Consequently, there arose what Stark describes as parallel churches, not so much of East and West, but of "Power and Piety."[18] The "Church of Power" was the one that stepped initially into the vacuum created by the

13. Stumph, "Development of the Church."
14. Stark, *The Triumph of Christianity,* 17:1.
15. Fletcher, *The Barbarian Conversion,* 38.
16. Coulton, *Medieval Village,* 259.
17. Coulton, *Medieval Village,* 259.
18. Stark, *The Triumph of Christianity,* ebook, ch. 17, p. 2.

demise of the Roman Empire, eventually shaping and informing almost every aspect of European life during the Middle Ages. Its religious observances gave rise to our calendar; its baptisms, confirmations, marriages, and funerals marked the most important moments in people's lives; and its teachings underpinned most of society's beliefs on ethics, the meaning of life, and even the afterlife.

This church included the great majority of priests, bishops, cardinals, and popes who ruled the church until Luther's Ninety-Five Theses spawned the Reformation. Stark describes these clergy mostly as "sensible and temperate men" but also "worldly," practical, and morally soft.[19] This was soon reflected in church careers determined by influence, commerce, and eventually heredity. Indulgences were not the only thing for sale—so were places of power within the church.

Having been established in direct succession to the apostle Peter, the papacy was now controlled by the aristocracy in competition with the Holy Roman emperors. Between 955 and 1057, there were a total of twenty-five popes, an average of one every four years. The local aristocracy appointed thirteen, the Holy Roman emperors twelve. One can hardly imagine why anyone in these times would seek the papacy, given that in a 140-year span between 872 and 1012, a third of the popes died violent deaths, many of them murdered by the feuding Roman elite.

Consider the Borgias who inspired Mario Puzo's Corleone family in *The Godfather* and the 2011 Showtime series *The Borgias*. The historical Borgias assumed prominence in the ecclesiastical and political affairs of the fifteenth and sixteenth centuries, producing two popes: Alfons de Borja, who ruled as Pope Callixtus III from 1455 to 1458, and Rodrigo Lanzol Borgia, as Pope Alexander VI, between 1492 and 1503. The TV Borgia's were pitched by its creators as "The Original Crime Family."[20]

Perhaps we should also be anticipating a new Showcase or Netflix series based on the life of a prominent Roman noblewoman named Marozia. Rodney Stark offers this historical trailer:

> Consider the making and unmaking of the popes by Marozia (890–937), a promiscuous and domineering Roman noblewoman of the powerful Theophylact family. When she was fifteen, Marozia became the mistress of Pope Sergius III (served 904–911), who had murdered Pope Leo V (served 903) to gain the papal throne and by whom Marozia had an illegitimate son.

19. Stark, *The Triumph of Christianity*, ebook, ch. 17, p. 3.

20. IMDb.com, "The Borgias."

> Marozia's mother was the mistress of Pope John X (served 914–928), whom Marozia conspired to have suffocated and replaced by Pope Leo VI (served 928), whom she quickly replaced with Stephen VII (served 928–931). Subsequently, when her son Alberic became ruler of Rome, he so feared her conspiracies that he had her imprisoned [where] she eventually died in her cell.[21]

Christianity's relationship with the state shifted further with the rise of Charlemagne. Under his rule, Christianity emerged even more strongly as a political movement and a religious one. Charlemagne viewed kingship as an ecclesiastical office and the kingdom as the church. Unlike the situation in Rome, where the emperor controlled church policy and activity, Charlemagne envisioned a Christian monarchy that would now control state policy and activity. In his eyes, there was no separation between church and state—the two became one. Secular law was replaced by Christian law, thus granting more power to the bishops than they had ever known. In 800, Pope Leo III crowned Charlamagne emperor of the Franks, securing the marriage of church and state (along with Charlamagne's commitment to defend the papacy). Sadly, like many well-intentioned marriages, the initial appeal of their alliance began to wane, and by the start of the eleventh century, church and state found themselves again in political and moral turmoil.

Earlier, we noted, "Royal decrees have their benefits." But they also have their consequences. In his article, "Building Composite Measures of Religion and State,"[22] Jonathan Fox compiled an extensive list with contributions from Chaves and Caan,[23] Chaves, Schrader, and Sprindys,[24] Gill,[25] as well as Norris and Inglehart,[26] of how the relationship between church and state has played out in many of our current political systems and cultural contexts:

> The constitution limits freedom of religion. · The constitution does not recognize freedom of religion. · A single official (established) state church exists. · The state favors one religion. · Religious organizations must register with the state or be designated by it to operate legally, or the government imposes

21. Stark, *The Triumph of Christianity*, ebook, ch. 17, pp. 6–7.

22. Fox, "Building Composite Measures," 13–19.

23. Chaves and Cann, "Religious Pluralism."

24. Chaves, Schraeder, and Sprindys, "State Regulation of Religion," 10879–77.

25. Gill, "Government Regulation," 287–316.

26. Norris and Inglehart, *Sacred and Secular*.

> restrictions on those organizations not registered or recognized. · The state issues legal permits for religious buildings. · The state appoints or approves church leaders, church leaders appoint or approve government officials, and/or church leaders have specific positions in the government. · The state pays church salaries directly. · The state subsidizes some/all churches. · The state provides tax exceptions for some/all churches. · The state bans clergy from all or some specified religions from holding public office. · The state owns some church property and buildings. · The state mandates some religious education in state schools, even though students can be exempted from this requirement with a parent's request. · There are reports of forced religious conversions. · The state restricts some denominations, cults, or sects. · The state restricts/bans some missionaries from entering the country for proselytizing purposes. · The state restricts/censors some religious literature entering the country or being distributed. · The state imprisons or detains some religious groups or individuals. · The state fails to deter serious incidents of ethno-religious conflict and violence directed against some minority groups. · The state is designated a country of particular concern for freedom of religion.[27]

While we will return to this tension in later chapters, it is enough at this point to remind ourselves that the marriage of religion and politics requires great care.

The Monastic Influence

While the "Church of Power" sought to dominate the political sphere, the "Church of Piety," comprised mainly of monks and nuns living in organized communities, also experienced significant growth. Ascetic practice in religion was not new to the Middle Ages. Our word for asceticism derives from the Greek *askeō*, meaning "to exercise" or "to train" and was typically associated with the practice of denying physical or psychological desires to attain a spiritual ideal or goal. We see examples in most of the world's great religions and cultures, including Egypt, the far East, and Indigenous cultures in Northern Europe, Australia, and North America. Characteristic of these movements has been the practices of fasting, prayer, and abstinence from sexual relations.

27. Fox, "Building Composite Measures," 8:13–19.

In the medieval church context, many of the early monastics were influenced by aesthetics like Benedict (480–543). These Christians vowed to live lives of chastity, obedience, and poverty, following periods of rigorous training and self-denial. The Benedictine rule, "work and pray," became the foundation for thousands of monasteries across Europe. Called the "Dark Ages" by many, this period in history appears to have been anything but dark when the influence of these communities is taken into account.

One of the monastic contributions many people are familiar with involves the preservation and copying of manuscripts. The monks appreciated the classical inheritance more than many modern students realize. Alcuin (c. 735–854), who was recognized by many at the time as the most learned person in Europe, described writings in his library at York by Aristotle, Cicero, Lucan, Pliny, Statius, Trogus, Pompeius, and Virgil. But the monastics did much more than preserve literacy. As Thomas Woods writes:

> They not only established the schools and were schoolmasters in them, but also laid the foundations for universities. There were the thinkers and philosophers of the day and shaped the political and religious thought. To them, both collectively and individually, was the due continuity of thought and civilization of the ancient world with the later Middle Ages and the modern period.[28]

Their monasteries became models of productivity and economic resourcefulness, introducing restorative agricultural techniques, teaching farming techniques, animal husbandry, as well as cheese and winemaking skills. The Cistercians, in particular, became well known for their development of mechanization and running factories using water-power to crush wheat, sieve flour, and prepare textiles.

Let's consider an example of technological innovation in the monasteries. In the late 1990s, an archaeometallurgist from the University of Bradford named Gerry McDonnel found evidence in Rievaulx Abbey's ruins in North Yorkshire, England, of a fascinating example of technological advancement. Rievaulx Abbey was one of the monasteries closed by King Henry VIII to confiscate church properties in the 1530s. McDonnell unearthed a remarkable discovery by exploring debris from the property and documentary evidence left behind from the monastery.

In offering an account of McDonnell's find, *Discover Magazine* writes that, in addition to divorcing wives and shutting down monasteries, King

28. Woods, "What We Owe the Monks."

Henry may also have "unwittingly delayed the industrial revolution"[29] by two hundred years. Typically, sixteenth-century furnaces were loaded with charcoal and iron from the top. Air would be pumped in, either with a hand or foot bellows, to feed the fire and separate the iron from ore. The material was then heated further and pressed to remove the mineral impurities known as slag. The slag left behind by primitive furnaces typically contains significant residues of ore. These early furnaces didn't get hot enough to separate the iron from the ore fully. But the slag McDonnell found at Rievaulx had much smaller percentages of iron.

Further convinced that the monks had built a more efficient furnace, he went looking and discovered a fifteen-foot-wide brick oven, situated below ground, with traces of steam that would likely have been used to drive the furnace's bellows. The larger furnace and water-powered bellows would have been enough to generate much higher temperatures. McConnell believes that the monks at Rievaulx were on the verge of building dedicated furnaces for the large-scale production of cast iron (one of the things that eventually gave rise to the eighteenth century's industrial revolution) and that the furnace he found was a prototype of the furnaces that wouldn't arrive until two hundred years later.[30]

Another of the monastic movement's contributions to society was its attention to charity. In the Rule of St. Benedict, Benedict advised: "All guests who come shall be received as though they were Christ, because he will say 'I was a stranger and you took me in.'"[31] As a result, monasteries became gratuitous inns and hospitals, providing a safe and peaceful place for travelers, pilgrims, the poor, and those who needed healing.

In some cases, religious brothers and sisters would go out at night looking for people who were lost or in need of a bed for the night. The story is told of a sixteenth-century hospital situated in the French Alps that would ring a special bell every night to direct travelers towards the abbey. In the nearby town of Aubrac, the people dubbed it "the bell of wanderers."[32]

As a testament to their caring, a historian from the Norman Abbey of Bec in Normandy wrote:

> Let them ask the Spaniards or Burgundians, or any foreigners whatever, how they have been received at the Bec. They will

29. Discover, "Henry's Big Mistake."
30. Woods, "What We Owe the Monks."
31. Meisel and del Mastro, *The Rule of St. Benedict*, 89.
32. Woods, "What We Owe the Monks."

> answer that the door of the monastery is always open to all, and that its bread is free to the whole world.[33]

A cursory reading of this material might suggest that the monastic life was preserved for men. But there are also numerous examples of women serving in cloistered orders, not the least of which was Hildegard of Bingen, who became revered as an abbess, visionary, mystic, healer, and composer. Born in Böckelheim, Germany, Hildegard was educated at the Benedictine cloister near Disibodenberg. Having experienced visions as a child, at the age of forty-three, she began to record and explore these further. Her record of these visions, entitled Scivias, written between 1141 and 1152, consists of twenty-six visions that are both prophetic and apocalyptic in form, addressing such topics as the church, the relationship between God and humanity, and redemption. A talented poet and composer, seventy-seven of Hildegard's lyrical poems are recorded for us, each with musical settings composed by her. Her writings include one on the lives of the saints and two works on medicine and natural history.

Hildegard's renown made her one of the most celebrated women in Europe. But not only did she have celebrity status—she also knew how to use it. As we learned earlier, many European monarchs wanted to dominate the church by controlling the appointment of bishops, thereby gaining influence over the Catholic leadership, the laity, and, of course, gaining access to church lands and riches. Using her notoriety, Hildegard began to speak out against these vices. Addressing King Frederick as one of her main opponents, she wrote to him, saying:

> I see you like a little boy or madman. . . . Beware therefore, that the Almighty King does not lay you low because of the blindness of your eyes, which fail to see correctly how to hold the rod of proper governance in your hand. See to it that you do not act in such a way as to lose the grace of God.[34]

In contrast to our modern perceptions of monastic life, Hildegard was never afraid of controversy or criticism. She never failed to stand up to the ecclesiastical or secular authorities for what she believed to be right.[35]

33. Woods, "What We Owe the Monks."

34. Baird, *Correspondence of Hildegard*, 78.

35. Campbell, "Prophetess and Pope," 22–35.

The German sociologist Max Weber defined power as "the ability to control others, events, or resources; to make happen what one wants to happen despite obstacles, resistance, or opposition."[36]

On the other hand, the *Merriam-Webster Dictionary* defines piety as "1) the quality or state of being pious, such as a) fidelity to natural obligations (as to parents), or b) dutifulness in religion, 2) An act inspired by piety, 3) A conventional belief or standard (orthodoxy)."[37]

At first glance, these definitions might lead us to see power described in this chapter as inherently harmful and piety as inherently positive. Consider for a moment, though, a conversation between Socrates and a man named Euthyphro. The Athenians revered Socrates as a wise man. But there were also men in authority who claimed that he was corrupting the Athenian youth with his teaching and that he did not believe in the gods, so they put him on trial. On his way to the courthouse, Socrates meets Euthyphro, a priest who was respected by those who had put Socrates on trial. Euthyphro was at the courthouse to try his father for murder. Socrates finds the scenario interesting and realizes that if Euthyphro can explain why he is prosecuting his father for murder, he might learn something about piety. If he can, this would help Socrates to defend himself. Euthyphro offers three definitions of piety, none of which satisfies Socrates. So, Euthyphro offers a fourth definition, which essentially says that piety is the knowledge of "how to sacrifice and pray." To this, Socrates replies, "if your definition is true . . . then piety is a trading skill between men and the gods."[38]

Power. Piety. Despite our first impressions, neither one is inherently right or wrong. Both have their merits and their pitfalls. It has been said that absolute power corrupts absolutely.[39] But if piety is "nothing more than a trading skill between men and the gods," cannot the same thing we said about power also be said about piety?

The challenges faced by the church in Canada suggest there may yet be a shift of axis waiting for us—a dramatic shift in perception and perspective—one informed by power and piety. In his 2021 inaugural speech, President Joe Biden asked Americans, "Will we lead through the example of our power or through the power of our example?" Is that

36. Wallimann, Tatsis and Zito. "On Max Weber," 231–35.

37. *Merriam-Webster Dictionary*, "Piety."

38. Rosen, "Piety and Justice."

39. Attributed to the British politician, Lord Acton, in the nineteenth century.

power the kind described by Max Weber, or is it something else? Is the kind of piety we need to be fashioned after the medieval monastics, or is there a new kind of reverence and devotion required?[40]

Biden asked his question of the American people, but it is also a question befitting the Canadian church. To many Canadian Christians, the church feels broken. They grieve its present, and they fear its future. Somewhere in the balance between power and piety lies an answer that perhaps our following chapters can help to address.

"Every light has its shadow,
and every shadow hath a succeeding morning."[41]

—NICOLAUS COPERNICUS

40. Biden, "Inaugural Address."

41. Copernicus, "15 Copernicus Quotes."

4

Brave New World

The Church Invades Turtle Island

When Jesus Christ came upon the Earth, you killed Him. The son of your own God. And only after He was dead did you worship Him and start killing those who would not.[1]

—TECUMSEH

It has often been said that, "History is written by the victors." Contemporary writers often attribute this phrase to Winston Churchill, the wartime Prime Minister of Great Britain, when he announced Germany's unconditional surrender at the end of the Second World War in Europe.[2] But were these words original to him?

In the 2019 movie *The Report,* Adam Driver stars as Dan Jones, a staffer with the United States Senate Intelligence Committee. The plot focuses on the Committee's investigation of the Central Intelligence Agency's (CIA) use of torture following the September 11 terrorist attacks in

1. Tecumseh, "Tecumseh Quotes."
2. Thacker, "Headmaster's Notes."

the United States.[3] Fearful that the CIA is about to destroy all copies of a pivotal internal review, Jones secretly removes a copy for investigation but is later threatened with prosecution for "stealing" that copy of the report. Later in the movie, Jones argues with his prospective lawyer over who first declared that the victors write history. The lawyer (portrayed by Corey Stoll) credits Winston Churchill, while Jones suggests Hermann Göring, Churchill's enemy during World War II. So, who was it? "The victorious Churchill or the vanquished Göring?"[4]

As it turns out, "neither of them."[5] While Churchill is still strongly associated with the phrase, there appears to be no documented instance in which he actually uttered those words. The closest Churchill comes seems to be in a speech given to the British House of Commons on January 23, 1948, where he states: "For my part, I consider that it will be found much better by all parties to leave the past to history, especially as I propose to write that history myself."[6] For his part, Göring is quoted at the Nuremberg trials saying, *"Der Sieger wird immer der Richter und der Besiegte stets der Angeklagte sein,"* which translates more or less to, "The victor will always be the judge, and the vanquished the accused."[7]

The Age of Faith?

The Middle Ages have often been described as the "Age of Faith." Historians tell us that during this time, most people believed what the religious authorities told them to believe.[8] But whose story is this? Regardless of who uttered the words first, winners and losers throughout the ages agree: the story that ends up in history books usually belongs to the winners.

Online encyclopedias and history primers describe the church as the center of medieval life. They point out that every community had a church building, while larger towns and cities had a cathedral. Church bells rang out the hours calling people to worship, teaching salvation, and offering it to anyone who followed its doctrines. The church building

3. On September 11, 2001, a series of four coordinated terrorist attacks by Al-Qaeda against the United States killed 2,977, and injured more than 25,000.

4. Phelan, "History is Written by the Victors."

5. Phelan, "History is Written by the Victors."

6. Phelan, "History is Written by the Victors."

7. Phelan, "History is Written by the Victors."

8. Murray, "Piety and Impiety," 83.

was the center of community activity; religious services were held several times a day. Their places of worship were host to town meetings, plays, and concerts. Merchants set up shop outside the building, while farmers sold their produce in the square. The church provided education; it cared for the poor and the sick. As William Manchester writes in his 1993 book, *A World Lit Only by Fire*, "There was no room in the medieval mind for doubt; the possibility of skepticism did not exist."[9]

While there is little doubt that the Catholic Church dominated the social and political life of the Middle Ages (as the Reformation churches later did in areas in which they wielded influence), theirs is not the only story that needs to be told. Religious life in the Middle Ages was hardly a model of orthodoxy. Not everyone was as faithful or committed as our history primers might have led us to believe.

As Joshua Mark suggests, Christianity did not immediately "win the hearts and minds" of the European people.[10] The process of Christianization amongst Europe's rural and common folk, typically referred to as pagans,[11] was slow. In fact, medieval churches were not necessarily the full-to-overflowing places reported by some. Rodney Stark notes that while there are few statistics on religious attendance during medieval times, "There are a surprising number of trustworthy reports . . . that the great majority of ordinary people seldom if ever went to church."[12] Stark cites the Dominican Prior Humbert of Romans (c. 1200–1277), who admitted that people in Italy "rarely go to church."[13] Sometime around 1430, St. Antonio recorded that Tuscan peasants seldom went to mass and that "very many of them do not confess once a year, and far fewer are those who take communion."[14] And St. Bernardino of Siena (c. 1380–1444) also wrote that even the few parishioners who did come to mass were usually late, and hurried out at the elevation of the Host[15] "as though

9. Manchester, *A World Lit Only by Fire*, 20.

10. Mark, "Religion in the Middle Ages."

11. The word pagan is derived from the Latin, *paganus*, meaning "countryside, rural or rustic"—the implication being that they came from the countryside where the old beliefs were still being practiced.

12. Stark, *The Triumph of Christianity*, ebook, ch. 15, p. 4.

13. Manchester, *A World Lit Only by Fire*, 20.

14. Coulton, *Medieval Panorama*, 193.

15. The elevation of the Host refers to a ritual raising of the consecrated bread and wine during the celebration of the Eucharist during mass. The reference implies that people were leaving the service before taking part in the sacrament.

they had not seen Christ, but the Devil."[16] In fifteenth-century England, the anonymous author of *Dives and Pauper*[17] lamented that "people these days . . . are loathe to hear God's Service. [And when they are forced to attend] they come late and leave early."[18] Another report from Saxony in 1574 tells the same story: "You will find more of them out fishing than at the service. . . . Those who do come walk out as soon as the pastor begins his sermon."[19]

There is considerable evidence that while medieval Europeans may have accepted most basic Christian doctrines, especially in the larger towns and cities, long-standing pagan beliefs and practices continued to intermingle with those of the new religion. Practices such as fortune-telling, dowsing, making charms and talismans or spells to ward off danger or bad luck were commonplace, while incantations were offered during the planting of crops or weaving of cloth. These practices persisted alongside going to church, the veneration of the saints, Christian prayer, confession, and acts of penance and contrition. As Gerald Strauss puts it:

> They practiced their own brand of religion, which was a rich compound of ancient rituals, time-bound customs, a sort of unreconstructable folk Catholicism, and a large portion of magic to help them in their daily struggle.[20]

Building on Strauss's description, Stark adds:

> Notice that Strauss did not include a list of popular divinities, neither pagan nor Christian. Although the people's religion did often call upon God, Jesus, Mary, and various saints, as well as upon some pagan gods and goddesses (and even more frequently invoked minor spirits such as fairies, elves, and demons), it did so only to invoke their aid, having little interest in matters such as the meaning of life or the basis for salvation.[21]

What mattered to them was the simple foot-in-mud, wind-in-face matters of everyday life, such as health, fertility, sex, weather, and good

16. Coulton, *Medieva Panorama,* 188.

17. *Dives and Pauper,* was a prose dialogue from the early fifteenth century in which a rich man requests doctrinal instruction regarding the Ten Commandments from a peasant, possibly a friar.

18. Stark, *The Triumph of Christianity,* ebook, ch. 15, p. 5.

19. Strauss, "Success and Failure," 49.

20. Strauss, "The Reformation, 211.

21. Stark, *The Triumph of Christianity,* ebook, ch. 15, p. 42.

crops. If religion did not speak to these things, it did not speak to them much at all. These coexisting synergies and contradictions are perhaps best illustrated in the liturgies of the day. Believing that right practice reflected right belief, the parish priests went about their business, celebrating the mass and offering contrition. Standing at their altars set apart from the congregation, they would witness the transformation of "bread and wine into the body and blood of Christ, far removed from the congregation of onlookers. The priest recited the mass in Latin, his back to the people, and whatever went on at the front had little to do with the people observing it."[22]

A more dramatic contradiction centers on the church's use of baptismal fonts. More than the altar, the font was seen by commoners as the focal point of their church lives. This is where life began, whether it was the celebration of birth through infant baptism or spiritual rebirth through baptism as an adult. Joshua Mark suggests, however, that in some churches, the baptismal font was large and deep enough for those accused of witchcraft to be bound and thrown in. If the person floated to the top, they were guilty. If they sank, they were innocent. Unfortunately, the innocent had to enjoy their exoneration post-mortem since not resurfacing meant, of course, that they had drowned.[23]

How the medieval peasant felt about this is largely a mystery. There appears to be little record of any public outcry, and the ritual itself (like executions) appears to have been a form of public entertainment. In fact, how the medieval peasant felt about anything seems unclear. Most were illiterate, so anything we read about their beliefs and behavior was most likely written in town and church records by clerics and priests. This silence is especially poignant when we consider the experience of women who worked alongside men in the fields, owned businesses, and participated in guilds and monastic orders. In many cases, women did precisely the same work as men but were still considered inferior. As scholar Eileen Power observes, the peasants of a town "went to their churches on Sundays and listened while preachers told them in one breath that a woman was the gate of hell and that Mary was the Queen of Heaven."[24]

22. Mark, "Religion in the Middle Ages."

23. Mark, "Religion in the Middle Ages."

24. Power, *Medieval Women*, 11.

The Burning Times[25]

This bias was especially evident in the burning of women as witches between 1550 and 1700, ironically a period also known to us as the "Enlightenment." Surprising, perhaps, since many of these women were also responsible for providing one of the most popular drinks of the day—beer. Humans have been drinking beer for almost 7,000 years, and the original brewers were almost always women. As Laken Brooks from the University of Florida writes, "From the Vikings to the Egyptians, women brewed beer both for religious ceremonies and to make a practical calorie-rich beverage for the home."[26] In fact, the Catholic abbess Hildegard von Bingen, whom we noted earlier, famously wrote about hops in the twelfth century, describing it as an essential ingredient in her own unique beer recipe

In Europe, beer offered an inexpensive way to consume and preserve grains. For the working class, it provided an important source of nutrients, full of proteins and carbohydrates. With beer representing such a common part of the family diet, fermenting was, for many women, a typical household task. Some of the more entrepreneurial women took their skills to market and began selling beer. Widows and unmarried women would use their fermentation prowess to earn extra money, while married women would work with their husbands, sometimes producing quite lucrative businesses.

When these women went to market, typically, they would be seen wearing tall pointy hats and standing in front of cauldrons. But as Brooks explains, "These women were no witches, they were brewers."[27] The tall pointy hats were meant to help them stand out in the crowd. They carried their beer in cauldrons. And those successful enough to have their own stores had cats, not as demon "familiars," but to scare mice away from the grain.

And just as women were taking hold of the beer markets in England, Ireland, and the rest of Europe, the Inquisition began. This fundamentalist movement, which originated in the sixteenth century, preached, among many things, stricter gender norms and condemned witchcraft. Male brewers saw this as an opportunity. To reduce their competition, many started accusing female brewers of being witches and using their

25. Read, *The Burning Times.*

26. Brooks, "Women Used to Dominate the Beer Industry."

27. Brooks, "Women Used to Dominate the Beer Industry."

cauldrons to brew up magic potions instead of beer. Unfortunately, the rumors took hold. Over time, it became increasingly dangerous for women to brew and sell beer because they would be misidentified as witches. Wrongly accused of witchcraft, these women were often ostracized in their communities, imprisoned, and even killed.

Before continuing, we need to set one misconception straight. Many of the women accused of being witches during the Middle Ages were not falsely accused. These women were not singled out because of some unfounded hysteria.[28] As Rodney Stark acknowledges, these women *were* "doing something"[29] that led them to be charged. What they were doing was magic. What the clerics and religious leaders failed to acknowledge was this—so was the church.

Church magic was common during the Middle Ages. Throughout Europe, there were sacred wells, springs, and shrines where people would come seeking miracles and blessings. Weather crosses blessed by priests were planted in fields to protect against wind and hail, and church bells were rung to drive away thunderstorms.[30] Priests were known for having a wide repertoire of incantations, prayers, and rites at their disposal to pray for rain, address people's needs, and especially to heal their illnesses. There were even priests who specialized in exorcisms.

Alongside this elaborate system of church magic was an extensive culture of folk magic, which also focused on healing and matters pertaining to home and agriculture. This non-church magic was carried out by local practitioners, who were often referred to as *wicces* or *wise ones.*[31] These wise ones would often perform non-magical functions as well.

28. In 1957, Turner and Killian developed the emergent norm theory which helps to describe the collective behavior that led to the persecution of witches. See Turner and Killian, *Collective Behaviour.*

29. Stark, *The Triumph of Christianity,* ebook, ch. 19, p. 33.

30. Flint, *The Rise of Magic,* 189.

31. The word now used for "witch" in English has it roots in the Old English word *wicche,* which did not initially differentiate between feminine or masculine. Later this became, *wicce, (a female magician or sorceress),* and *wicca, (a male sorcerer, wizard or magician).* It was not until the sixteenth century that our modern word, "witch," with a "t," first appeared, now referring almost exclusively to women. The subtler meaning of these words, however, is not quite as clear. Often, they were used in association with words like *cunning* and *wise.* The word *cunning* comes from the Old English word, *conning,* meaning "learned, or possessing knowledge." "Wise" comes from the Old English *wis,* meaning "learned, sagacious, cunning; sane; prudent; discreet; experienced; having the power of discerning and judging rightly." See https://www.etymonline.com/search?q=witch.

Such was the case for midwives, who combined their practical skills and knowledge of magical spells to deliver babies.

The problem, as Stark suggests, was that "all magic works sometimes."[32] This meant that some of the sick who would go to their priests for healing, recovered. But so did some who turned to their local *wicces*. For the church, this prompted a serious theological concern: if church-magic works because of God's power, why did non-church magic work as well? Where did that power come from? Those in the church concluded that there could be only one answer. If their power did not come from God, it must be from Satan. Therefore, anyone who practiced non-church magic must have entered into a pact with the devil.

For centuries, women in many cultures have found themselves at this kind of social disadvantage due mainly to patriarchal and misogynistic views on menstruation. These views have portrayed women's periods as everything from unclean and embarrassing to evil. In Jewish law, women were considered ritually "unclean" during what was known as their *niddah* and were prohibited from having sexual intercourse during menstruation. During this time, ancient (and modern Orthodox) Jewish women had to be physically separated from others so as not to contaminate men with their touch. Even the objects they touched during this time had to be blessed by a rabbi before being used again.[33]

Pliny the Elder, a first-century Roman philosopher, suggested that menstruating women could stop hailstorms, calm winds, and prevent lightning—not to mention, kill bees, dim mirrors, and blunt weapons. He also thought that menstrual blood drove dogs mad. Medieval Europeans believed the ashes of burnt toads would lessen menstrual flow, that period-sex led to "monsters" being born, and that menstrual blood could cure leprosy.[34]

From this chauvinistic and discriminatory milieu in the fifteenth century, an infamous witch-hunting manual known as the *Malleus Maleficarum* (The Hammer of the Witches) emerged. This document suggests that women's lack of intelligence made them more susceptible to demons, in addition to all of their other perceived shortcomings.[35] One section reads:

32. Stark, *The Triumph of Christianity*, ebook, ch. 19, p. 32.

33. Stein and Kim, *Flow*.

34. Delaney, Lupton and Toth, *The Curse*.

35. Broedel, "The Malleus Maleficarum."

> Just as through the first defect in their [women's] intelligence, they are more prone to abjure their faith; so through their second defect of inordinate passions . . . they inflict various vengeances through witchcraft. Wherefore it is no wonder that so great a number of witches exist in this sex.[36]

In the town of Ellwangen, in southwest Germany, more than 400 people, most of them women, were accused of witchcraft and killed between 1611 and 1618. In Bamberg, the number killed between 1624 and 1631 was 300. In France, nuns were accused of being possessed by Satan and appearing in the form of priests. Perhaps the best known of these incidents involves the Ursuline monastery in Loudun, France, in 1636, which became the subject of Aldous Huxley's twentieth-century book, *The Devils of Loudun.*[37]

In 1603, Scotland and England's kingdoms united under James VI of Scotland (James I of England). James was widely known for a particular fascination with the occult. Shortly after assuming the throne of England, he released *Daemonlogie,*[38] which explored the subjects of witchcraft and non-church magic. He was so obsessed with the "dark arts" that he even succeeded in convincing Parliament to pass legislation ruling witchcraft to be a crime punishable by death.

The popularity of James's book heightened public anxiety to such a degree that towns and villages began seeking the services of professional "witchfinders," who would travel from place to place, identifying witches for their neighbors to burn.[39]

One such "witch-hunter" was Matthew Hopkins.[40] While historians know little of Hopkin's early years, he emerged onto the scene in 1644 after over-hearing several women discussing their "meetings with the devil." Of the twenty-three women he accused of witchcraft, four were said to have died in prison, while nineteen were later convicted and hanged. Spurned on by his apparent success in defense of the church, in 1645, Hopkins took up the title of Witch-Finder General, claiming to have been officially commissioned by Parliament to persecute witches. Together,

36. Farrell, "Medieval Witch Image."
37. Huxley, *The Devils of Loudun.*
38. James I, *Daemonlogie.*
39. Levack, *The Witch Hunt*, 59.
40. Deacon, *Matthew Hopkins*, 186.

with his group of "lady-prickers," they would travel the towns and villages of eastern England, trying and examining women for witchcraft.

The witch-hunters, or "lady-prickers," played a vital role in weeding out witches from the community. The procedure was rooted in the belief that every witch's body had a "witch's mark." This mark was identifiable because the witch would not feel any pain or bleed when that spot on her body was pricked. To try them, these "lady prickers" would strip the accused women of their clothes, locate their witch's mark and prick them to obtain evidence to be used in the trials.[41] A decent living was to be made by unmasking witches. So, Hopkins, and others, developed intricate means of extending their efforts, designing knives with retractable or blunt blades to ensure the "witches" would not bleed when "tested."[42]

However, Hopkins's favorite confessional method was the infamous "swimming test," a version of the church's "ordeal by water" described earlier in this chapter. This simple but effective test involved tying the accused's arms and legs to a chair before throwing them into the village pond. If the person sank and drowned, they would be innocent and received into heaven. If they floated, they would be tried as a witch. Between 1644 and 1646, Hopkins and his associates, using these methods, are believed to have been responsible for the deaths of 300 women. Between 1550 and 1700, historians estimate that as many as 80,000 people were tried for witchcraft. About half of them are believed to have been killed, with most of them being burned alive. And while this number includes some men, the vast majority were women.

In 2018, Peter Leeson and Jacob Russ from George Mason University published a unique and compelling argument as to why this phenomenon occurred when it did—and to the extent it did. In "Witch Trials," they suggest that these medieval trials reflected an economic principle known as "non-price competition" between the Catholic and Protestant churches vying for their share of the member market.[43]

In 1517, the Reformation split the church in two. The Catholic Church found it no longer had control of the entire market, while the Reformers were looking to build confidence in their "confessional" brand. Each tradition looked to strengthen its influence on believers, and the

41. Pihlajamaki, "Swimming the Witch," 355–58.

42. Deacon, *Matthew Hopkins*, 190.

43. Leeson and Russ, "Witch Trials," 2067.

witch trials became the arena of choice.[44] The more witches they exposed, the holier they would appear. And the holier they appeared, the greater the likelihood of attracting followers to their side.

Accordingly, the data shows that the witch-hunts began to accelerate after the Reformation and following the spread of Protestantism. Leeson and Russ argue that, for the first time since the early days of Christianity, the Reformation offered large numbers of Christians a religious choice: stay with the old church or switch to the new. "And when churchgoers have a religious choice," they write, "churches must compete."[45] Their analysis suggests that the "witch-craze" was most intense between 1555 and 1650 when the Catholic-Protestant rivalry was at its peak. It was during this time that the opposing traditions experienced "peak competition for Christian consumers." We see evidence of this in the Catholic counter-reformation (c. 1545–1648). During this time, Catholic leaders pushed back against the successes that Protestants were experiencing in converting Catholics to new ways of worship throughout much of Europe.[46]

Leeson and Russ explain that the two traditions would target key regional battlegrounds during this period, in much the same way as the Democratic and Republican parties in the United States focused their attention during the 2020 Presidential election. This theory explains why nearly 40 percent of all European convictions for witchcraft occurred in Germany—the Reformation's birthplace. In Scotland, where different branches of the Protestant Church were in competition, they witnessed the second-highest number of witch trials with 3,563 people tried. In contrast, Spain, Italy, and Ireland—which remained Catholic strongholds—collectively represented only 6 percent of the European witch trials.

By around 1650, the number of trials had begun to decline, and by 1700 they had all but disappeared in Europe. Leeson and Russ attribute this to a series of treaties in 1648, which brought peace to Europe's Holy Roman Empire, and closed a catastrophic period in European history where religious wars killed approximately 8 million people.

"Unfortunately," Leeson and Russ conclude, "the use of terror to impress a message upon a population has not abated. The phenomenon we document—using public trials to advertise superior power along some

44. Leeson and Russ, "Witch Trials," 2070.

45. Doward, "Europe's Wars of Religion."

46. Leeson and Russ, "Witch Trials," 2072–75.

dimension as a competitive strategy—is much broader than the prosecution of witches in early modern Europe."[47]

Brave but Not-So-New

Around the time that the church in Europe was rehearsing this well-worn tale, European monarchs had set their sights on the "new world" with a remarkably similar story. A policy known as the "Doctrine of Discovery"[48] provided a framework for Christian explorers to claim uninhabited territories in their monarch's name. Endorsed by a series of Papal Bulls in the fifteenth century, this framework included a concept known as *Terra Nullius,* a Latin expression meaning "land belonging to nobody."[49]

But as we now know, the territories that these explorers set out to discover were not so empty. Nor were they new. In fact, when Columbus arrived in the Americas in 1492, it is estimated that as many as 100 million Indigenous people were living here—roughly one-fifth of the world's population at the time. Hardly *Terra Nullius!* And yet, we can quickly see how this understanding would spark centuries of Indigenous oppression. As Allen Jorgenson, associate dean at Waterloo's Martin Luther College University writes:

> Behind the Doctrine of Discovery, and its nefarious implementation was the presumption that the peoples indigenous to the Americas were spiritually, intellectually and culturally inferior. At its best, colonialism was a parochial effort to form native children into good citizens of empire; at its worst it was a demonic design intended to enslave or slaughter sub-humans in expanding the insatiable reach of empire.[50]

Witness King Henry VII of England's commission of John Cabot on March 5, 1496. Cabot and his three sons were authorized to set out for "all parts of the eastern, western and northern sea . . . to find, discover and investigate whatsoever islands, countries, regions or provinces of heathens and infidels, in whatsoever part of the world placed, which before this time were unknown to all Christians."[51]

47. Leeson and Russ, "Witch Trials," 2094.
48. Assembly of First Nations, "Dismantling the Doctrine of Discovery."
49. Indigenous Corporate Training, "Christopher Columbus."
50. Jorgenson, "Embodying Truth."
51. Jones and Condon, "Cabot and Bristol's Age of Discovery," 29.

Terra Nullius provided the authority. But it was money that provided the motivation. As Cabot described it, his primary goal was to reach China and Japan by sailing west across the Atlantic. Like Columbus, with whom he is believed to have sailed on the historic 1492 voyage, Cabot knew that the Orient had a vast supply of goods that Europeans wanted, like silk and spices. The problem was that these items were extremely expensive. Vast distances between source and market sometimes meant these items would take more than a year to arrive. Import merchants had the cost of transporting the goods as well as any duties levied by countries they had to pass through. And then, of course, there was the profit they needed to make. The result was that some items could cost as much as ten times what they cost in the Orient. So, if a European merchant could avoid all of that by sailing to those countries directly, he could buy the items at source, ship them home at low cost, and make a sizeable profit.[52]

For his part, the king would receive one-fifth of all the profits. Jones and Condon explain that the grant gave Cabot the sole right to "exploit his product" as with any modern patent.[53] This arrangement meant that English subjects could only sail to Cabot's "discovered" lands with his permission. But the grant provided more than this. Since Cabot's ships would be sailing under the king's colors,[54] foreign powers would know that Cabot was under the king's protection and to expect retaliation if they interfered. So, while Henry VII did not pay for Cabot's expedition, the legal and political guarantees afforded Cabot were significant.

During the 1960s, Alwyn Ruddock, an historian and lecturer at the University of London, uncovered documents that cast new light on how the voyages came about and the church's role in the venture. While the king's grant was issued to the explorer, these grants could be assigned to others, in whole or in part. This arrangement resembles the way modern venture capitalists buy shares in an enterprise from an entrepreneur who has a patent. Cabot would sell part of his rights to the profits in exchange for the money needed to launch his expeditions.

52. Jones and Condon, "Cabot and Bristol's Age of Discovery," 35.

53. Jones and Condon, "Cabot and Bristol's Age of Discovery," 29.

54. "Sailing under the king's colour's" refers to the flying of flags and banners that would identify their ship to others as serving under a particular monarch. Typically, when ships returned from battle or an expedition, they would return with their flags at full mast to indicate victory or a successful journey. If they had suffered defeat, or been unsuccessful on their journey, they would return with their flags lowered to half mast. Hence the phrase, "passed with flying colours."

Along with the investment of Bristol merchants, Ruddock found that a significant portion of Cabot's funding came from Italian banks based in London. She also suggested that one of his primary brokers was an Augustinian friar from Milan named Giovanni Antonio de Carbonariis. According to Jones and Condon, this was "no ordinary friar."[55] Carbonariis was responsible for collecting the pope's taxes in England, and his involvement provides a likely explanation as to how Cabot was able to gain access to the king and secure his approval. In addition to his financial and political support, Ruddock's research suggests Carbonariis may also have sailed on Cabot's third expedition in 1498.[56]

While Columbus had sailed south to the Canary Islands before heading to the Caribbean, Cabot headed north of Ireland before going west, making landfall on June 24th. The exact location remains a subject of considerable debate for historians. Still, Cabot's *New Founde Land* is believed to have been somewhere in what is now southern Labrador, northwestern Newfoundland, or possibly Cape Breton Island.

Few records of the journey remain. Our best accounts are found in a letter written by a London merchant named John Day, under the alias of Hugh Day. Day's letter, written in the winter of 1497–98, was discovered in Spanish archives in the mid-1950s and is believed possibly to have been written to Christopher Columbus. Having accompanied Cabot on the expedition, Day tells of going ashore but never venturing "more than a crossbow's shot" onto the land. He reports seeing two running figures in the woods that might have been human or animal. Their investigations uncovered an unstrung bow, a snare used for capturing game, and a needle for making nets. The only other record of note was that Cabot had found an enormous source of fish. In December of 1497, following Cabot's return, the Milanese ambassador to England heard Cabot describe the sea as "swimming with fish, which can not only be taken with the net, but in baskets let down with stone."[57]

When Cabot arrived in what is now Canada, he wasn't the first person to set foot here—millions of Indigenous people had lived here for centuries. Nor was he the first European to arrive on the continent—the Vikings at L'Anse aux Meadows had been the first to accomplish that. Yet, when Cabot's ship, the *Matthew*, landed on Canada's east coast, he set

55. Jones and Condon, "Cabot and Bristol's Age of Discovery," 33.

56. Jones and Condon, "Cabot and Bristol's Age of Discovery," 33.

57. Roberts, *Unnatural History*, 33.

in motion what would soon become another complex relationship between church and people in a brave but, not-so-new world. The lands he had discovered were not, as he would later boast, the home of the "Great Khan" of China,[58] but rather that of the Beothuk and Innu.

The Kingdom of Saguenay

Thirty-seven years after Cabot's voyage, the French explorer Jacques Cartier continued Europe's western migration. Departing Saint-Malo on April 20, 1534, with two ships and sixty-one men, Cartier reached the coast of Newfoundland twenty days later. On the 26th of June, they reached the Magdalen Islands, and three days later arrived at what are now the provinces of Prince Edward Island and New Brunswick. Cartier sailed from there to Chaleur Bay, where, on July 7, he recorded an encounter with a group of Mi'kmaq:

> Some of these savages came in nine canoes to the point at the mouth of the cove, were we lay anchored with our ships. And being informed of their arrival we went out with two longboats to the point where they were at the mouth of the cove. As soon as they saw us they began to run away, making signs to us that they had come to barter with us, and held up some skins of small value, with which they clothe themselves. We likewise, made signs to them that we wished them no harm, and sent two men on shore, to offer them some knives and other iron goods, and a red cap to give to their chief.[59]

Cartier's account of the exchange represents the first historical record of trade between the French and North America's Indigenous peoples. It was also Cartier who appears to have first used the Huron-Iroquois word *Kanata,* meaning village or settlement, to refer more generally to the territory he had "discovered."

After this, Cartier's records describe going ashore to erect a thirty-foot cross, claiming the land for France's king:

> On [Friday] the twenty-fourth of the said month [July], we had a cross made thirty feet high, which was put together in the presence of a number of savages on the point at the entrance to this harbour, under the crossbar of which we fixed a shield

58. Jones and Condon, "Cabot and Bristol's Age of Discovery," 36.

59. Cook, *The Voyages of Jacques Cartier,* 21.

> with three fleurs-de-lys in relief, and above it a wooden board, engraved in large Gothic characters, where was written, long live the King of France. . . . When we had returned to our ships, the captain, dressed in an old black bear-skin, arrived in a canoe with three of his sons and his brother, but they did not come so close to the ships as they had usually done. And pointing to the cross he made us a long harangue, making the sign of the cross with two of his fingers, and then he pointed to the land all around about, as if he wished to say that all this region belonged to him, and that we ought not to have set up this cross without his permission.[60]

The people Cartier encountered were Iroquois from the village of Stadacona, near present-day Quebec City. Led by their chief, Donnacona, they had come with a group of about 200 people to fish and hunt. As the ship's records describe, Donnacona objected to the cross they had erected. Cartier responded to this protest by seizing Donnacona, but later appealed to the chief by offering gifts from the "old world." Returning to France, Cartier arrived with two "trophies": Doagama and Taignoagny, the sons of Donnacona, whom he had persuaded to come with him. While the record uses the word "persuaded," it is unclear whether "being persuaded" meant going willingly or under duress. Again, "victors vs. losers!"

In 1535, Cartier returned to North America with Donnacona's sons, three ships, and about 110 people. Traveling through the Gulf of St. Lawrence and into the St. Lawrence River, one of Donnacona's sons guided them up what he knew as *Kaniatarowanenneh,* to the village of Stadacona. Hoping to explore the surrounding region, the French decided to spend the winter there. However, against the advice of Donnacona, Cartier agreed to sail upstream towards Hochelaga, now the city of Montreal, where he arrived on October 2, 1535. Nearly 2,000 Indigenous people were living there at the time. A mountain overlooked the island and village that he named Mont-Royal. Deterred from traveling further by the rapids situated north and south of the island village, Cartier returned to harbor on the Saint-Charles River near Stadacona. Feeling betrayed by Cartier's journey to Hochelaga, Donnacona broke off relations with Cartier, leaving the French to endure the winter themselves. From mid-November on, the ships were ice-locked, and in December, the French found themselves suffering from scurvy. Cartier's journal records that of the 100 French that were afflicted, twenty-five died. On May 3, Cartier

60. Cook, *The Voyages of Jacques Cartier,* 80.

planted a cross where they had wintered, and on the same day, abducted ten Iroquois men, with Donnacona and his sons, Doagama and Taignoagny among them.[61]

By the Rivers of Babylon

What occurred on the banks of *Kaniatarowanenneh* that day would set in motion some of the most consequential events in the history of "[the Iroquois] nation, a second nation from another world, and a third nation that did not exist."[62] Like the Israelites who, following their expulsion from God's promised land, sat by the rivers of Babylon "and wept," so that moment would initiate a relationship between the church and Canada's First Nations that, to this day, is fraught with tears.

Colonialism is often described as the policy or practice of acquiring full or partial political control over another country or nation, occupying it with settlers, and exploiting it economically. During the late Middle Ages, European countries strove to conquer the Americas, Africa, and much of Asia. In the beginning, their goal was to gain access to resources, including gold, silver, furs, fish, and spices, that would support the feudal societies that existed throughout much of Europe at the time.

At the heart of this expansion was a view of capitalism that appeared to focus on the acquisition of goods and services with little regard for the human cost. Two main types of colonialism grew out of Europe's hunger for profit: one based on the exploitation of labor; and another on the displacement of Indigenous people by settlers. In places like India, the Caribbean, and South Africa, a small number of Europeans assumed authority over much larger Indigenous populations. In order to make their profits, the colonizers took advantage of the labor that the conquered people could provide. The colonizers' goal was to take the wealth produced by the miners, farmers, and later, factory workers. A prime example of this occurred during the 1800s in India, where Indigenous farmers were forced to grow cotton, which was later shipped to Britain to be processed in factories and sold to generate excessive profits.[63]

61. Cook, *The Voyages of Jacques Cartier*, 28.

62. A prose depiction of the encounters between Donnacona and Cartier. Tindall, "Donnacona."

63. Woroniak and Camfield. "Choosing Not to Look Away."

Colonialism in Canada was different. Here, and in places like the United States and Australia, it took the form of "settler" colonialism. Europeans settled permanently on Indigenous land, systematically displacing its inhabitants until the latter were outnumbered. Unlike the "worker" colonialism experienced elsewhere, the primary goal of settler colonialism was to separate the people from their land, bury the culture rooted in their relationship with the land, and eventually eliminate the land's Indigenous societies so that the settlers could live there themselves.

Christianity and colonialism are often closely associated, not so much because they were part of the same medieval milieu, but because one would often use the other, at least in part, as a means to achieve its own ends. In his 2019 article, "Christian Missions and Colonial Empires Reconsidered," Edward Andrews, writes that Christian missionaries were initially portrayed as "visible saints, exemplars of ideal piety in a sea of persistent savagery."[64] What if we also suppose that Leeson and Russ's theory of "non-price competition" is as true for Turtle Island[65] as it was for medieval Europe during the witch hunts? Wouldn't this mean that the church's participation in the colonization of North American also represents an attempt by Catholics and Protestants to gain their respective share of an expanding market?

The irony is striking! When Israel found itself in the wilderness, they built a tabernacle to carry God's presence with them because God no longer had any home. When they reached Canaan, the promised land, they built a temple because God had come home. Yet, when Israel's descendants arrived in this "new land," they displaced its people—for whom the land was sacred—so they could use it for themselves. In Canada, Indigenous people lamented colonialism's disrespect for life and the relationships between living things and the natural world. Under colonialism, the land was not treated as something that "humans should live in a respectful relationship with,"[66] but simply as a resource to exploit. Colonial capitalism would not have survived without access to Indigenous lands. For Canada's First Nations, this remains as true today as it did in the sixteenth and seventeenth centuries.

64. Andrews, "Christian Missions," 1.

65. Turtle Island is the name many Algonquian- and Iroquoian-speaking people in the northeastern part of North America use to refer to the continent.

66. Woroniak and Camfield. "Choosing Not to Look Away."

The award-winning Cherokee writer Thomas King[67] reminds us that any conversation about colonialism and Canada's First Nations begins with the land. In his 2012 book *the Inconvenient Indian,* King writes: "Land. If you understand nothing else about the history of Indians in North America, you need to understand that the question that really matters is the question of land."[68]

The people of Canada's First Nations have lived on this land for nearly 12,000 years. Maybe longer.[69] Before European contact, First Nations communities[70] were healthy, self-sustaining societies with highly developed social, political, and economic systems. As in Europe, no one culture defined the people of this continent. While each of them shared many things in common, they also demonstrated wide variations in social organization, food resources, housing, tools, modes of transportation, and language—as well as spiritual beliefs.

Often their social structures were informed by the land they occupied. For example, the Woodland nations who inhabited eastern Canada's dense forests tended to be hunters and trappers, who relied on an intimate knowledge of animals' habitats and seasonal migration. In contrast, the Iroquois First Nations, who occupied the Great Lakes and St. Lawrence River region, tended not to migrate much. They learned to take advantage of the fertile soil in what is now southern Ontario and Quebec to plant crops of corn, beans, and squash. This allowed them to form permanent communities, which were often much larger in size than the hunting and gathering nations. Their sedentary lifestyle also gave rise to highly structured political systems. The Huron-Wendat, for example, developed a three-tiered system consisting of village councils, tribal councils, and a council of the confederacy.

The Pacific Coast Nations, who relied primarily on fishing for food and economic strength, were also known for a highly developed aristocracy that was regarded as superior by birth. The basic social unit for nations in this part of the country was based on extended family groups, whose members drew their lineage from a common ancestor. Most of these families had their own emblems featuring animals or supernatural beings that were believed to be their founders. The most famous method

67. Thomas King was the 2014 winner of the RBC Taylor Prize in Non-Fiction for Canadian literary excellence.

68. Quoted in Epp, "Land is the Hearth of the Matter."

69. Findlay and Sajecki, "Canada's First Peoples."

70. Canada, "First Nations in Canada."

of displaying these symbols was on a totem pole consisting of all the ancestral symbols belonging to a particular lineage.

Historically, each of these cultures had its own religious and spiritual customs and practices. Despite differences, the vast majority shared a belief system based on animism, a faith in the spiritual dimensions that intertwine with the physical world. Central to their teachings was a belief that people should live in harmony with the natural world and everything in it. The oral traditions that they passed from generation to generation would outline for their children how the world came into being and their place in it. They were urged to give thanks for everything in nature since their own survival, and the survival of their people, depended on it.

The arrival of explorers like Cartier and Cabot, and the world they brought with them, changed all of that. It was not long before a network of competing colonies, sponsored by European colonial authorities, pushed to expand their own influence on the North American continent. While many European countries, including the Spanish, Dutch, and Portuguese, were involved, the British and French quickly became the dominant powers. Soon after the founding of these colonies, the two European powers cemented their alliances with the First Nations to support their commercial interests, fueled mainly by the fur trade. The English aligned with the Haudenosaunee (Iroquois confederacy) and the First Nations of the Allegheny Mountains. The French aligned with the First Nations of the St. Lawrence, which included the Huron, Algonquin, Odawa, and Montagnais, and in Acadia with the Mi'kmaq, Maliseet, and Passamaquoddy. While the First Nations quickly adapted to this new commerce, which brought them European goods such as iron and firearms, the degree of profit experienced soon caused the competing groups to clash, often violently.

In the early 1700s, this tumultuous period appeared to come to an end in Montreal with a treaty signed between France and forty First Nations known as the "Great Peace." Prior to this treaty, Haudenosaunee leaders had also agreed with the British to sell their lands around the Great Lakes in exchange for British protection and the continued right to hunt and fish in perpetuity. The understanding was that in these agreements, the various peoples inhabiting the continent would share the lands as "one dish with two spoons."[71]

71. Government of Canada, "First Nations in Canada."

One Dish, One Spoon

It would take almost three hundred years for Canada and its government to admit that our country has not lived as "one dish with two spoons." If anything, it would be more accurate to say that Canadians, along with our colonial predecessors, have only lived as "one dish with one spoon"—all the while holding the other spoon behind our backs.

The writing was already on the wall in 1867 when the British North American colonies of Canada,[72] Nova Scotia, and New Brunswick united to form the Dominion of Canada. With confederation, voters' rights were granted only to British male subjects over the age of twenty-one who held property. Women, of course, were notable by their exclusion. It was not until 1918 that Canadian women gained the right to vote.[73] Aboriginal men, however, did gain the right to vote, but with one, not-so-small, condition.

Through a process called "enfranchisement," First Nation's men could vote as long as they surrendered their treaty status. This "status" represented the legal recognition of a person's First Nation heritage. With it came a certain number of rights, including the right to live on Indigenous reserves. For Indigenous people, "having their say" in any real way meant giving up their identity. This "enfranchisement" also applied to a much larger group of Indigenous men and women who automatically lost their native status for one of several reasons. These included losing status for completing university or, for women, marriage to a non-status man. Indigenous men who served during the Second World War were given the right to vote without losing their status, but only if they agreed to move off native reserves.[74]

It was not until 1960, under the Conservative government of Prime Minister Diefenbaker, that Canada's Indigenous people gained the right to vote without restriction. The Parliamentary Hansard for January 19, 1960, records Diefenbaker's words as follows:

> The provision to give Indians the vote, is one of those steps which will have an effect everywhere in the world—for the reason that wherever I went last year on the occasion of my trip to

72. At the time of Confederation, what had formerly been known as the Province of Canada was divided into the Provinces of Ontario and Quebec, so that the new Dominion was made up of four provinces.

73. Sangster, *100 Years of Struggle.*

74. Canada, "First Nations in Canada."

> Commonwealth countries, it was brought to my attention that in Canada the original people within our country, excepting for a qualified class, were denied the right to vote. I say that so far as this long overdue measure is concerned, it will remove everywhere in the world any suggestion that color or race places any citizen in our country in a lower category than the other citizens of our country.
>
> I say this to those of the Indian race that in bringing forward this legislation the Minister of Citizenship and Immigration (Mrs. Fairclough) will reassure, as she has assured to date, that existing rights and treaties, traditional or otherwise, possessed by the Indians shall not in any way be abrogated or diminished in consequence of having the right to vote. That is one of the things that throughout the years has caused suspicion in the minds of many Indians who have conceived the granting of the franchise as a step in the direction of denying them their ancient rights.[75]

While this represented a significant step forward in Canada's relations with its First Nations, it would still be another thirty-eight years before Canada's government would apologize for its oppression of Canada's Indigenous peoples. On January 7, 1998, in an address to members of the Royal Commission on Aboriginal People, along with Elders and Chiefs of Canada's First Nations, Minister of Indian Affairs and Northern Development Jane Stewart offered the following:

> Sadly, our history with respect to the treatment of Aboriginal people is not something in which we can take pride. Attitudes of racial and cultural superiority led to a suppression of Aboriginal culture and values. As a country, we are burdened by past actions that resulted in weakening the identity of Aboriginal peoples, suppressing their languages and cultures, and outlawing spiritual practices. We must recognize the impact of these actions on the once self-sustaining nations that were disaggregated, disrupted, limited or even destroyed by the dispossession of traditional territory, by the relocation of Aboriginal people, and by some provisions of the Indian Act. We must acknowledge that the result of these actions was the erosion of the political, economic and social systems of Aboriginal people and nations.
>
> One aspect of our relationship with Aboriginal people over this period that requires particular attention is the Residential School system. This system separated many children from their

75. Diefenbaker Centre, "Enfranchisement of the Aboriginal Peoples."

> families and communities and prevented them from speaking their own languages and from learning about their heritage and cultures. In the worst cases, it left legacies of personal pain and distress that continue to reverberate in Aboriginal communities to this day. Tragically, some children were the victims of physical and sexual abuse.
>
> The Government of Canada acknowledges the role it played in the development and administration of these schools . . . and to those of you who suffered this tragedy at residential schools, we are deeply sorry.[76]

Later, in 2015, Canada's Truth and Reconciliation Commission echoed these words:

> For over a century, the central goals of Canada's Aboriginal policy were to eliminate Aboriginal governments, ignore Aboriginal rights; terminate the Treaties; and, through a process of assimilation, cause Aboriginal peoples to cease to exist as distinct legal, social, cultural, religious entities in Canada.[77]

And all of it beginning with a cross and an abduction of the banks of the *Kaniatarowanenneh*. The place could just have easily been the River Thames, the Seine, the Euphrates, the Nile, or any one of a number of rivers that have, at one time or another, fallen under the authority of a western monarch. The story was still the same; rulers conquering others in the name of their gods. Lands were seized, entire nations were displaced, and the movement of people was restricted. Languages were banned. Spiritual leaders were persecuted, rituals were forbidden, and objects of spiritual value were confiscated or destroyed. "In its dealing with Aboriginal people," the report concludes, "Canada did all these things."[78] Canada and its people participated in cultural genocide.

Donnacona "Discovers" Europe

Upon their arrival in France, the monk and historian André Thevet claimed to have had a long conversation with the chief.[79] Later, Donnacona was brought before the king, François I. Whether he considered

76. Stewart, "Statement of Reconciliation."
77. Truth and Reconciliation Commission, *Honouring the Truth*, 1.
78. Truth and Reconciliation Commission, *Honouring the Truth*, 1.
79. Thevet and Dorat, *Les singularitez de la France antarctique*, 407.

it a matter of diplomacy or self-preservation, Donnacona shared with him stories of Saguenay's mines, rich with gold and silver, and stores full of cloves, nutmeg, and pepper. On March 25, 1539, Thevet records that three of the Iroquois men that Cartier had brought back with him were baptized, though he does not identify them. While Donnacona appears to have been treated well in France at the king's expense, he never returned to Stadacona. Despite Cartier's promise to return him after "twelve moons," the Iroquois chief died before Cartier could mount his third voyage. In fact, French accounts suggest that all but one of the Iroquoians whom Cartier brought back to France died—a little girl whose name and story remain unknown.[80]

In October of 1540, François I ordered Cartier to return to Canada. He was to serve as chief navigator to Jean-François de La Rocque de Roberval, a Huguenot courtier and friend of the king, who would later be named the first lieutenant governor of French Canada. The goal of discovering a route to the Orient had been abandoned. The goal now was to find the riches of Saguenay and establish a permanent settlement on the St. Lawrence River.

Few records exist from Cartier's return and the winter of 1541–42. But from the accounts of returning sailors, it is clear that Cartier was not well received. Having failed to return Donnacona, Cartier had established himself as *persona non grata*. The result was that early in 1542, the Iroquois attacked Cartier's settlement, killing about thirty-five of the settlers. Convinced that he no longer had the resources to protect his base or go in further search of Saguenay, Cartier returned to France. Spending the remainder of his life in Saint-Melo, Cartier died on September 1, 1557, the victim of an epidemic. Ironically, the "treasures" of diamond and gold that Cartier believed he had returned from North America with turned out to be nothing more than quartz and pyrite.[81] To this day, Cartier's mistake remains a part of French folklore with the saying, "*Faux comme un diamant du Canada*" which means "as fake as a Canadian diamond."[82]

Albert Einstein once wrote, "You cannot use an old map to explore a new world."[83] The story of Canada's earliest explorers and its earliest peoples serves as a striking illustration of this truth. In a tale as dystopian

80. Trudel, "Donnacona."

81. Burrage, *Early English and French Voyages*, 911–12.

82. Blackwell, "No Longer Fake"; Pelletier, "Faux comme diamants du Canada."

83. Einstein, "Inspiriting Quotes."

as Aldous Huxley's *Brave New World*, Cartier's planting of a cross at the mouth of the St. Charles River and same-day abduction of ten Iroquoians in the name of the French monarch highlights for us the juxtaposition of faith and oppression that had long existed in Europe and indeed throughout the "Old World." While the geography may have been new to Cartier and his crew, they still found themselves in ancient territory.

Suffer the Little Children

When I started writing this section, a line from a hymn I had remembered from my childhood kept playing inside my head:

> When mothers of Salem
> Their children brought to Jesus,
> The stern disciples drove them back
> And bade them to depart;
> But Jesus saw them ere they fled,
> and sweetly smiled and kindly said,
> "Suffer little children
> To come unto Me."[84]

The verse recalls the Gospel passage[85] where Jesus' disciples are frustrated that some adults have brought their children with them. The children are distracting them and getting in the way of what the disciples believe are more important spiritual matters. Jesus responds angrily towards them, essentially saying to the disciples: "Why are you stopping them? Let them come. If the kingdom of heaven belongs to anyone, it belongs to them." Somewhere in all of this, it seems that the church got it wrong—at least where Canada's Indigenous children are concerned.

In Canada, the term "Indigenous" includes First Nations, Inuit, and Métis people. Schools for Indigenous children had existed in the French and British colonies for more than 300 years. Starting in New France, Catholic missionaries had instituted the first boarding schools for Indigenous children as early as the seventeenth century. A royal decree dictated that authorities carry out a policy of "Frenchification" that was intended to

84. The hymn "When Mothers of Salem" was written by William Medlen Hutchings for an anniversary service of St. Paul's Chapel Sunday School in Wigan, England in 1850. It was first published in the *Juvenile Missionary Magazine* of June 1850. See https://hymnary.org/text/when_mothers_of_salem_their_children_bro.

85. Mark 10:31–36; Luke 18:51–57.

create a single race.[86] French leaders imagined this would occur through the creation of blended communities made up of French immigrants and enculturated Indigenous people. Dissatisfied with their strategy's lack of success, the French eventually abandoned this approach, favoring one that promoted segregated settlements or *reducciones*. Integral to this strategy was a series of boarding schools that taught religion, reading, writing, and French. This policy struggled as well. Parents resisted sending their children. Many of those who did attend ended up running away, while those who stayed often died from European diseases.

When the English defeated the French in 1760, they also assumed responsibility for "managing" the territory's Indigenous people. Unlike the French, the British were not as inclined to launch a missionary campaign. They were more concerned with developing military alliances. The phrase "keep your friends close, and your enemies even closer" comes to mind. During most of this time, the British Imperial government's official policy had been to value "friendship in times of war," rather than make any attempt to reclaim Indigenous people from "a state of barbarism and introducing amongst them the industrious and peaceful habits of a civilized life."[87]

However, in 1830, Sir George Murray, Britain's secretary of state for the colonies, introduced a radical change to the government's longstanding policy. Due to increased settlement and a subsequent loss of wildlife, particularly in Upper Canada, Murray proposed a "more enlightened course."[88] To this end, the Department of Indian Affairs encouraged "in every possible manner the progress of religious knowledge and education generally amongst the Indian Tribes."[89]

There is little reason to suggest that Murray had anything but Indigenous Canada's best interests at heart. Nevertheless, as John Milloy writes in his bestselling book, *A National Crime*, "As with many tragedies, this journey, too, began with good intentions."[90] This "policy of civilization," as it was known, called for tribes to be located on serviced settlement sites on reserves, complete with houses, barns, churches, and schools. A

86. Milloy, *A National Crime*, Part 1, 2:4.

87. Milloy, *A National Crime*, Part 1, 2:2.

88. Milloy, *A National Crime*, Part 1, 2:2.

89. For those wanting to explore Canadian policy on this topic more directly, Milloy recommends: Tobias, "Protection, Civilization, Assimilation"; Miller, *Skyscrapers Hide the Heavens*; and Dickason, *Canada's First Nations*.

90. Milloy, *A National Crime*, Part 1, 2:2.

cooperative effort between Protestant missions, the Department of Indian Affairs, and band councils, the program was also meant to provide agricultural training and everything else necessary to adopt a "settler life." Through new farming methods, commercial fishing, grist, and sawmilling, these communities would come to achieve self-sufficiency in the growing "modern" economy.

As part of this plan, the Methodists in Upper Canada began to develop "Indian missions" as early as the 1820s, opening not just churches, but schools as well.[91] The Anglican Missionary Society followed with missions in the Grand River area and, then, in the early 1840s, the Roman Catholics established a mission at Wikwemikong on Manitoulin Island.

Formal government involvement in residential schools seems to have first been put forward by Sir Peregrine Maitland, governor of Upper Canada. In 1820, his proposal imagined most of the "civilizing" ideas and practices that would emerge over the next three decades. While Maitland called for the conversion of hunters into settled agriculturalists, under the Department of Indian Affairs and missionaries' supervision, his goal was to focus his policies on children. He believed that, in "prosecuting such a plan, little perhaps can be expected from the grown-up Indians, its success, therefore, will chiefly depend upon the influence which it may acquire over the young."[92]

Writing again in *A National Crime,* Milloy describes for us Maitland's design for the "School Houses of Instruction and Industry":

> The school was designed to prepare the child for life within an Aboriginal community that would itself be remodelled to approximate as nearly as possible a respectable, industrious settler community. All children would be boarders, divorced from the impediments of "savage" existence, plainly clothed and simply fed. They would be taught the precepts of religion, the social manners of a polite settler, and the basic skills of reading, writing, and arithmetic. But more to the purpose, they would be instructed in the essential skills of settlement. The boys would be employed at "trades or on the farms and the girls in making clothes, taking care of Dairies, etc." The graduates would be models of industry and correct deportment, enthusiastically

91. For a history of the early Methodists in Canada, see Carrol, *Case and His Contemporaries.*

92. Quoted in Milloy, *A National Crime,* Part 1, 2:5.

> and efficiently taking up their responsibilities in a new Aboriginal society they were helping to create.[93]

Maitland's proposal remained mostly theory until he partnered with the Methodists and the Mississauga's of the Credit River to build a community with twenty homes and a school. While still primarily in its development phase, Maitland's plan proved significant, becoming a model upon which George Murray fashioned his "civilized society."

Despite some initial "success" with these settlements, a two-year review conducted in 1842 by Sir Charles Bagot concluded that the communities had only achieved a "half-civilized state."[94] A subsequent study headed up by Sir E. Head determined that "Any hope of raising the Indians as a body to the social and political level of their white neighbours, is yet a glimmer and distant spark."[95]

As negative sentiments began to grow, so did calls for a shift in government policy. The *Bagot Commission Report* had stressed that further progress in native communities would only occur if "the civilizing system was amended to imbue Aboriginal people with the primary characteristics of civilization, industry and knowledge."[96] And in the commission's opinion, the key to success was education. While emphasizing the need to maintain some reserve schools, the commission recommended introducing "as many manual or Industrial schools" as possible. These centralized boarding schools, located off-reserve, would provide training for boys in animal husbandry, agriculture, and mechanical trades. At the same time, girls would receive training in "domestic arts and science," which included dairying cattle, needlework, and cooking. Milloy notes that it was by such instruction that "the material and extensive change among the Indians of the rising generation [would] be hoped for."[97] Lawmakers believed that with non-Aboriginal teachers and isolated from the influence of their parents, Indigenous pupils would "imperceptibly acquire the manners, habits, and customs of a civilized life."[98]

Following confederation in 1867, the Government of Canada formalized its role in residential schools with an act of Parliament. In 1876,

93. Milloy, *A National Crime,* Part 1, 2:7–8.
94. Milloy, *A National Crime,* Part 1, 2:2.
95. Special Commissioners, "Report of the Special Commission," 21:3.
96. Milloy, *A National Crime,* Part 1, 2:4.
97. Milloy, *A National Crime,* Part 1, 2:4.
98. Quoted in: Milloy, *A National Crime,* Part 1, 2:7.

the Indian Act gave the federal government full control over most aspects of Indigenous life, and by 1880 residential schools became federally mandated with the passage of the Residential Schools Act. Speaking in defense of the government's policy, Canada's first prime minister, Sir John A. Macdonald (sounding frighteningly like the priests and bishops of the Middle Ages), told the House of Commons:

> When the school is on the reserve the child lives with its parents, who are savages; he is surrounded by savages, and though he may learn to read and write his habits, and training and mode of thought are Indian. He is simply a savage who can read and write. . . . [T]he only way to [change] that is to put them in central training industrial schools where they will acquire the habits and modes of thought of white men.[99]

The government's intention could not have been more explicit: separating children from their parents and sending them to residential schools was done not to educate them, but "to break their link to their culture and identity."[100] The institution of residential schools was part of a coherent government policy to assimilate Indigenous people into Canadian society against their will. These laws required Indigenous families, without exception, to send their children as young as four to these schools. RCMP officers were used to forcibly remove children from families who would not comply.

The schools were often located in isolated areas or islands, making it difficult for children to escape and find their way back to their families. When possible, the children's families would camp near the schools to catch a glimpse of their children, only to be dispersed and later driven away by the RCMP.[101]

While the government had mandated these schools, it was the churches that administered them. Approximately 50 percent were Catholic, while the Anglican, Methodist, Presbyterian, United, and Baptist churches operated the remaining schools. Children were not allowed to speak their language or practice any of their cultural traditions. Those found doing so would be beaten or punished in some way.

As early as 1900, the federal government had started receiving reports that up to 50 percent of children were dying in these residential

99. Truth and Reconciliation Commission, *Honouring the Truth*, 2.

100. Truth and Reconciliation Commission, *Honouring the Truth*, 2.

101. Jessica O'Neill (historian), Facebook post June 28, 2021.

schools. To investigate, the Department of Indian Affairs hired Dr. Peter Bryce, a founding member of the Canadian Public Health Association and author of Canada's first public health act, as their chief medical officer. In 1907, he submitted his report documenting a 40–60 percent mortality rate at these schools, due mainly to tuberculosis. While tuberculosis was already endemic in the general population, Bryce identified residential schools as an ideal environment for the transmission of tuberculosis. Bryce suggested that it was "almost as if the prime conditions for the outbreak of epidemics had been deliberately created."[102]

Two modern experts agree. Lena Faust, a PhD student at McGill University's International TB Centre, and Courtney Heffernan from the Tuberculosis Program Evaluation and Research Unit at the University of Alberta emphasized that although there was a TB epidemic at the time, it was greatly exaggerated by the conditions in these schools. They write:

> TB is a communicable infectious disease directly shaped by inequity at the individual and population level. It is well-established that social determinants of health, including malnutrition and poor ventilation, contribute to the development and spread of TB, and these conditions were common in residential schools.[103]

Bryce had found that death rates in residential schools were far greater than amongst school-age children throughout the rest of Canada.[104] To address these alarming numbers, as well as the rampant physical, emotional, and sexual abuse he had observed,[105] Bryce made several recommendations for improvements to school buildings, the children's diets, and that TB nurses be present on site. However, on the grounds that these changes would be too expensive, Bryce's recommendations were quickly dismissed. Not only did the government fail to implement his suggested changes, but eventually, the Department of Indian Affairs terminated Bryce's research funding, prevented him from presenting at academic conferences, and finally pushed him out altogether.

Not to be silenced, in 1922, Bryce published his findings in, *The Story of a National Crime: An Appeal for Justice to the Indians of Canada.* Bryce described the government's role in establishing and perpetuating

102. Canadian Press, "TB at Residential Schools."

103. Faust and Heffernan, "Residential School Deaths."

104. Canadian Press, "TB at Residential Schools."

105. Bryce reported that as many as 90 percent of all residential school children were suffering from severe physical, emotional, and sexual abuse.

conditions that had led to the high number of student deaths in residential schools and the government's deliberate decision not to take action. In it, he wrote, "This trail of disease and death has gone on almost unchecked by any serious efforts on the part of the Department of Indian Affairs."[106]

Despite Bryce's efforts, residential schools remained open for another ninety years.[107] Hardly surprising when we recall the words of deputy minister of Indian affairs Duncan Campbell Scott in 1920, two years before the release of Bryce's book. Speaking to a parliamentary committee, Scott outlined the government's policy, stating that, "Our object is to continue until there is not a single Indian in Canada that has not been absorbed into the body politic."[108]

For many twenty-first-century Canadians, Scott's declaration strikes painfully at our sensibilities, disrupting and dismantling any lingering thoughts that somewhere in this storyline, Canada was justified in its actions towards the people of its First Nations. But if any doubt remains, let us draw one final connection between Canada's "School Houses of Instruction and Industry" and youth indoctrination in Germany of the 1920s and 1930s.

Hovering above the gate at the entrance to Auschwitz, the infamous German death camp, is a sixteen-foot wrought-iron sign that reads, *Arbreit Macht Frei*—"Work makes one free." Beginning in the 1920s, the Nazi party began to employ a practice frighteningly similar to the one used in Canada with Indigenous people, targeting German youth as a means to influence society. German officials developed the Hitler Youth *(Hitlerjugend)* and the League of German Girls *(Bund Deutscher Mädel)* to introduce Nazi ideology and policy to children and youth. When the Nazis assumed power in January of 1933, the Hitler Youth movement had approximately 100,000 members. By the end of that same year, there were more than 2 million. By 1937, membership in the Hitler Youth had grown to 5.4 million and by 1940 to 7.2 million, representing 82 percent of German youth between the ages of ten and eighteen.

Through these organizations, the goal of the Nazi party was to dismantle the country's existing traditions and social structures through its youth. Gradually, the leadership began to impose conformity on its youth. German youth wore the same uniforms, sang the same Nazi songs,

106. Bryce, *Story of a National Crime.*

107. Tenant, "Pushed Out and Silenced."

108. Truth and Reconciliation Commission, *Honouring the Truth,* 3.

and participated in the same activities. By 1936, membership in Nazi youth groups became mandatory for all boys and girls between the ages of ten and seventeen. After-school meetings and weekend camping trips were used to train children to become faithful members of the Nazi party and future leaders of the National Socialist state.

Belonging to these organizations meant a significant time commitment—and with time came even more influence. Increasingly, these activities interfered with other priorities, such as church and school, eventually eroding the influence of parents, teachers, and religious leaders. Nazi officials even used the Hitler Youth and the League of German Girls to gather information on what was happening in their schools, churches, and families.

Schools were pivotal in this system. Nazi educators celebrated the "merits" of Aryan races while labeling Jews, Blacks, and homosexuals as cultural parasites incapable of creating culture or civilization.[109] After 1933, the Nazis purged its school systems of Jewish teachers and anyone they found to be "politically unreliable." In the classroom, as with the Hitler Youth, class instruction aimed to produce "race-conscious, obedient, self-sacrificing Germans who would be willing to die for Führer and Fatherland."[110]

Hitler understood the advantage of influencing young people at the most vulnerable and impressionable stages of their development. More than this, he understood the value of removing them from the influence of their parents, some of whom opposed his advancing regime. The Third Reich knew that families (private, cohesive groups that were sometimes difficult to sway politically) were an obstacle to their goals. The Hitler Youth offered a way to contest that. In 1938, Hitler said:

> These boys and girls enter our organizations at ten years of age, and often for the first time get a little fresh air; after four years of the Young Folk they go on to the Hitler Youth, where we have them for another four years. . . . And even if they are still not complete National Socialists, they go to Labor Service and are smoothed out there for another six, seven months. . . . And whatever class consciousness or social status might still be left . . . the Wehrmacht [German armed forces] will take care of that.[111]

109. Bytwerk, "The Jew as World Parasite."

110. United States Holocaust Memorial Museum, "Indoctrinating Youth." Holocaust Encyclopedia. Accessed on Feb. 2, 2021: https://encyclopedia.ushmm.org/content/en/article/ctrinating-youth.

111. Quoted in United States Holocaust Memorial Museum, "Indoctrinating Youth."

One of These Things Doesn't Belong Here

In the children's television favorite *Sesame Street,* there is a segment that helps children identify something that seems out of place. The accompanying song begins:

> One of these things is not like the others,
> One of these things just doesn't belong,
> Can you tell which thing is not like the others
> By the time I finish my song?

By the mid-1940s, policy-makers in Ottawa were increasingly concluding that the residential school system did not belong in Canadian society. In a surprising about-face, the Department of Indian Affairs released a statement indicating that it was "the firm opinion of this Department that the children will receive better care in their own homes under the guidance of their parents than they would in residence."[112] In May of 1946, a special joint committee of the House of Commons and the Senate began an extensive review of the department's mandate to prepare amendments to the Indian Act. Following two years of hearings and reviewing more than "400 briefs from Indian bands, organizations, other groups, and individuals," it released its report with twelve major recommendations. While supporting the idea that assimilation still offered the best possible solution to the "Indian problem," committee members also expressed their sympathy to Indian "aspirations." As a result, the committee delivered some surprisingly progressive recommendations, including granting limited self-government to First Nations communities and establishing a commission to investigate treaty violations and land claims.[113]

Why, then, did Canada's residential schools persist so stubbornly for another four decades? After the Second World War, the focus in many of Canada's residential schools had shifted from "providing opportunities for academic learning to that of a child caring institution."[114] Increasingly, residential schools had become part of a governmental welfare system that Indigenous communities relied on for support. If the government shut them down, society would have to find another means of providing support, demanding resources that the government wasn't sure it wanted to commit.

112. Milloy, *A National Crime.* Part 2, 9:1.
113. Milloy, *A National Crime.* Part 2, 9:1.
114. Quoted in Milloy, *A National Crime,* Part 2, 2:10.

As the federal and provincial governments continued to grapple with the question of how to support the welfare of Indigenous children, it also found itself in:

> the anomalous position of having to administer a group of [residential] schools which have a degree of independence of operation permitting them to pursue policies which are diametrically opposed to those of the Federal Government, particularly with respect to segregation and welfare. The tension created by this internal conflict is damaging to the Indian education program and confusing to the Canadian public.[115]

The tension, of course, had to do with the conflicting interests of the church. In 1959, the Anglican Indian School Administration expressed its concerns in a letter to the minister of citizenship and immigration:

> The old spirit of co-operation of Church and Government working together for the good of the Indians [sic] children has been lost; . . . more and more, Indian Affairs Branch is beginning to control the greater amount of detail in school operations, with the result that our Principals are tending to become simply servants of the Government.[116]

The letter continued, "The pendulum [has] now swung too far in the opposite direction." In conclusion, the letter prayed for a return to their previous relationship, where the church "had more freedom in the making of decisions as they affect[ed] individual schools."[117] As one senior Anglican insisted, residential schools remained "a definite step forward in Indian education and tend[s] to the more speedy assimilation of the Indian into full Canadian citizenship."[118] While the government grappled with fixing a broken system—the church was trying its best to preserve it. The church was losing influence—and didn't like it one bit.

This relationship remained in place until 1969. When the government formally ended its relationship with churches, many argued that this represented a growing secularism within western culture and throughout Canada that did not bode well. As the principal of the Qu'Appelle Residential School put it:

115. Quoted in Milloy, *A National Crime,* Part 2, 10:9.

116. Quoted in Milloy, *A National Crime,* part 2, 10:10.

117. Quoted in Milloy, *A National Crime,* Part 2, 10:10.

118. Quoted in Milloy, *A National Crime,* Part 2, 10:10.

> Satan and his legion, making a review of their positions came to the conclusion that they were losing ground the world over and the Indian population was not exempt, therefore they changed their strategy, adopted modern tools and went on the attack seven times stronger. What is this strategy? Or, to put it in modern words, what is this policy? To them religion must be done away with in all schools. A formula had to be found to lure the Indians away from denominational schools. . . . Now what are the tools the devil uses to implement his policy? He hides himself behind the faces and hypocritical views of some white-men with influential positions within the educational channels of our society.[119]

While the government had initiated residential schools as a means to assimilate Canada's Indigenous people, it was churches that made it possible. Both parties assumed that western culture and the Christian faith were superior to Indigenous culture and spirituality. In 1942, John House, the principal of the Anglican residential school in Gleichen, Alberta, illustrated this belief when he championed a campaign outside the school to have two Blackfoot chiefs deposed for supporting traditional dance ceremonies.[120] In 1947, Roman Catholic official J. O. Plourde told a federal committee that since Canada was a country of churches, he could see no reason why residential schools "should foster aboriginal beliefs."[121] George Dorey of the United Church told the same committee that he doubted whether there even was such a thing as "native religion."[122] In a 2012 report, the Truth and Reconciliation Commission concluded that to "both Protestant and Catholic Missionaries, Aboriginal spiritual beliefs were little more than superstition and witchcraft."[123]

By the time Canada's last residential schools closed in 1996, more than 150,000 First Nation, Métis, and Inuit students had passed through the doors of Canada's 132 residential schools. But the story of Canada's residential schools extends far beyond the legislation that governed it or the political ideology that led to it. For the children who lived in these schools, all that mattered was their experience of it. For most of Canada's Indigenous children, life in these schools was harsh, lonely, and alien.

119. Milloy, *A National Crime*, Part 2, 10:22.

120. Truth and Reconciliation Commission, *Honouring the Truth*, 3.

121. Truth and Reconciliation Commission, *Honouring the Truth*, 5.

122. Truth and Reconciliation Commission, *Honouring the Truth*, 5.

123. Truth and Reconciliation Commission, *They Came for the Children*, 15.

In these schools, children were separated from their families and communities, sometimes by force. They lived in and attended classes in these schools, often year-round. Staff members were limited in number, poorly trained, and inadequately supervised. The buildings were poorly located, poorly built, and poorly maintained.[124]

In describing her first memory of attending the school in Fort Albany, Ontario, Rachel Chakasim told the Truth and Reconciliation Commission:

> I saw violence for the first time. I would see kids getting hit. Sometimes in the classrooms, a yardstick was being used to hit. A nun would hit us. Even though our hair was short as it is, the nuns would grab us by the hair, and throw us on the floor of the classroom. . . . We never knew such fear before. It was very scary. I witness as other children were being mistreated.[125]

Beverly Anne Machelle remembers that even after two of her brothers committed suicide, she wasn't allowed to talk to her sister: "I wasn't allowed to talk to my brothers, and I had three brothers there. Two of those brothers committed suicide. Yeah, it really hurt not to be able to, and I couldn't even talk to my sister."[126]

Lydia Ross told the commission: "My name was Lydia, but in the school [where] I was, I didn't have a name. I had numbers. I had number 51, number 44, number 32, number 16, number 11, and then finally number one when I was just about coming to high school. So, I wasn't, I didn't have a name. I had numbers."[127]

And finally, the words of Julianna Alexander, who remembers her experience at the Kamloops school:

> You know they were trying to tell me [that in] this church, or this place we're in, you know, I had to do, I had to be this perfect, perfect person or whatever. And yet at the same time, that's not what I saw. Because I thought to myself, well, if you're a priest and nun, how come you're doing this to this child, or you're doing this to me, and I would say it out loud, and I'd get more lickings.[128]

124. Truth and Reconciliation Commission, *Honouring the Truth*, 3.
125. Truth and Reconciliation Commission, *The Survivors Speak*, 139.
126. Truth and Reconciliation Commission, *The Survivors Speak*, 94.
127. Truth and Reconciliation Commission, *The Survivors Speak*, 66.
128. Truth and Reconciliation Commission, *The Survivors Speak*, 89.

These are the stories of the children who survived. But in May 2021, media outlets shocked Canadian society with the traumatic news that a survey of the grounds at the former Indian Residential School in Kamloops, British Columbia, had revealed the remains of 215 buried children. The Catholic Church operated the Kamloops Indian residential school on behalf of the Canadian Government from 1890 to 1969 when the federal government took over its administration and continued to operate the building as a residence for a day school until closing it in 1978.

Reporting on the findings, Tk'emlúps te Secwépemc Chief Rosanne Casimir stated: "To our knowledge, these missing children are undocumented deaths. Some were as young as three years old. We sought out a way to confirm that knowing out of our deepest respect for those lost children and their families, understanding that Tk'emlúps te Secwépemc is the final resting place of these children."[129]

One month later, Chief Cadmus Delorme of the Cowessess First Nation revealed the discovery of 751 unmarked graves at the former Marieval Indian Residential School, 160 km east of Regina. The Marieval school operated from 1898 to 1997 in Saskatchewan's Qu'Appelle Valley.[130] In an interview with CBC News following the discovery, Pamela Hart, executive director of the Native Women's Resource Centre of Toronto, summarized the grief of Canada's First Nations: "I think that a spirit bigger than us here is ensuring that these tiny spirits, tiny babies are being found. They deserve that, the families deserve that, the Nations deserve that."[131]

While the discoveries at Kamloops and Marieval have opened the eyes of many Canadians to the atrocities of Canada's residential school system, the story is far from over. Canada's residential schools closed in 1996, but Indigenous children are still being taken away from their families. Currently, there are more First Nations children in foster care than at the height of the residential school program. According to the 2016 Canadian census, 7.7 percent of all children aged fourteen and under are Indigenous. But 52 percent of the children fourteen and under who are in foster care are Indigenous. The 2011 National Household Survey shows that 38 percent of Indigenous children in Canada live in poverty, compared to 7 percent of non-Indigenous children.[132] Indigenous chil-

129. Dickson and Watson, "Remains of 215 Children."

130. Taylor and Neustaeter, "Cowessess First Nation."

131. Brown, "Discovery of 751 Unmarked Graves."

132. Canada. "Reducing the Number."

dren continue to suffer because of the systems originally put in place by the Canadian government, administered by Canadian churches, and accepted by the settler people of Canada.

Truth and Reconciliation

In October 1960, six months before Indigenous people gained the right to vote, Prime Minister John Diefenbaker said, "There can be no dedication to Canada's future without a knowledge of its past."[133] On June 1, 2008, almost half a century later, the Truth and Reconciliation Commission opened the door a crack towards realizing that future by committing to hear and document the stories of Canada's residential school survivors and to reflect on the lasting impact of the schools on all Canadians.

In 2015, the Commission's final report acknowledged that still "too many Canadians know little or nothing about the deep historical roots of these conflicts." "This lack of historical knowledge," the report continues, "has serious consequences, not only for First Nations, Inuit and Métis peoples but for all Canadians."[134] History tells us that people and nations who persist in telling only the "winner's" story cannot move forward. For governments, these attitudes continue to lead to poor public policy decisions. For society, it reinforces racist attitudes and fuels civic distrust between Indigenous people and other Canadians—and between all Canadians.

And what of our churches? What implications do these acknowledgments have for the church's place in Canadian society, and how can we begin to live in right relations with our country's First Nations? The Truth and Reconciliation Commission defines reconciliation as "an ongoing process of establishing and maintaining respectful relationships."[135] The report continues:

> A critical part of this process involves repairing damaged trust by making apologies, providing individual and collective reparations, and following through with concrete actions that demonstrate real societal change.

133. John Diefenbaker, quoted in the *Toronto Star*, October 8, 1960.
134. Truth and Reconciliation Commission, *Honouring the Truth*, 8.
135. Truth and Reconciliation Commission, *Honouring the Truth*, 16.

A critical step in demonstrating change has been the development of specific and tangible responses to the Commission's *Calls to Action*. Of the ninety-four recommendations put forward by the Commission, there are four that specifically address the church's relationship with Canada's First Nations.[136] Call to Action #60 from the report states:

> We call upon leaders of the church parties to the Settlement Agreement and all other faiths, in collaboration with Indigenous spiritual leaders, Survivors, schools of theology, seminaries, and other religious training centres, to develop and teach curriculum for all student clergy, and all clergy and staff who work in Aboriginal communities, on the need to respect Indigenous spirituality in its own right, the history and legacy of residential schools and the roles of the church parties in that system, the history and legacy of religious conflict in Aboriginal families and communities, and the responsibility that churches have to mitigate such conflicts and prevent spiritual violence.

Calls to Action 73, 74, and 75 address the need for churches to work with Aboriginal communities and former residential school students to establish and maintain an online registry of cemeteries and burial plots, to inform the families of children who died at residential schools of the location of these plots, to ensure the protection of these sites, to honor families' wishes for appropriate commemoration ceremonies and markers, and to facilitate reburial in their home communities as requested.

In a 2015 response to the Truth and Reconciliation Commission's initial report, the leaders of the Anglican Church of Canada, Presbyterian Church in Canada, the Roman Catholic Entities Parties to the Settlement Agreement, the United Church of Canada, and the Jesuits of Canada, issued the following statement:

> Beginning in the 19th century and continuing until the late 1960s, our churches were partners with the Government of Canada in running Indian Residential Schools. Notwithstanding the good intent and care of many who worked in the Schools, it is clear that Indian Residential Schools, in policy and in practice, were an assault on Indigenous families, culture, language and spiritual traditions, and that great harm was done. We continue to acknowledge and regret our part in that legacy.[137]

136. Truth and Reconciliation Commission, *Calls to Action*, 111.

137. Anglican Church, *Response of the Churches*.

Since then, religious denominations have responded with independent apologies, policy directives, and statements on how they have complied with the recommendations to date. They have developed educational tool kits for church members and facilitated focus groups. The various denominations have adopted land acknowledgments, advocated for Indigenous rights, and partnered in development projects that can lead to more sustainable life and work for Indigenous peoples.

But is this enough? The discovery of 215 Indigenous children's bodies on the Kamloops Indian residential school grounds highlights the challenge of whether it can, or ever will be, enough. According to Mary-Ellen Turpel-Lafond, director of the Indian Residential School History and Dialogue Centre at the University of British Columbia in Vancouver, the Truth and Reconciliation Commission had heard that only fifty deaths occurred at the Kamloops school. The discovery confirmed what Indigenous people had known for years. Still, Canadians could not admit that many Indigenous children who were removed from their families and taken to these schools never returned.

Speaking to the CBC's *Early Edition,* Turpel-Lafond added that because federal agents often moved children around from school to school, it is possible that many of these children were also from other First Nations communities. There are "massive ongoing problems" with historical records, she said, including those "held by certain Catholic entities that they will not release" that have made it hard to understand exactly what happened. "There may be reasons why they wouldn't record the deaths properly and that they weren't treated with dignity and respect," continued Turpel-Lafond, "because that was the whole purpose of the residential school . . . to take total control of the Indian children, to remove their culture, identity, and connection to their family."[138]

How does a nation begin to speak of reconciliation when confronted with the unreported deaths of more than a thousand children? And to the decades of ongoing cultural genocide that it points to? In a letter to the *Toronto Star,*[139] Jan Wood Daly highlights the immense challenge this poses in a country that persists in singing "our home and native land" as part of its national anthem. "National anthems," she writes, "hold a unique power. They have the ability to inspire, instill devotion and unify a country." Anthems say something about a country's people and what

138. Dickson and Watson, "Remains of 215 Children."

139. Jan Wood Daly, "Canada Is the Home."

that country stands for. Because of that, "national anthems can also create discomfort, resentment and division." As settler descendants, she says, we belong to a legacy of belief and practice that has appropriated someone else's native land in order to make it our own. This land is *not* our native land, and as long as we continue presumptively to treat it as such, there can be no reconciliation.

Canadian church-goers have joined the groundswell of response. In the days and weeks that followed the burial ground discoveries, they wore orange ribbons, edited their Facebook Frames with First Nations motifs, and placed shoe totems on the steps of government and public buildings as acts of solidarity. On September 30, 2021, they donned orange shirts, attended vigils, and participated in blanket ceremonies as part of Canada's first National Day of Truth and Reconciliation.[140] These are critical first steps. Nevertheless, as Indian Residential Schools Survivor Society co-chair Rick Alec laments, a deeper question for Canadian Christians remains: "My Creator," says Alec, "is asking their God why their disciples would do this to us?"[141]

In 1957, Canadian sociologist Anthony Parel wrote a compelling article entitled "Christianity and Colonialism." While he was writing primarily on the missionary efforts of the church in Asia, it offers some critical insights for our discussion here. First, most contemporary views of Canada's European colonization involve the meeting of two groups, two cultures, and two ways of life that involved the intersection of Western and non-Western ways of life. In one sense, that is true. But in another sense, this understanding continues to demonstrate our colonial bias by suggesting that the cultures present in North America prior to European colonization can be defined by their opposition to, or contrast to, Western ways of life. By introducing "non" as a modifier for Western ideologies, we belie our sense of neutrality.

Secondly, our assumption that Canada's First Nations can collectively be described as a *homogenous culture* in contrast to Western culture fails to adequately express the breadth and diversity of Canada's Indigenous peoples. For example, there are currently 630 First Nation

140. The bill to create a statutory holiday in response to recommendation #80 of the Truth and Reconciliation Commission's ninety-four calls to action received royal assent on June 3, 2021. "The day honours the lost children and Survivors of residential schools, their families and communities." Canada, "National Day of Truth and Reconciliation."

141. Dickson, "Residential School Survivors Society."

communities in Canada, representing more than fifty nations and fifty distinct Indigenous languages. Imagine trying to describe Europe, Africa, or Asia as a single, easily-definable, homogenous culture. Or even more poignantly, the appropriateness of representing Europe, Africa, or Asia as "non-North American." Continuing to see Canada's First Nations with this kind of narrow vision does not hold true to the TRC's calls to action. This kind of "non" language can only serve to perpetuate colonial attitudes within our borders. But can we also begin to see how it undermines our capacity, individually as Christians and collectively as the church, to see and treat anyone who falls outside the Christian "norm" as equals, whether that is because of religion, culture, race, age, gender, or sexual orientation. Describing individual and cultural groups by *who they are not* fails to recognize *who they are.*

Thirdly, the ideology behind much of colonialism, namely the lust for wealth, inextricably casts Christianity in a negative light. To the people of Canada's First Nations, it made the intentions of European and later home-grown Christian missionaries, if not perplexing, ineffective at the very least. We have no further to look than the recollections of Marcel Guiboche, who, when he testified before the Truth and Reconciliation Committee, offered these words:

> A sister, a nun started talking to me in English and French, and yelling at me. I did not speak English, and didn't understand what she, what she was asking. She got very upset, and started hitting me all over my body, hands legs and back. I began to cry, yell, and became very scared and this infuriated her more. She got a black strap and hit me some more.[142]

The identification of Christianity with Western culture, and its subsequent evaluation based on the impressions left behind by the colonizers and their missionaries, remains one of the strongest barriers to right relations between Canada's churches and our country's First Nations. Any interpretation of what it means to believe in and worship the "One True God" that we translate as "my way or the highway" is doomed to fail.

More liberal Christians typically take a different approach At this end of the spectrum, there are Christians who affirm that Christ was just like any other of the world's great religious leaders and that his divinity has merely been ascribed to him by Christian piety. But, we may protest, if Christ is no more divine than Buddha or Krishna, does it not also follow

142. Truth and Reconciliation Commission, *The Survivors Speak*, 48.

that Christianity is no more absolute than either Buddhism or Hinduism? And if this is the case, does this not make the conversion from one faith to another unnecessary? To this, Indigenous people might respond, as Gandhi maintained, that a Hindu has only to be a better Hindu, a Christian a better Christian, and a Muslim a better Muslim.

At the risk of heading too far down a theological rabbit hole, can we ask—is that a debate we feel confident enough to enter? If the church in Canada currently finds itself in decline and Canada's First Nations are seeking to restore a more equitable place in Canadian society, what would it look like for each of us to begin with Gandhi's assertion, and seek each other's assistance in doing so? And what of our dialogue with others who do not fit the Christian "mold"?

The point to be made here is that before Christians, regardless of their theological orientation, go criticizing the spirituality of others, they first examine their own faithfulness and expressions of spirituality as advised by Jesus in Matthew 5:3–5:

> Why do you look at the speck of sawdust in your brother's eye and pay no attention to the plank in your own eye? How can you say to your brother, "Let me take the speck out of your eye," when all the time there is a plank in your own eye? You hypocrite, first take the plank out of your own eye, and then you will see clearly to remove the speck from your brother's eye.

Moreover, in taking this approach, Christians might open themselves to the possibility of deepening their own faith through the teaching and lessons of others.

There is one final point around which I find my own thoughts still emerging. They focus on how the church perceives its own place in society. When Cartier arrived in the Gulf of St. Lawrence and planted his cross on Iroquois land, he signified the dominance that his belief system held in society. Considering what followed, we might well suggest he assumed too much. My impressions of the Canadian church are that it no longer suffers from the over-inflated view of itself that it might have once had, but rather a deflated one. The comments of denominational leaders, pastors, and church-goers who are a part of my daily work seem to suggest a church that is grieving its loss of influence, its loss of privilege, and, as a result, finds itself in what seems very much like a place of exile.

Does any of this sound familiar? Does any of it resonate with the story that Indigenous Canadians have been telling us for centuries?

Let me be clear. I am not suggesting that the decline our churches have experienced over the last five or six decades comes anywhere close to the experience of Canada's First Nations. I *am* suggesting, though, that the challenge created by, and the reflection demanded by, the Truth and Reconciliation Commission's *Calls to Action* leaves the Canadian church with some difficult questions—ones that go further even than our right relations with Canada's First Nations. It asks us: Who have we been? Who have we become? And who do we want to be?

In 2019, Indigenous Corporate Training, an Indigenous company that advises Canadian Corporations on understanding Indigenous issues, published *Four Common Barriers to Reconciliation with Indigenous Peoples.*[143] The four factors they address are 1) Denial, 2) Apathy, 3) Misconception and 4) Being Overwhelmed. Their advice holds as true for the Canadian church as it does for corporate Canada.

Denial

Some people do not want to accept the hard truths about Canada and our governments' actions towards the people of Canada's First Nations, let alone the church's role in it. Similarly, many Christians do not want to acknowledge the hard truths that Canada's churches face at present, not the least of which is the privilege we have enjoyed in Canadian society and the negative impacts that has had.

Apathy

The absence of emotional engagement makes reconciliation difficult. The experience of 150,000 Indigenous children in Canadian residential schools is not just "their" history. It is *Canada's* history. And as Christians in Canada, it is also our history. The intergenerational impacts of poorer health, lower levels of education, employment, income, and higher incarceration rates are very much a part of our present and our future without reconciliation.

In 2014, the Royal Canadian Mounted Police (RCMP) released a report indicating that between 1980 and 2012, 1,107 Indigenous women and girls had been murdered—and that at least 105 Indigenous women

143. Indigenous Corporate Training, "Four Common Barriers."

and girls remained missing under suspicious circumstances.[144] In 1980, Statistics Canada reported that 9 percent of female homicide victims were Indigenous. By 2015, that number had risen to 24 percent.[145] The National Inquiry into Missing and Murdered Indigenous Women and Girls, published in 2017, notes that while homicide rates for non-Indigenous women had been going down, homicide rates for Indigenous women were going up. The likelihood of violent death for Indigenous women is also significantly higher than for non-Indigenous women. The report cites Dr. Tracy Peter, whose research indicates that Indigenous women are twelve times more likely to be murdered or go missing than other women in Canada and sixteen times more likely than Caucasian women. In Manitoba and Saskatchewan, Indigenous women are nineteen times more likely than Caucasian women to be murdered or go missing.[146]

In June 2019, Statistics Canada reported that Indigenous Canadians die by suicide at a rate three times higher than non-Indigenous Canadians. In 2015–16, Indigenous people represented only 5 percent of the population but almost 25 percent of the federal prison population. Aboriginal youth accounted for 46 percent of the admissions while representing only 8 percent of the general youth population in ten reporting jurisdictions.[147]

If Canadian society continues to see the harm done by residential schools and abuses currently experienced by Indigenous people as "their issue" or as an "Indigenous issue," or even as the "previous generations'" issue, we will never achieve reconciliation. Similarly, if the church in Canada wishes to live off the coattails of its predecessors—or blame them for its current struggles—today's church will only drive itself further into exile.

Misconceptions

The Merriam-Webster Dictionary defines "misconception" as "a wrong or inaccurate idea or conception."[148] Three of the most commonly-held misconceptions about Indigenous Canadians are that they receive free housing, free post-secondary education, and do not pay taxes. Canadians

144. RCMP, "Missing and Murdered Aboriginal Women."

145. The National Enquiry into Missing Women, *Interim Report*, 7.

146. The National Enquiry into Missing Women, *Interim Report*, 8.

147 Anand, "The Institutionalization and Suicide Crisis."

148. Merriam-Webster (online version), "Misconception."

who build their impressions of Indigenous people on these assumptions are unlikely to see the need for reconciliation. In their eyes, these benefits create an unfair advantage for Indigenous Canadians over non-Indigenous Canadians.

What do these benefits look like? Concerning housing, Aboriginal people living on reserve lands can apply for social housing programs offered through the Canada Housing and Mortgage Corporation (CMHC). Bands and First Nations that meet CMHC lending criteria can apply to a bank for conventional mortgage funds to finance social housing construction. The band then rents these units to its members and maintains the mortgage.[149] How much these individuals pay (or do not pay) is determined by their agreement with band leaders—not the federal or provincial government.

With respect to education, the federal government provides educational support to Indigenous students through what is known as the Post-Secondary Student Support Program (PSSSP). Only "status Indians"—people formally recognized by the federal government as "Indian"—are eligible for funding under this program. To put this in perspective, Statistics Canada estimates that only about half of Canada's Indigenous people have formal status.[150] This requirement means that only half of Canada's Indigenous people qualify for post-secondary educational support. Students have to apply for funding from their home community. Often, the demand for funding far exceeds the money that local bands receive for post-secondary education from the federal government. For those who do receive funding, the money often comes with strict conditions. Students have to reapply to their band every year, maintain a certain grade-point average, submit a career outline, not miss classes and enroll in a minimum of four courses per semester. Students who have their funding suspended for any reason often have to wait a minimum of two years before they can reapply. Due to restrictions at the local level, some students only have their tuition and books covered. Like many non-Indigenous students, most First Nations students have to work or apply for loans to cover living expenses.[151]

149. Indigenous Corporate Training. "Myth #3."

150. Statistics Canada, "Projections of Aboriginal Population."

151. Assembly of First Nations, "First Nations Post-Secondary Fact Sheet"; Monkman, "Debunking the Myth"; Cull, Hancock, McKeown, Pidgeon and Vedan, "Myths that Impact."

A third misconception holds that Indigenous Canadians do not have to pay taxes. This is not true. All Canadians are required to pay taxes. Similarly, all Canadians have options to reduce their taxable income, depending on their circumstances. Section 87 of the Indian Act outlines the benefits that apply to Status Indians. Note again that these benefits apply only to the 50 percent of Indigenous Canadians who hold formal status. Having status enables Indigenous Canadians to avoid taxes on personal and real estate income if it is earned or located on a reserve. Any income earned on property owned off-reserve is taxed whether the individual has status or not.[152]

Holding onto misconceptions such as these does not contribute to reconciliation. Pursuing right relations with Canada's First Nations means setting aside our assumptions and misconceptions about Indigenous Canadians—and listening to their story in their words. But the learning goes deeper than that. Canadians have misconceptions about Indigenous Canadians, but we also have misconceptions about the church—even those of us who belong to it. What assumptions do we make? What misconceptions do we hold in our local congregations about other religious traditions and society in general? In my work with churches and religious leaders, I often hear phrases like, "We are too old," "There are not enough young people," "Society has grown too secular," "There's too much religious and cultural diversity," and "We're not having as much impact as we used to." Often these statements are based on assumptions and half-truths—not fact. Holding onto misconceptions that have no basis in fact does not allow us to move forward.

Being Overwhelmed

Reconciliation is a daunting task. Something that has been dysfunctional for centuries is not going to be repaired overnight—or even years. It is likely to take decades. And it is going to take long-term commitment on the part of everyone involved.

Similarly, religious institutions and systems that have been in decline for years will take time to refresh and renew. Reconciliation is hard. It requires setting sail for a brave new world, not knowing what exactly awaits us. And that's daunting. Whether reconciliation needs to occur in your local congregation, your community, or amongst senior leaders

152. Intuit Turbo Tax, "Do First Nations Residents."

in your denomination, the enormity or complexity of the task is not a reason to back away from contributing or taking part. The truth is that the face we put on for the world matters; the words we choose and the choices we make, matter. Perhaps now more than ever:

> "A man can smile and smile, and be a villain."
>
> —ALDOUS HUXLEY (*BRAVE NEW WORLD*)

5

Steeplechase

The Canadian Church in the Twentieth Century

"I sought to hear the voice of God and climbed the topmost steeple,
But God declared: 'Go down again—I dwell among the people.'"

—JOHN HENRY NEWMAN

IN MID-EIGHTEENTH-CENTURY BRITAIN, CHURCH steeples stood as prominent landmarks, rising above the British countryside's trees and rolling hills. With the country's agricultural land increasingly being marked off by its owners, hunters, especially upper-class ones who enjoyed fox-hunting, had to learn to jump hedges, stone walls, fence rails, and creeks to track their prize. Faster horses and faster dogs were also being bred, commonly leading to arguments over whose horses were the most accomplished. To prove their claims, owners would hold races across the countryside. The first of these recorded races were held in 1752 in County Cork, Ireland. Following a disagreement over whose horse was best, Cornelius O'Callaghan put his horse up against one owned by Edmund Blake. The four-and-a-half-mile race was staged from Buttevent Church to St. Leger Church—and the steeplechase was born.[1]

1. Charlotte Steeplechase Foundation, "About Steeplechasing."

Similar races were held across England and Ireland from the mid-eighteenth century onward. One of England's earliest recorded races was held in 1790 between horses owned by Mr. Loraine Hardy and the Hon. Mr. Willougby. From Melton Mowbray to Dalby Wood, the nine-mile race was staged, with a prize of 1,000 guineas being awarded to the winner. None of these early races had a set course; the rider was free to select his own route from "point-to-point." It was not until later that flags were used to mark required obstacles along an agreed-upon course. In 1813, one six-mile race held in County Roscommon, Ireland, listed the obstacles as including "six walls five feet high and several yawning ditches."[2]

The first known steeplechase held over a prepared track with built fences (as opposed to natural obstacles) is believed to have been held in Bedford, England, in 1810. The three-mile race had eight fences, four to six feet in height. The first recognized national competition was held on March 8, 1830,[3] and by 1840, there were more than sixty sanctioned races in various parts of England.[4] Not long after, North America's first major steeplechase competition was held in Montreal in 1840. Captain Walter Jones of the Queen's Light Dragoons was Canada's sole competitor, riding against riders from various British regiments.[5] The event was won by Colonel White of Britain's 7th Hussars.[6]

Confederation Confusion

By the end of the century, a different kind of steeplechase was well underway in Canada. At the time of confederation, the church, while prominent in the spiritual and social lives of most Canadians, was, as John Webster Grant records, "small, immature, and in some cases still largely dependent on external aid."[7] Unlike the United States, where the Constitution is enshrined in the minds of many as a quasi-religious document, institutional religion was relatively absent from Canada's confederation story.

At the time, political rhetoric linking the United States with a divine power had surfaced on a large scale with the outbreak of the Civil War

2. Thoroughbred Heritage, "Steeplechasing Notes."
3. Charlotte Steeplechase Foundation. "About Steeplechasing."
4. Thoroughbred Heritage. "Steeplechasing Notes."
5. Cooper, *History of the Montreal Hunt.*
6. American Turf Register. "Steeplechase in Montreal."
7. Grant, *Church in the Canadian Era*, 46.

in 1861. A Pennsylvania clergyman named M. R. Watkinson urged that the phrase "In God We Trust" be placed on all American coins at the outset of the war to support the North's cause. "Such language," Watkinson wrote, would "place us openly under divine protection."[8]

The church's role in Canada's nation-building and political process was far more subtle. If the fathers of confederation had put their trust in anything, it was in Sir Sandford Fleming's promise of uniting Canadians from coast to coast by rail. At the same time, the church was left to grapple with the vast territory it now had in which to operate.

As John Webster Grant writes:

> Even when they were not responding consciously to the challenge of confederation, the churches had to deal with the new situation it brought into being. They had to cope with the expanded scale of the nation, represented most dramatically by the acquisition of the northwest. They had to bridge the chasms separating the people of its various regions, now linked by railway and telegraph. They had to come to terms with its emerging self-awareness, still largely devoid of ideological content. The problems of Canadian existence, although seldom at the centre of the church's conscious concern, constituted the framework within which all important decisions were made and all major enterprises undertaken.

Born of political and economic necessity and "fathered by politicians and railway promoters,"[9] the new dominion would still rely on churches in ways similar to its colonial days—even if the churches didn't know it.

With confederation taken care of and denominational claims in the east more or less assigned, the new dominion set its eyes upon the west. In 1869, the Canadian Government negotiated the purchase of Rupert's Land from the Hudson's Bay Company, and on July 15, 1870, the expansive territory became part of Canada. In what John Webster Grant describes as an "almost forgotten transaction,"[10] the British Government also transferred the McKenzie basin, which had never been of much interest to the Hudson's Bay Company, and in 1871 British Columbia, was added to the dominion.

It is one thing to declare the birth of a nation; it is quite another to move it towards maturity. The new land needed not only to be claimed

8. Mislin, "In God We Trust."

9. Grant, *Church in the Canadian Era*, 24.

10. Grant, *Church in the Canadian Era*, 30.

but populated. As early as the 1840s, concerns had been expressed that without further investment from the Hudson's Bay Company and the people who would follow, the vast western territories would be annexed by its American neighbors to the south. With "new management" in place, inhabiting the land became paramount. In the late-nineteenth century, Canada's population was heavily weighted in its five eastern provinces: Quebec, Ontario, New Brunswick, Prince Edward Island, and Nova Scotia. Eastern Canada had some large urban centers, but the country's future depended largely on attracting farmers to the west. Concerned about the population imbalance, the government began to actively promote western settlement. And it is here that the churches would play a crucial role.

By the time the Hudson Bay transfer had been consummated, several faith groups had already planted their flags in the west. The Catholics and the Anglicans showed the strongest western presence, with the religious authorities in many communities holding as much or more sway than the politicians. Prominent amongst this list was A. A. Taché, a Catholic bishop who claimed to have descended from La Veréndrye, the French "discoverer" of Manitoba. Having arrived in 1845, in what at the time was simply called the "North-West," Taché had been responsible for building a sizeable establishment on the Red River, persuading many of the local Métis to settle in well-defined parishes.[11] The Anglicans, under Bishop Machray, had built both a cathedral and college to support the evangelistic and educational aims of the denomination. They were followed by the Presbyterians and Methodists and later by the Baptists, who opened a mission in Winnipeg in 1873.

However, it was the arrival of another religious group in Manitoba that would set the west's direction and reinforce the Canadian government's persistent colonial principles. In 1874, several thousand Mennonites left Russia to settle along the Red River. In her book, *One Quilt, Many Pieces: A Guide to Mennonite Groups in Canada,* Margaret Loewen Reimer describes how the Russian government's increasingly restrictive policies and its persecution of many sectarian groups led to the migration of close to 18,000 Dutch and low-German Mennonites to North America. Anxious to populate the west, Alexander Mackenzie's Conservative government offered several unusual concessions. The promise of land, cultural and educational autonomy, self-governing communities,

11. Grant, *Church in the Canadian Era,* 30.

and guaranteed exemption from military service were more than enough to attract about 7,000 of these Mennonites to southern Manitoba. While these policies would later expose both the Mennonites and the government to hostility from the public, the Mennonite's passion and skill for farming factored significantly in opening up the prairies and much of Western Canada to future settlement.

As expansion continued across Saskatchewan and Alberta, the irony of MacKenzie's sales pitch to the Mennonites and other European religious groups became increasingly evident. As Catholic and Protestant groups continued to erect their spires on land still populated mainly by Canada's First Nations, the government offered large blocks of land to religious and ethnic minorities from Europe who wanted to maintain their way of life *and* seek greater freedom in the new world.[12] Many of these immigrants belonged to sectarian groups, like the Doukhobors, who had resisted assimilating even in their countries of origin. So, while the Canadian government continued its expansive policies enforcing the assimilation of Canada's First Nations, it was also inviting "alien" settlers with the government's express permission to maintain their culture, language, and customs!

And come they did. To these land-hungry homesteaders, the Canadian government offered idyllic descriptions of "blue skies, golden crops, happy, friendly neighbors and independence."[13] The government's promotional materials included detailed color maps of each of the four western provinces, showing surveys of township borders and where land was available, along with descriptions of their proximity to rivers, towns, roads, and railways. Between 1896 and 1914, more than two million settlers from Europe and the United States responded, pouring into the prairies. In 1896, only 17,000 immigrants had arrived in Canada. But by 1901, the annual number had risen to close to 50,000, bringing the total number of immigrants to about 700,000—or about 12 percent of Canada's population of five million people at the time. In 1906, Canada welcomed nearly 200,000 immigrants. In 1913, the number had risen to 400,870, still a record for Canadian immigration in one year. And even that number may have been understated.

In 1901, Canada's Department of the Interior highlighted a unique challenge in documenting accurate immigration figures. In an extract

12. Mackinnon, *Canada and the Minority Churches*, 20.

13. Chandler, "Selling the Prairie Good Life."

from the 1901 Immigration Report to the House of Commons, the minister explained:

> As explained on many previous occasions, the Board of Trade returns do not give any accurate idea of the emigration from the United Kingdom to Canada. All the 2nd class and steerage passengers on the various steamers are included as emigrants, whether they are going out for the first time or not, and the emigrants are classified as going to the United States or Canada according to the place at which they land. For instance, a great many emigrants go to Canada, especially eastern Canada, via the United States, but they are all regarded in the returns as emigrants to the States, while those who go to the States via a Canadian port are returned as emigrants to Canada. The disadvantage under which Canada labours in this respect has been accentuated this year, inasmuch as all the emigrants travelling by the Dominion steamers to Portland are classified as United States emigrants, while in former years when landed in Halifax and Montreal were returned as settlers in Canada.[14]

Fields without a Farmer

The country's expanding immigration levels were the church's blessing and its curse. More people meant, of course, more people to fill Canadian churches. Many of the denominations who had established themselves early on prairie land had the advantage of offering receptive church homes to anyone looking. Their problem was keeping pace. Soon the fields were full to overflowing with new settlers—and not enough churches or clergy to tend to the flock. A survey conducted just after World War I suggested that half of Alberta's children were growing up unchurched.[15]

Also complicating the Canadian church's mission was a shifting ethnic mix brought about by the country's liberal immigration policies. The Catholic Church felt threatened since the majority of immigrants had Protestant roots. The Protestants felt threatened because the influx of new immigrants pushed Catholic and Orthodox Canadians into communities traditionally dominated by Protestants. Equally challenging were the nation's changes in ethnic composition.

14. Swiggum and Kohli, "1901 Immigration Report."

15. Grant, *Church in the Canadian Era*, 94.

At the time, churches, especially the Protestant ones, found themselves at the apex of their power and influence. They finally appeared to be reaping the benefits of a "church-going, Sabbath-keeping population."[16] As "self-appointed custodians of the national conscience,"[17] they had a dream of national greatness defined by adherence to a strict moral code, and the nation's advancing ethnic and religious diversity threatened that.

In remarks eerily similar to those of the earliest colonizers, we read Methodist Chaplain Wellington Bridgeman's words regarding central Europeans. "These people carry an innate morbid passion to shed blood." A prominent Presbyterian official was quoted as saying, "It may be taken for granted that a considerable percentage of new arrivals are, morally, socially and intellectually of a decidedly lower type than the average Anglo-Saxon." And finally, John Stark, in an address to the Baptist Convention of Ontario and Quebec, said, "All that is choicest and best in our national life is trembling in the balance."[18]

Despite these tensions, Canadian churches still felt bound to serve. As John Webster Grant writes:

> If his presence constituted a problem, the immigrant was also a fellow-human in need, a brother for whom Christ had died. Almost without exception churchmen argued that everything possible should be done to ease the way of the newcomer and to improve conditions under which he lived.[19]

And while all churches took on pastoral work in immigrant communities, they were inclined to work mostly with their own members. Western Roman Catholics expressed a natural affinity for immigrants from Europe, especially Poland and Germany. The Presbyterians and Baptists ministered mainly to the Dutch and Hungarians. Denominations that held a strong missionary presence in China and India gravitated towards these populations, particularly in British Columbia. The Japanese, who had relatively few ties to existing denominational groups, developed their own churches.[20]

John Webster Grant outlines three ways that the Canadian government relied on churches, especially Protestant ones, to advance their

16. Grant, "The Reaction of WASP Churches," 6.
17. Grant, "The Reaction of WASP Churches," 6.
18. Grant, "The Reaction of WASP Churches," 6–7.
19. Grant, *Church in the Canadian Era*, 96.
20. Grant, *Church in the Canadian Era*, 96.

immigration aims. First, they recognized the affinity that Canadian churches had for these immigrants as "strangers in a foreign land,"[21] recalling the experience of their Hebraic ancestors. A second motive was to offer the gospel to those who seemed to be without faith, much like the colonizers had viewed Canada's native peoples. It should not go unnoticed that Protestants tended to include Catholic and Orthodox Christians in this group. And as far as the Canadian government was concerned, a third and crucial motive was the Protestant desire to plant Canadian ideals in Canada's newcomers. Why spend time and resources on "naturalizing" or "Canadianizing" its recent arrivals when the church would do it for them?[22]

For Roman Catholics, assimilation into Canadian life was far less important than integration into church life. Until the end of the nineteenth century, most Canadian Catholics, including those in the west, spoke French, as did the entire hierarchy that oversaw them. Canada's wave of immigration changed all of that. The French remained the single largest Catholic group, but by no means did they dominate as they had previously.[23] Here, the challenge became one of building a home for English and European Catholics within the church while preserving the Catholic Church's role as a champion of the French language and culture within an officially bilingual confederation.

Falling Stocks

The stock market crash of 1929 introduced a worldwide crisis that put any further notions of Canadian church expansion on hold. World War I had already dramatically slowed Canada's immigration numbers. Canadian churches shifted their focus to stabilization and maturation, both with their evangelical endeavors (for many, through the exercise of the social gospel) and institutionally, as evidenced by the union of Methodist and Presbyterian traditions to form the United Church of Canada in 1925.

Canada was hit particularly hard. Its heavy dependence on raw material and farm exports, combined with a crippling prairie drought, produced a widespread loss of jobs and family savings. During the "Dirty Thirties," wages fell by 42 percent, and by 1933, a third of the labor force was out of work. Hardest hit were the prairie provinces, where church

21. Gen 15:13.

22. Grant, *Church in the Canadian Era*, 97.

23. Grant, *Church in the Canadian Era*, 97.

expansion had been the greatest. In the rural prairie areas, two-thirds of the population required government assistance.

The churches, like most institutions at the time, were pressed into operating on smaller budgets. Ministers and priests absorbed much of the shortfall, with salaries cut by a third to a half in some cases.[24] Many ministers were asked to expand their geographical areas of responsibility, seminary and denominational staff were cut, and many welfare ministries were turned over to secular agencies. The United Church accumulated a debt of $1.7 million trying to keep its ministries afloat. The Anglican Church came close to bankruptcy with a devastating and much-publicized loss of much of its capital investments.[25]

Despite their financial challenges, churches continued to respond to the most immediate needs of those suffering in their communities. In a variety of collaborative efforts, Protestants and Catholics cooperated with each other and with agencies like the YMCA, the federal government, and the railways. In the particularly hard-hit prairies, churches responded by sending carloads of clothes and food to the most severely-afflicted areas.

For the church, this was a time of both loss and gain. Many congregations saw themselves grow steadily smaller as young people left in search of jobs. They met in buildings increasingly in need of maintenance and repair. Sunday School rolls highlighted the decline in birth rates while increasing numbers of clergy broke down physically or emotionally under the strain of offering spiritual and material support. At the same time, adversity seemed to spawn a renewed interest in exploring faith more deeply. Individual congregations and denominational leaders were challenged to rethink their priorities and "rid themselves of some persistent illusions."[26] Canadians in general were discovering that the church meant more to them than they realized or perhaps had been willing to admit.

The Second World War

It is often argued that the Great Depression ended dramatically with the start of the Second World War and the explosive spending that Western governments mobilized to respond to the fascist threats of Germany, Italy, and Japan. There are some economists, however, who suggest that

24. Grant, *Church in the Canadian Era,* 136.

25. Grant, *Church in the Canadian Era,* 137.

26. Grant, *Church in the Canadian Era,* 148.

the Depression ended, and prosperity was restored, not with increased spending, but with the reduced spending, taxes, and regulations that came about at the *end* of the Second World War.

By the beginning of the war, high unemployment rates had already begun to slow, but this was mainly due to the military enlistment of several thousand Canadians. Canada's Gross Domestic Product or GDP increased markedly during the war. Still, spending on military weaponry and tactical resources hardly amounted to improved living standards for working people, at least not in the short term. During the war, many Canadians still experienced economic suffering and reduced standards of living. The difference now was that they believed it was for a good cause.[27]

While church attendance saw little rise during the war years, the war itself was often framed in righteous terms. The moral terminology used by churches, ministers, and denominational leaders linked the national war cause with a larger spiritual cause. Worship became one of the ways that Canadian citizens could participate in the war. Buying victory bonds, accepting rationing, working in weapons factories, paying more in income tax, recycling rubber, glass, old saucepans, and toothpaste tubes all became religious acts of faith.

It was not until after the war, though, that Canada began to experience significant economic relief. With an iron and steel industry that had fostered aircraft manufacturing, ship-building, and weaponry, Canada was transformed from a rural economy based on agriculture to one focused on household consumption, business development, and international trade.

Canadians had not responded to the Second World War by flocking to church. It was not until the "boys" came home that the Canadian church experienced what might be described as an adolescent growth spurt. Soon after the end of the war, until about 1960, men and women who had shown little more than a cursory interest in church life before going off to war demonstrated a new-found enthusiasm in attendance and most things religious. Membership, attendance, and financial support all resumed the upward trend that the church had experienced in the early part of the century.

The first signs of renewal were in the Sunday Schools, with numbers exploding as war veterans tried to ensure their children would inherit

27. Ferrara, "The Great Depression."

the same "Christian" values they had fought for. John Webster Grant describes this time:

> When ministers suggested that children were likely to take Christianity seriously only if they saw evidence of their parents' interest, young couples took the hint and began to attend church with unaccustomed regularity. They sometimes found sermons difficult to understand, and the next step was enrollment in study groups. Indeed, the range of possible activities seemed to be almost limitless. Women's organizations flourished, men's clubs came alive, and service projects abounded. Many church buildings were rarely out of use during waking hours.[28]

The result was that many church buildings could not even begin to accommodate the resurgence. Many church properties had suffered from a lack of attention and resources during the Depression. And in many of the rapidly expanding suburbs, churches did not yet exist. Denominational officials and extension committees toiled fervently to identify sites, tender architects, and raise funds. Between 1945 and 1966, the United Church alone built 1,500 new churches.[29]

One community, in particular, highlighted this trend. In 1951, amidst a severe post-war housing shortage, industrialist E. P. Taylor announced the development of Don Mills as Canada's first "model" community. The community was to be built on 2,000 acres of farmland, situated northeast of downtown Toronto at Don Mills Road and Lawrence Avenue East. Fashioned after the "Garden City" model that had emerged in the United Kingdom late in the nineteenth century,[30] the design envisioned features that would define not only the form and style of suburban sprawl but the business practices of those who would develop them. The plan was to build the community in quadrants around its major intersection, with regional shopping at its center and each quadrant containing a school, a church, and a park.[31] Occupying the four corners of the quadrant were Donway Baptist Church,[32] Donway United Church, Church of the Ascension (Anglican), and St. Mark's Presbyterian Church. Shortly after, St. Bonaventure Catholic Church would follow.

28. Grant, *Church in the Canadian Era*, 161.

29. Forest, "The Present," 64.

30. Stern, Fishman, Tilove. *Paradise Planned*, 48.

31. Sewell, "Don Mills," 264–60.

32. The author grew up in Don Mills, attending Donway Baptist Church from 1961 to 1985 and Don Mills Collegiate from 1976 to 1979.

It is difficult to overestimate the influence of Don Mills on suburban development and church life in Canada. Don Mills defined the basic design of many Canadian neighborhoods. Some direct descendants include Erin Mills, Meadowvale, and Bramalea in the Toronto area, Bow River in Calgary, and Kanata in the Ottawa area.[33] In Canada, a "church on every corner"[34] was just as common as a "pub on every corner" in industrial England.[35] In these new communities, people went to churches to congregate, not just for worship, but also for Scouts and Guides, Cubs and Brownies, Saturday afternoon children's movies, bridge clubs, pot-luck meals, and badminton nights, concerts, and daycares.

The mid-twentieth-century steeplechase was no longer about seeing who could race fastest from one steeple to another, but rather who could build the next steeple the fastest. Some faith traditions were able to take advantage of the religious boom more readily than others. Denominations with centralized resources often found themselves better situated than those that depended on local initiative. The Lutherans, for example, were able to take advantage of "mission developers" from the United States. In contrast, congregational traditions like the Baptists relied more heavily upon individual "parent-congregations" to raise funds and plant new congregations.

John Webster Grant points out that the response varied in terms of locality and class. The religious boom of the 1950s "was largely a phenomenon of suburbia, where families with small children were most heavily concentrated and where the effects of increased affluence were most widely felt."[36] But in small towns, inner-cities, and rural areas, the church saw little growth. Popular amongst the middle-class, it struggled to connect with blue-collar families and those living on the margins of society. What appeared to be a massive return to religion was somewhat deceptive. Spire-filled neighborhoods were filled partly by emptying old ones, and Sunday Schools owed their appeal as much to rising birth rates as they did to religious fervor.

33. Sewell, "Don Mills," 264–60.

34. The corner of Fourth Avenue East and Tenth Street East in Owen, Sound, Ontario represents one of many Main Street examples of church on every corner. Known locally as Salvation Corners, the four corners are occupied by First Baptist Church, Church of the Nazarene, St. George's Anglican Church and Georgian Shores United Church. https://www.owensoundtourism.ca/en/explore/Historic-Walking-Tour.aspx.

35. O'Connor, *A Pub on Every Corner.*

36. Grant, *Church in the Canadian Era,* 161.

A sense of nostalgia also factored significantly. Men and women who had been involved in the war effort saw an opportunity to rejoin the mainstream of Canadian life. They wanted to make up for lost years, and they were prepared to work hard for it. They wanted to forget the interruption of their lives. For many, church and church life represented a return to normalcy:

> Couples who had been separated during wartime worried about saving their marriages. Men who had grown up during the depression worried about holding their jobs. A near-obsession with material security developed, and many stories were told of applicants who showed more interest in minute details of pension plans than in possibilities of future advancement. Anxious people looked to the church for help in achieving personal stability and consolidating their position in the community.[37]

Undoubtedly, many were concerned about spiritual security, too, although few seemed willing to talk about it.

The Comfortable Pew

As the 1960s emerged, Canada sought to make its independent mark on the world. In trying to distance itself from its old-fashioned British parent, the still-young nation also tried to take a step back from big-brother America by defining a culture of its own. A new flag was in the works. Under Prime Minister Lester Pearson, Canada had assumed prominence as an international peace-keeper. Canada welcomed more than 100,000 American Vietnam draft dodgers into the country. Canadian artists like Joni Mitchell, Neil Young, Gordon Lightfoot, and The Guess Who shone on the international stage, and Canadians played integral roles in designing the lunar module that in 1969 landed astronauts Neil Armstrong and Buzz Aldrin on the moon. As far as the church was concerned, its pews were still comfortable, and the biggest complaint of most church pastors "was that they heard so few complaints."[38]

Despite the prevalence of new church construction, cracks in the foundation were already starting to appear. As early as 1958, the United Church of Canada's moderator had noted that despite Canadians' personal interest in religion, there also appeared to be an "endless relativity

37. Grant, *Church in the Canadian Era*, 163.

38. Grant, *Church in the Canadian Era*, 184.

in faith and morals."[39] To stay relevant, denominations in Canada and abroad explored how best to modernize their message. In 1959, the Anglicans had issued a revised *Common Book of Prayer.* In 1962, Pope John XXIII consecrated the teachings of Vatican II. The year 1964 saw the approval of a new *Book of Common Order* by the Presbyterians and a combined effort with the United Church to introduce a new hymn book.[40]

At the time, United Church leaders were also working with the Baptists to develop a new curriculum for use in Christian education. The two denominations had decided to pursue the project's development together as early as 1952. According to Dr. William Wood, one of the Baptist readers assigned to the project, the editorial board had set out to produce a contemporary set of three annual books. The curriculum's first year focused on the Old Testament, the second year on the New Testament, and the third on the history and the purpose of the church. Admittedly, the third year was going to present some challenges for the committee since the history and polity of the two denominations were somewhat different. Fortunately for the committee (or unfortunately, depending on your point of view), the Baptists never got that far, pulling out of the project, objecting to the "modernism" it portrayed. Subsequently, the denomination voted to destroy all copies of the curriculum in their possession.[41]

Moving ahead on their own, the United Church introduced its materials in 1962 with more than 600,000 copies of the adult study book[42] sold that first summer. While sales of the new curricula materials surpassed the total enrollment in United Church Sunday Schools, the response in many United Church congregations was mixed. Some Sunday School teachers resigned, finding the resources too "liberal" for their liking. Some members abandoned the United Church for more conservative congregations, while many congregations reported an enthusiastic response from most members.[43]

In addition to these internal developments, two additional factors were influencing Canadian society more broadly. The first of these was

39. Grant, *Church in the Canadian Era,* 184.

40. Grant, *Church in the Canadian Era,* 18.

41. Personal conversation with Dr. Wm. R. Wood. Retired minister and past president of the Baptist Union of Western Canada and the Baptist Convention of Ontario and Quebec.

42. Mathers, *The Word and the Way.*

43. Grant, *Church in the Canadian Era,* 187.

Pierre Berton's best-selling book, *The Comfortable Pew.*[44] In 1963, the Anglican Church's Department of Religious Education asked Berton, Canada's best-known journalist at the time, to look critically at the church and to write a book about what he saw. Berton was a self-professed agnostic who had grown up in the Anglican Church but left the church in his early twenties when it no longer seemed relevant to his own experience.

As William Kilbourn writes in his introduction to *The Restless Church: A Response to the Comfortable Pew,* "Anglicans in 1963 were beginning to speak a good deal about becoming 'a listening Church' and engaging in dialogue with the world."[45] And listen, they did. Smashing Canadian records, with more than 170,000 copies in print in Canada alone after its first year, it was hard not to! The release of *The Comfortable Pew* caused a storm of controversy in the press and amongst countless church leaders. Kilbourn continues:

> It was the subject of hundreds of newspaper editorials, articles, and cartoons, and several dozen radio and television programs. . . . [T]here can scarcely be a Protestant church or parish hall in the county in which the name of the book or its author was not mentioned in 1965, and in some, at times, it almost seemed as if people were talking about nothing else.[46]

The Comfortable Pew was described as everything from "clear, fresh and penetrating to trite, dated, and confused."[47] It was recommended as required reading by some, and fodder for the fire by others. For Berton's supporters, the book aptly named the church's loss of relevance—and struggle to know how or where to rediscover it. For some of his detractors, it went too far. And for others, not far enough.

The challenge that Berton did not go far enough in his critique is perhaps best expressed by Lotte and Werner Pelz. Lotte, a teacher, and Werner, an Anglican vicar, wrote:

> We who are also trying to find the "something" of great price that so many—believers and unbelievers alike—still, surprisingly, expect to find hidden somewhere behind or beyond religion, cannot help agreeing with almost every one of the accusations Pierre Burton hurls at the ecclesiastical set-up. There

44. Berton, *Comfortable Pew.*
45. Kilbourn, ed., *The Restless Church*, vii.
46. Kilbourn, *The Restless Church,* viii.
47. Kilbourn, *The Restless Church,* viii.

> is, however, a quaint, old-world look about the arguments of one so eager to drag the church from the bronze into the aluminum-plastic age, to make it play its cymbals, lutes and harps before microphones, T.V. cameras and newspaper editors. Surely his objections have been stated 50, 100, even 200 years ago and have not substantially increased in depth and acumen since the days of Voltaire. One is a little disappointed in Mr. Berton for having missed an opportunity for having apparently forgotten—like many other objectors and defenders—to re-read Nietzsche, Marx, Jeremiah, Isaiah and that much misunderstood Man of Nazareth who, during the last 2500 years, have attacked religion on a much profounder level.[48]

Where Berton did succeed was in bringing about a serious attempt by many to study some of the issues he raised—and actually engaging people in debate in "a country where ideas are not normally taken seriously and are more apt to be praised, blasted, or ignored than carefully examined."[49] In the wake of the book's release, religious leadership, institutional models, theology, and practice were all up for review. The steeple was no longer quite so visible—and the chase had become a whole lot muddier.

The Sixties Scoop

Simultaneously, as Canada sought to establish its identity on the world stage, it was expanding its attempts to undermine and eliminate Canada's First Nations' aboriginal identity. And the church was running alongside.

Beginning in 1951, the Canadian Government revised the Indian Act to give jurisdiction over the welfare of Indigenous children to the provinces. For close to a century, First Nations communities had been subject to a devastating set of federal policies that had resulted in systemic poverty, poor health, high death rates, and extreme socioeconomic barriers. With no additional funding and most Aboriginal communities under-serviced, under-resourced, and still under the control of the Indian Act, most provincial welfare agencies opted to remove children from their homes, rather than invest in community resources and supports.

From 1960 to the 1980s, provincial governments followed in the federal government's footsteps, considering the removal of Indigenous children the fastest and easiest way to address their "welfare." This

48. Pelz and Pelz "The Uncomfortable Few," 103.

49. Kilbourn, *The Restless Church*, ix.

practice, known as the "Sixties Scoop," saw more than 20,000 First Nations children taken from their homes, often without their family's consent, and taught to disregard their own culture, language, and identity. In 1983, Patrick Johnston submitted a report to the Canadian Council on Social Development entitled, *Native Children and the Child Welfare System.*[50] He described the practice not as an isolated response to inferior Indigenous parenting, but as an extension of Canada's paternalistic policies that sought to assimilate Indigenous communities and their children.

Many of the young, mostly white, social workers employed by the provinces were shocked by what they found: families living in dilapidated and crowded homes, many of which had been designed by Canada's Department of Indian Affairs. There was no indoor plumbing. They encountered rampant poverty and alcohol addiction and a relaxed communal parenting style completely foreign to their own experience. They considered it in the child's best interest to "rescue" them from this perceived neglect and place them in white, middle-class homes with all the material comfort and opportunity they could provide.[51] As Raven Sinclair, an associate professor in the Faculty of Social Work at the University of Regina, writes:

> Children were apprehended by the thousands, in questionable circumstances, with economic incentive rather than neglect or abuse emerging as the motive for removing children from their homes. . . . The white social worker, following on the heels of the missionary, the priest, and the Indian agent, was convinced that the only hope for the salvation of the Indian people lay in the removal of their children.[52]

It was not until 1980, with the introduction of the Child, Family and Community Services Act, that social workers were even required to notify band councils of a child's removal from their community.

Federal initiatives such as the Adopt Indian Métis Program aggressively advertised Aboriginal children in catalogs, marketing them to (mostly) white adoptive parents, including many in churches across the country.[53] In 1959, only 1 percent of the children in care were Aboriginal. By 1970, more than a third of children in care were Indigenous, even

50. Johnston, *Native Children and the Welfare System*, 99.

51. Fournier and Crey, *Stolen from our Embrace*, 30.

52. Sinclair, "Identity Lost and Found."

53. Bokma, "Adoptees Seeking Redress."

though Indigenous Canadians made up only 4 percent of the overall population.[54] Approximately 70 percent of the children apprehended were placed into non-Aboriginal homes, where their birth heritage was mostly denied.

Many of the children responded to the fostering and adoption in the same way they had to residential school; they ran away, did poorly in school, and grew up confused about and ashamed of their heritage. Many children floated from foster home to foster home or lived in institutional care. Some were emotionally and sexually abused by their foster and adoptive parents. Many turned to drugs, alcohol, crime, and suicide. Even those adopted into the most privileged of homes—including the son of former Prime Minister Jean Chrétien and his wife Aline—had lives marked by addiction and incarceration.[55]

In 1985, Justice Edwin Kimelman released a highly critical review of the apprehension of Indigenous children entitled, *No Quiet Place: Review Committee on Indian Métis Adoptions and Placements.* Popularly known as *The Kimelman Report,* it concluded that cultural genocide had taken place in a "systemic, routine manner," calling the government's policy one of "wholesale exportation" or what can hardly be described as anything less than human trafficking.

These children have often been called "the lost generation."[56] Caught between a world in which they had been raised but did not fit in and an ancient native culture into which they had been born but denied access, many had no sense of who they were. They were taken from their homes. Their names were changed. Many had their personal histories erased because of incomplete, falsified, sealed, or missing adoption records. In some cases, people who had fought to win back their Indigenous status discovered that the Canadian government had registered them as deceased under their original identity. Canadian society had succeeded not only in killing the "Indian within the child," but erasing some of them from history altogether.

Money is a strong motivator. By putting Indigenous children up for adoption, the treaty status and corresponding benefits of thousands of Indigenous children were buried. By downloading the responsibility for these children's welfare onto the provinces, who in turn downloaded

54. Truth and Reconciliation Commission, *The Came for the Children.*

55. Bokma, "Adoptees Seeking Redress."

56. Bokma, "Adoptees Seeking Redress."

responsibility onto Canadian families, various levels of government saved millions. As Jeffrey Wilson, the Ontario lawyer who argued a class-action suit on behalf of the Sixties Scoop plaintiffs, states: "Adoption is the cheapest form of childcare[;] . . . somebody on some level saved a lot of money."[57]

In December of 2018, the federal government approved an $800 million settlement to compensate survivors of the Sixties Scoop for the loss of culture, language, and identity. Fifty million dollars of the award was dedicated to establishing a "Sixties Scoop Healing Foundation" with a focus on healing, wellness, language, culture, and commemoration. An additional $750 million was to be distributed in equal, individual payments to survivors themselves.[58]

The Sixties Scoop, however, is about much more than money saved and money paid out—especially where the church is concerned. While the Sixties Scoop refers to a certain period in Canadian history, it points to a deep disconnect between the values that churches of various denominations have *claimed* and the lives they have *lived out*. The ideology behind the church-led residential school system was intended to "civilize" Aboriginal people and assimilate them into "Canadian" society. The child welfare intervention that began in the late 1950s, and was pitched as a means of resolving the ills of the residential school system, demonstrated that residential schools were only the tip of the iceberg of what is a deep void in the church's understanding of human equity.

In chasing steeples, the church has often succeeded in undermining the identity of others and losing sight of its own. Steeples that stood tall across the rural countryside and later on suburban street corners were intended to act as markers. They were meant, literally, to stand for something. There is a childhood rhyme using hand actions many of us learned that goes like this: "Here is the church and here is the steeple. Open the doors and see all the people." Now that the pews are not so full, the steeples are failing, and the buildings beneath them are closing, where does that leave us?

The church in Canada now finds itself between a rock and a hard place. The obstacles before us are as difficult as they have ever been. Scripture tells us we have been called God's children by adoption,[59] and yet

57. Bokma, "Adoptees Seeking Redress."

58. Griffin, "Sixties Scoop Survivors."

59. Gal 4:4–5.

by endorsing an inequitable school and welfare system that still removes Indigenous children from their families, we have also participated in an adoption scheme that has gone terribly wrong. Amnesty International describes the Sixties Scoop survivors as living in a diaspora, something Christians, through our Judaic ancestors, know all about—or at least we should. Some would say that this is where the Canadian church finds itself now—scattered and separated, if not from its homeland, from its identity. And while Christians in Canada have played a significant role in separating Indigenous people from their homes, culture, and identity, perhaps as people who now find ourselves in our own diaspora, we are discovering ways of learning from and identifying with those we have wronged.

In John 8:32, Jesus says to his disciples, "You will know the truth, and the truth will set you free." In this passage, Jesus does not say, "Tell the truth in order to make yourselves good, right or righteous, and others evil, wrong or unrighteous." He does not say, "Tell the truth by creating your own 'facts' or by using 'facts' as weapons against others." Truth goes deeper than that. When we fail to tell the truth, we do not just cause others to lose their freedom—we lose our own.

On January 6, 2021, insurrectionists in the United States stormed the Capital Building in Washington, DC. After the riots, the media narrative was about the "Big Lie" that motivated the demonstrators. The lie was about the 2020 American election being stolen, a claim for which there was no evidence. However, underneath the "Big Lie" was an even "Bigger Lie"—that one way of life, one culture, or race is superior to another.

The lie that some of God's children are superior and others are inferior is not exclusive to the United States. It is a lie that lives and breathes in Canada as well. And even in its churches. According to the Bible, idols separate people from God. But the idol of mostly white, mostly Western culture has done just that. And tragically, we have believed it. Steeples built on lies will inevitably crumble. Reconciliation needs truth. Colonialism, patriarchy, and racial superiority are lies. They are all expressions of idolatry that need to be removed from Canadian churches. As Desmond Tutu and Nelson Mandela in South Africa preached, there can be no reconciliation or unity without truth and "no future without forgiveness."[60]

Telling the truth is the responsibility of every Canadian Christian. It is not good enough to seek changes in government policy, applaud truth and reconciliation commissions, and sigh in relief at the financial awards

60. Tutu, *No Future without Forgiveness.*

made to Aboriginal Canadians as though that somehow lets the Canadian church off the hook. Telling the truth means humbling ourselves and acknowledging what lies we have been telling. It means working to detoxify the racism and privilege that we have exercised. It means listening to the hurt we have caused, learning how our prejudice is both personal and systemic, and accepting deeply the truth of Paul's First Letter to the Corinthians, when it says, "If one part of the body suffers, then all the parts suffer with it." Canada's Christians need to face the truth. And we need to face it together.

In June of 2021, many Canadians urged governments and municipalities to cancel or scale back July 1st Canada Day celebrations as a way of facing this truth. Reflecting the sentiment of many, Angela White, executive director of the Indian Residential School Survivors Society told CBC reporters:

> This Canada Day is different for all Canadians, not just the Indigenous population. This Canada Day should be, in my opinion, a moment or a pause for grieving and the ability to rebuild and acknowledge those past with a better future with us rooted in it.[61]

Pursuing a slightly different angle, Chief Cadmus Delorme of the Cowessess nation put it this way:

> We all inherited this. Nobody today created residential schools. Nobody today created the Indian Act. Nobody today created the Sixties Scoop. But we all inherited this. And if we want to say we're proud Canadians, then we will accept the beautiful country we have today, and we will accept what we all inherited . . . so that our next generation won't inherit this. We will make them more as dreamers.[62]

In many ways, that is all Canada's First Nations have been asking for. Speaking at the 50th anniversary of the Canadian Music Industry's Juno awards in June of 2021, eighty-year-old Indigenous Canadian folk icon Buffy Sainte-Marie shared this impassioned appeal, saying:

> This broadcast is coming from the Dish with One Spoon Territory. The Dish with One Spoon is a peace and friendship treaty amongst the Anishinaabe, the Mississauga, and the Haudenosaunee people that binds them to share the territory and protect the land. Treaties across Canada invite Canadians

61. Vermes, "Cancel Canada Day."

62. CBC News, "Cowessess First Nation Chief."

and newcomers into meaningful relationships with the original people of this country in the spirit of peace, friendship, and respect. The recent discovery of even more remains of residential school indigenous children, this time in Kamloops, is shocking to some people and a revelation. But it's not news to Indigenous people. The genocide basic to this country's birth is ongoing, and we need to face it together. And I ask for your compassion.[63]

63. Sainte-Marie, "The Genocide."

6

Just a Brick in the Wall

Declining Attendance and Shifting Values

Daddy's flown across the ocean
Leaving just a memory
Snapshot in the family album
Daddy what else did you leave for me?
Daddy, what'd'ja leave behind for me?!?
All in all it was just a brick in the wall.
All in all it was all just bricks in the wall.

—PINK FLOYD—THE WALL (PART 1)

IN 1979, THE BRITISH Rock Group *Pink Floyd* released their epic Rock Opera, *The Wall.*[1] With more than 30 million copies sold worldwide, the album explores the life of Pink, a jaded rock star whose self-imposed isolation from society becomes the cornerstone of a symbolic wall. Recalling those lyrics, it is hard not to imagine some readers wondering if, in addition to writing about his childhood, Roger Waters was not also writing about the church and its relationship with God. While many Christians at

1. Waters, "Another Brick in the Wall (Part 1).

the time were actively resisting Friedrich Nietzsche's widely quoted assertion that "God is dead," increasing numbers were also starting to believe that if God wasn't dead, God had at least left the building.

Losing Their Religion

Shortly after the Second World War, 67 percent of Canadians attended worship services every week, with the majority of these people attending Christian churches.[2] By the mid-1950s, Gallup had already begun to report declines in church attendance.[3] By the mid-1960s, national weekly attendance was hovering around 50 percent.[4] By 1974, numbers in United Church Sunday Schools had dropped to less than half of what they had been eight years before, despite hopes that the New Curriculum would boost enrollment. Between 1965 and 1975, Protestant weekly attendance fell from 32 percent to 25 percent.[5] In the Catholic Church, attendance at weekly mass across the country had dropped from 83 percent to 61 percent, with even more significant declines recorded in the province of Quebec.[6] John Webster Grant highlights how dramatic some of these numbers were. Membership in the church-sponsored social movement *la Jeunese Ouvrière* dropped from almost 31,000 in 1961 to just 3,000 ten years later. Between 1962 and 1972, 14 percent of the country's 6,000 priests abandoned the priesthood. During that same period, the number of men serving in Catholic orders was cut in half, and the number of women in Catholic orders declined by 22 percent. In 1968–69 alone, financial giving in Catholic parishes dropped by 20 percent.[7]

For a short time during the mid-1970s and '80s, places of worship seemed to experience an attendance reprieve. Declines leveled off, and still, around one-third of Canadians could be found attending worship in any given week. But by the time R.E.M.'s Grammy-award-winning song, "Losing My Religion," hit the charts in 1991, Canadians were reflecting the group's sentiments in droves. By 2007, Ipsos Reid[8] was reporting that

2. Gee and Veevers, "Religiously Unaffiliated Canadians."
3. Grant, *Church in the Canadian Era,* 227.
4. Hiemstra and Stiller, "Religious Affiliation."
5. Grant, *Church in the Canadian Era,* 229
6. Grant, *Church in the Canadian Era,* 227.
7. Grant, *Church in the Canadian Era,* 227.
8. Hiemstra and Stiller, "Religious Affiliation."

only 20 percent of Canadians were attending worship weekly, and by 2019, the number had dropped to 16 percent.[9]

Attendance and Denomination

While most Christian traditions have seen their attendance at worship drop, not all have shared this decline equally. A 2013 poll conducted by the Evangelical Fellowship of Canada and pollster Angus Reid shows that between 1996 and 2013, the number of French Catholics who said they attend mass weekly fell from 16 percent to just 5 percent (see Fig. 4). The number of English-speaking Catholics attending church once a week fell from 33 percent to 19 percent. For mainline Protestants, weekly attendance figures dropped from 20 percent to 10 percent. Evangelicals, the only major Christian group to measure above the national average, still fell nine percentage points from 49 percent to 40 percent.

Figure 4: Weekly Worship Attendance of Canadians by Faith Tradition

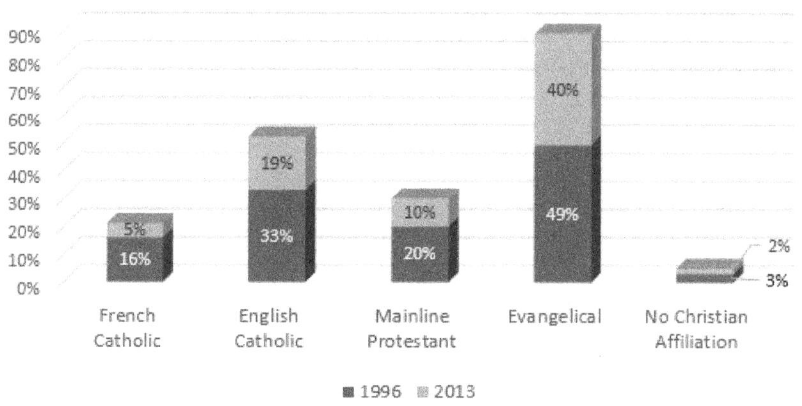

Source: Hiemstra, R., 2014; Angus Reid, 1996; Angus Reid/EFC, 2013.

In 2019, updated monthly figures from the General Social Survey showed that 16 percent[10] of Canadians attend religious group activities

9. Cornelissen, "Religiosity in Canada, 1985 to 2019," 3.

10. Cornelissen, "Religiosity in Canada, 1985 to 2019," 3.

at least once a week[11] and 7 percent at least once a month.[12] Thirty–one percent of individuals who identify as Christian participated in religious group activities at least once a month. Jehovah's Witnesses (86%), Latter-Day Saints (80%), Anabaptist groups (75%), Pentecostals, and other Charismatic groups (72%) take part in monthly religious activities well above the average. Other faith traditions such as Buddhists (15%), Anglicans (19%), United Church (19%), and Jews (24%) are well below the average (see Table 1).

11. Note the change in language by Statistics Canada from attending *worship* once a month to attending *religious group activities* once a month.

12. Cornelissen, "Religiosity in Canada, 1985 to 2019," 3.

Table 1: Different Forms of Religiosity by Faith Tradition (2017 to 2019)

Affiliation	Share of Population	In groups at least once a month	In groups less than once a month, but individual once a week	In groups or individually at least once a month during the year	No group participation or individual religious practices	Religious or spiritual beliefs somewhat or very important1	Religious or spiritual beliefs not very important or not important at all1
	Percentage						
Buddhist	1.4	15	17	45	23	67	33
Christian (total)	63.2	31	16	24	29	68	32
Christian (no other specification)	10.3	44	15	20	20	77	23
Anabaptist	0.5	75	10[N]	8[N]	6[N]	93	7[N]
Anglican	3.8	19	17	28	39	62	38
Baptist	1.4	54	12	15	19	86	14
Catholic	32	25	17	27	31	62	38
Christian Orthodox	1.4	26	19	34	21	73	27
Jehovah's Witness	0.4	86	5[N]	5[N]	4[N]	98	2[N]
Latter-Day Saints	0.3	80	7N	7N	6N	96	4N
Lutheran	1.2	31	15	26	28	66	34
Methodist and Wesleyan	0.3	46	12N	19	23	87	13N
Pentecostal / Charismatic	0.8	72	9N	8N	12[N]	94	6N
Reformed and Presbyterian	1.4	35	12	20	33	69	31
United Church	3.8	19	15	26	39	64	36

Table 1: Different Forms of Religiosity by Faith Tradition (2017 to 2019)

Affiliation	Share of Population	In groups at least once a month	In groups less than once a month, but individual once a week	In groups or individually at least once a month during the year	No group participation or individual religious practices	Religious or spiritual beliefs somewhat or very important1	Religious or spiritual beliefs not very important or not important at all1
				Percentage			
Other Christian related tradition	4.4	35	17	18	31	73	27
Hindu	1.7	31	23	34	12[N]	79	21
Jewish	1	24	9	49	18	70	30
Muslim	3.7	42	23	15	19	82	18
Sikh	1.4	48	12[N]	36	4[N]	84[N]	16
Indigenous	0.2	22[N]	34[N]	15[N]	29[N]	83	17[N]
Other religions / spiritual tradition	1	24	30	25	20	79	21
TOTAL REPORTED RELIGIOUS AFFILIATION	73.7	32	16	25	27	69	30
NO REPORTED RELIGIOUS AFFILIATION	26.3	2	7	17	74	21	79

N—strong sampling variability, estimate to be used with caution.

1—data on the importance of religious beliefs are for GSS cycles, 31, 34, and 34 only

Note: minimum and maximum margin of error at 95% probability

Source: Statistics Canada, General Social Survey, cycles 31–34, 2017 to 2019.

Attendance and Age

Differences in worship attendance are influenced in part by differences in religiosity between younger and older generations.[13] In general, the younger the person, the less likely they are to participate in group religious activities, individual religious or spiritual activities, and value religious or spiritual beliefs in their everyday lives.[14] Participation can also change over time. Cornelissen reports that the frequency of group and individual religious activities declines with age in almost every age cohort.[15]

Figure 5 shows how participation for different age groups varies across the country.

Figure 5: Religious Participation of Canadians by Region and Year of Birth

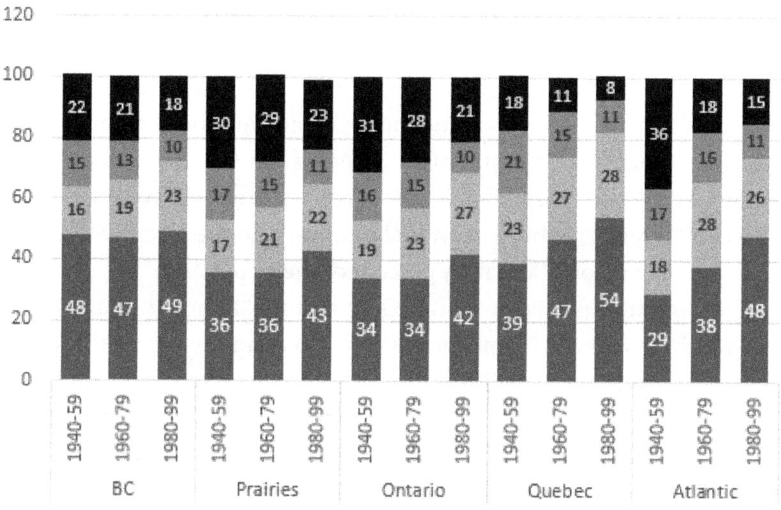

Note: some columns do not sum to 100% due to rounding

Source: Statistics Canada, General Social Survey, cycles 31 to 34, 2017 to 2018

13. Bibby, Thiessen, and Bailey, *Millennial Mosaic*, 181.
14. Cornelissen, "Religiosity in Canada, 1985–2019," 6.
15. Cornelissen, "Religiosity in Canada, 1985–2019," 7.

Currently, adults born between 1940 and 1959 show the highest rates of monthly participation. Worship attendance is highest in the Atlantic provinces, where 36 percent of adults born during this period participate in religious group activities at least once a month. The number falls to 31 percent in Ontario, 30 percent across the prairies, 22 percent in British Columbia, and 18 percent in Quebec. At the opposite end of the scale, Canadians born between 1980 and 1999 show the highest levels of non-participation. Quebecers lead the way, with 54 percent of residents aged 20 to 39 showing no group or individual participation. British Columbia follows Quebec at 49 percent, the Atlantic provinces (48%), the Prairie provinces (43%), and Ontario (42%).[16]

Attendance and Immigration

Before the 1980s, Canada's immigrant population was relatively small, mostly European and overwhelmingly Christian. In recent years, however, Canada's welcoming policy has encouraged rising numbers of immigrants, with close to half of all immigrants (9.4% of the Canadian population) having arrived since 2001.[17] Canada currently leads G8 countries, with 22 percent of residents born outside the country. In the United States, immigrants make up only about 13 percent of the population.[18]

Immigration is vital to Canada's economy,[19] although many Canadians would also like to blame the church's attendance woes on those high numbers of immigrants. With increased numbers also comes increased diversity. Most immigrants (56%) who arrived in the 1970s were Catholic or Protestant, while only a quarter were affiliated with other world religions such as Judaism, Hinduism, Islam, Buddhism, and Sikhism. Since 2001, about 39 percent of new Canadians (four in ten) have belonged to these religious minorities, equaling the number of new immigrants who identify as Protestant or Catholic. Currently, immigrants from Asia, Africa, and the Middle East represent half of Canada's immigrant population. In comparison, only 30 percent of United States immigrants come from these regions. With immigrants making up more than a fifth of Canada's

16. Cornelissen, "Religiosity in Canada, 1985–2019," 6.
17. Statistics Canada, "Census Profile, 2016 Census."
18. Pew Research. "Canada's Changing Religious Landscape."
19. Picot, "Immigrant Economic and Social Outcomes," 6.

population, it is not surprising that their religious beliefs would influence Canada's overall religious makeup.

Figure 6: Religious Affiliation of Canadian Immigrants by Decade of Arrival

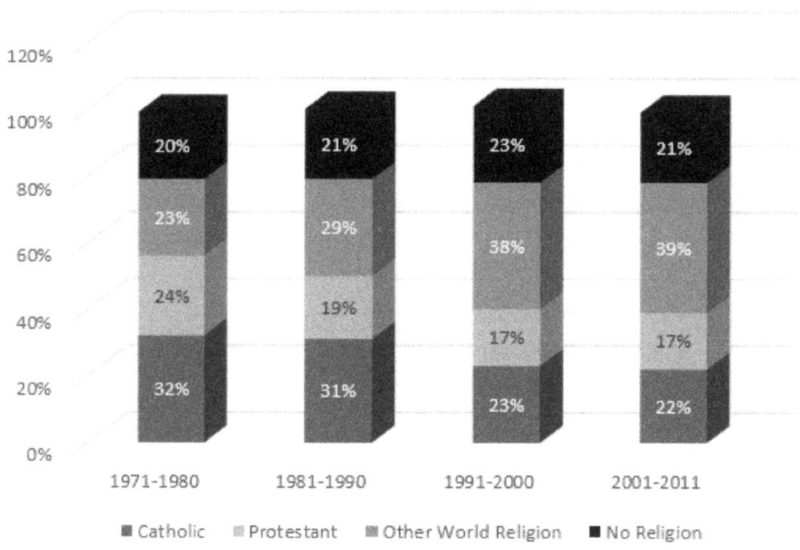

Source: 2011 National Household Survey

But while immigration may be contributing to Canada's religious diversity, it does not appear to be supporting Canada's declines in religious attendance overall. If anything, religious attendance is higher among immigrants than among the general population and has remained that way for several years. In 2016, 47 percent of immigrants reported attending religious services at least once a month, up slightly from 43 percent in 1998. In contrast, in 2016, only 23 percent of native-born Canadians said that they attended religious services at least once a month, down from 31 percent in 1998.[20]

Affiliation and Religiosity

Declines in religious attendance make the headlines. But attendance numbers aren't the only religious statistic that has been in decline. In

20. Pew Research, "Canada's Changing Religious Landscape."

1971, 88 percent of Canadians identified as Christian. Fifty years later, that number has fallen to 68 percent.[21] Put it another way, Canada had almost 19 million Canadian Christians in 1971. In 2019, there were 25.6 million Christians, an increase of only 6.6 million Christians in a country whose population had increased by more than 15.6 million.

Only 23 percent of Canadians participate in religious group activities at least once a month, while 30 percent said they engaged in personal religious or spiritual activities like prayer and meditation at least once a week (see Table 2). One in five Canadians (18%) who report a religious affiliation take part in religious group activities rarely, never engage in spiritual or religious activities on their own, and find religious or spiritual beliefs to be of little or no importance in how they live their lives.

Table 2: Religiosity of Canadians Aged 15 and Older (2017 to 2019)

Indicator of Religiosity	TOTAL %	Male %	Female %
Religious Affiliation			
Yes	68	64	72
No	32	36	28
Frequency of participation in group religious activities			
At least once a week	16	14	18
At least once a month	7	7	8
At least once a year	24	24	25
Not at all	53	55	50
Frequency of religious or spiritual activity on one's own			
At least once a day	20	15	24
At least once a week'	10	9	12
At least once a month	7	6	7
At least three times a year	4	4	4
Once or twice a year	7	6	7
Not at all	53	60	46
Importance of religious or spiritual beliefs in everyday life			
Very important	29	25	33
Somewhat important	25	22	28
Not very important	17	18	16
Not important at all	29	35	23

Source: Statistics Canada, General Social Survey, cycle 34, 2019

21. Cornelissen, "Religiosity in Canada 1985 to 2019," 1.

Women are more likely than men to report religious affiliation (72% to 64%) or to acknowledge the importance of religious or spiritual beliefs to how they live their lives (61% to 47%). Women are also more likely than men to be involved in group religious activities, especially private religious or spiritual practices (36% to 24%).

Measures of religiosity also vary significantly from region to region (see Fig. 5). High levels of non-affiliation and lower attendance have characterized British Columbia for decades. For example, in 1985, 25 percent of provincial residents aged fifteen and older reported no religious affiliation, compared to 9 percent in the rest of Canada. As early as 1901, census data showed, even then, a higher proportion of British Columbians with no religious affiliation (1.5% vs. 0.16% in the rest of Canada).[22] They were also less likely than Canadians in eastern provinces to attend church or other places of worship.[23] Between 2017 and 2019, 40 percent of British Columbia residents reported having no religious affiliation, and 47 percent indicated they had no group or individual religious activities in the previous year.

Non-affiliation in British Columbia was even more evident amongst younger people. For example, from 2017 to 2019, more than half (53%) of people born between 1980 and 1999 reported no religious affiliation. This compared to 38 percent of those born between 1960 and 1979 and 27 percent of people born between 1940 and 1959. Surprisingly, perhaps, these generational affiliation differences did not appear to affect religious or spiritual activity levels. The percentage of people who took part in a religious group activity at least once a month ranged between 18 and 22 percent. The percentage of individuals who did not participate in group or individual religious activities throughout the previous year was more or less the same across cohorts, ranging from 47 to 49 percent.[24]

Quebec distinguishes itself with the highest proportion of people who report religious affiliation and say their religious beliefs are not very important or not at all important (40 percent compared to anywhere between 15 and 25 percent in other regions). Quebec also had the lowest percentage of people participating in group religious activities at least once a month (14 percent compared to numbers ranging from 21 percent to 32 percent in other provinces). This low rate of participation relates

22. Cornelissen, "Religiosity in Canada, 1985 to 2019," 10.

23. Marks, "Exploring Regional Diversity in 1901," 247–54.

24. Cornelissen, "Religiosity in Canada, 1985–2019," 11.

significantly to dramatic changes amongst Catholics in Quebec. Some, including Wilkins-Laflamme, have used the term "cultural Catholicism"[25] to describe this combination of affiliation, low value of belief, and low religious participation. Between 1985 and 2019, Catholics aged fifteen and older declined from 87 percent to 62 percent. At the same time, the percentage of people who affiliated with traditions other than Catholic doubled from 9 percent to 18 percent. We see these distinctions at play regarding participation as well. From 2017 to 2019, monthly group participation rates for Catholics were 14 percent and 26 percent for those reporting a religious affiliation other than Catholic. Quebecers born between 1980 and 1999 (19%) were half as likely as those born between 1940 and 1959 (39%) to participate in religious group activities at least once a month or religious activities on their own at least once a week.[26]

Typically the Atlantic provinces have tended to be the most religiously stable. However, the most recent General Social Survey findings uncover some significant differences between older and younger age groupings in this region. For example, between 2017 and 2019, 36 percent of those born between 1940 and 1959 participated in religious group activities at least once a month. This compares to 15 percent of those born between 1980 and 1999. More strikingly, almost half (48%) of those in the youngest age group had not participated in a religious group activity in the year before, showing rates similar to those observed amongst young people from the same age cohort living in British Columbia. Similar differences were found in terms of religious affiliation and the importance given to religious or spiritual beliefs. In the case of Ontario and the prairie provinces, changes in affiliation and attendance have been more inclined to reflect the kinds of changes reported nationally.[27]

Perhaps the most dramatic change on the Canadian religious landscape is the rise of "religious nones." In their book, *None of the Above: Nonreligious Identity in the U.S. and Canada,* Thiessen and Wilkins-Laflamme describe these religiously unaffiliated individuals as the "fastest growing religious 'tradition' in the United States and Canada, and much of the modern Western world."[28] In 1971, religious nones made up less than 4 percent of the population. Today, they make up 32 percent.

25. Wilkins-Laflamme, "Religious-Secular Polarization," 166–85.
26. Cornelissen, "Religiosity in Canada, 1985 to 2019," 12.
27. Cornelissen, "Religiosity in Canada, 1985 to 2019," 9.
28. Cornelissen, "Religiosity in Canada, 1985–2019," 1.

The relationship between declining attendance and religious affiliation is a little bit like asking, "Which came first, the chicken or the egg?" On the one hand, individuals who become less inclined to identify with one tradition or another are less likely to attend religious services. On the other hand, as declining attendance becomes more "normal" and there are fewer social reinforcements to attend worship regularly, people are less likely to see themselves as religious. And round and round it goes. Thiessen and Laflamme explain further:

> As fewer people say they identify or are involved with a religious group, the social acceptance towards such a declaration increases, which in turn normalizes the "no religion" option for others in society. This process is aided when those with little religiosity have children of their own and raise their children without explicitly religious socialization. It is unlikely in these circumstances for people to suddenly "take up" religious affiliation or belief, if for no other reason than they lack the social environments (e.g., family, education, politics, and media) to expose or teach them about such options.[29]

In 2017, Angus Reid avoided the question of affiliation or attendance by asking Canadians whether they were inclined to embrace religion, reject it, or whether they found themselves somewhere in between. They found that while more Canadians are still more inclined to embrace religion (30%) than reject it (26%), the vast majority of Canadians (44%) find themselves somewhere in between (see Fig. 7). The 30 percent of Canadians who said they embrace religion was down 15 percent from Bibby's observations in 1985.[30]

29. Thiessen and Wilkins-Laflamme, *None of the Above,* 60.

30. Bibby, *Fragmented Gods.*

Figure 7: Religious Leanings of Canadians

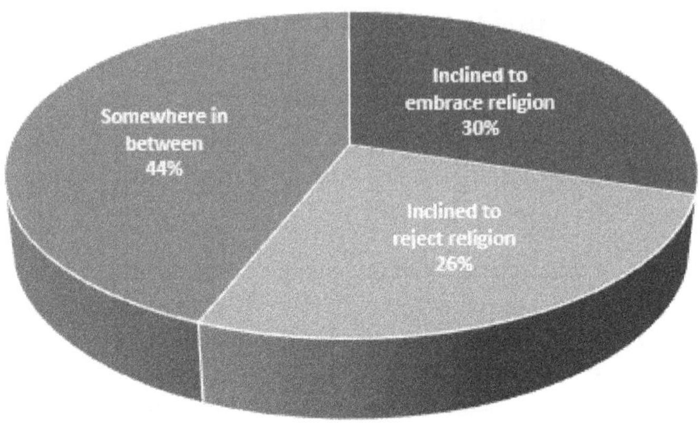

Source: Angus Reid 2017

Those who identify as "in-betweeners" still hold many conventional religious beliefs and sometimes still engage in spiritual practices, including worship attendance—but do not see themselves as devout. Of those who say they are still inclined to embrace religion, only slightly more than half report attending services at least once a month. And yet, pollsters also found that while those who embrace religion may not be attending worship as often as in the past, still close to nine in ten continue to pray individually (86%), read scripture (45%), feel strengthened by their faith (79%), and claim to experience God's presence (68%). More Canadians than not still believe in the existence of God or a higher power, in heaven, in angels, and life after death (see Table 3). Even a third of those who feel ambivalent towards religion would still prefer a religious funeral when they die.[31]

31. Bibby et al., *The Millenial Mosaic*, 176.

Table 3: Select Conventional Beliefs of Canadians by Generation

Percentage of people who believe	All	Millennials (1986—plus)	Xers (1966–85)	Boomers (1946–65)	Pre-Boomers (Pre-1946)
God or a higher power exists	73	66	72	76	80
God or a higher power cares about you personally	61	53	59	63	70
Jesus was the Divine Son of God	59	50	57	63	68
They have experienced God's presence	47	44	46	48	54
In life after death	66	70	66	65	59
In heaven	63	62	62	65	64
In hell	42	46	44	39	35
In angels	62	59	62	64	58
They have been protected from harm by an angel	56	52	55	60	57

Source: Bibby et al., 2019

God may have left the building, or at least be on the way out the door, but there certainly does not appear to be any evidence of God's imminent demise. So, if it is not God's absence that threatens the church's survival, but the emergence of religious "nones"—who are they?

As we have already seen, the rise of Canada's religious "nones" spans many different demographic groups. They include men and women, domestic and foreign-born, well and not-so-well educated, and young and old. At the same time, there are some significant differences in the rates of disaffiliation within each of these groups. Thanks to the important work of Thiessen and Laflamme,[32] Bibby, and others,[33] we know that Canada's religious nones are most likely to be young, unmarried men, between the ages of twenty-five and forty-four, were born in Canada, live in British Columbia, and have completed a post-secondary education (see Table 4).[34]

32. Thiessen and Wilkins-Laflamme, *None of the Above.*

33. Reginald Bibby and the Angus Reid Group in Canada as well as the Pew Research Center in the United States have been instrumental in helping map a picture of religious belief and values along with trends in religious attendance and affiliation.

34. Pew Research, "Canada's Changing Religious Landscape."

Table 4: Select Trends in Disaffiliation (1971 to 2011)

% who describe themselves as disaffiliated	1971	1981	1991	2001	2011
Canadian Population	4	8	13	17	24
Younger adults (Ages 25 to 44)	55	9	15	20	29
Middle-aged adults (Ages 45 to 64)	4	5	9	14	20
Senior adults (ages 65 and older)	2	3	6	9	12
Men	5	9	15	19	26
Women	3	6	11	15	22
Married	4	7	11	15	19
Unmarried	5	8	15	19	27
College graduate	12	12	14	18	23
Some college or less	4	6	12	16	21
Born in Canada	4	7	13	17	25
Foreign-born	7	10	14	18	20

Source: Bibby et al., 2019

Regionally, the highest percentage of religious nones are found in Western Canada, particularly British Columbia. For example, 53 percent of those in the province born between 1980 and 1999 are religiously unaffiliated (see Fig. 8). Thirty-nine percent of prairie residents in the same age cohort were religiously unaffiliated, followed by Ontario at 36 percent, the Atlantic provinces at 33 percent, and Quebec at 30 percent.

Figure 8: Religious Affiliation of Canadians by Region and Year of Birth

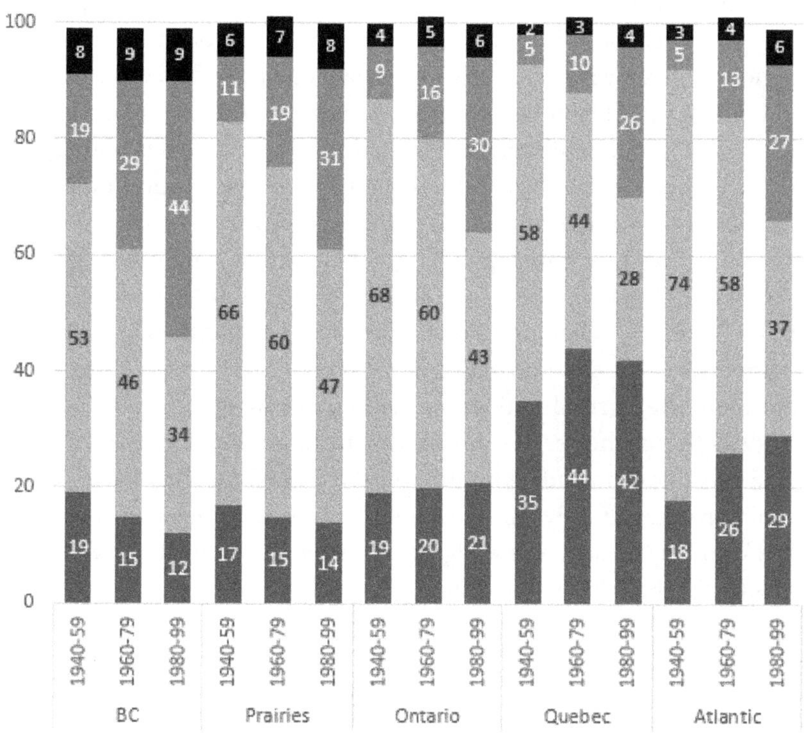

Note: some columns do not sum to 100% due to rounding.
Source: Statistics Canada, General Social Survey, cycles 31, 32, and 34, 2017 to 2019.

Canadians often find themselves looking to the United States for comparisons. In many respects, our two countries are similar when it comes to religious nones. But as Thiessen and Laflamme have observed, the proportion of religious nones grew earlier and more quickly in Canada than in the United States. Only recently has the number of American nones begun to rise sharply. In Canada, almost half (49%) of those who claim to be unaffiliated are under age thirty-five. In the United States, the number is about 44 percent. Similarly, 57 percent of all religious nones in

Canada are male, compared to 54 percent in the United States.[35] Canada's nones are also more likely to be born outside the country (18%) than in the United States (12%). When looking specifically at adults aged twenty-five to forty-four, Thiessen and Laflamme point out that America's religious nones are more likely to be unmarried (45%) than Canada's religious nones (31%). Similarly, religious nones are less likely than affiliated individuals to have children (Canada and the United States both 43%). With traditional family structures, taught and valued by most organized religious groups, these two factors perhaps come as no surprise.[36]

What may be surprising is the apparent lack of connection or influence that higher education, rural living, or visible minority status have on the number of religious nones. In both Canada and the United States, it appears as though almost as many religious nones have a university education, live in rural settings, or identify as belonging to a visible minority as those who see themselves as part of a religious tradition. Two small exceptions include education in the United States, where slightly more nones have a university education (34%) than religious Americans (30%), and in Canada, where slightly more religious affiliates live in rural areas (15%) than do religious nones (12%).[37]

How to Make a Religious None

Our previous section describes the prototypical religious none. But it is also helpful to explore some of the factors contributing to their dramatic rise in North America.

It Has Become Socially Acceptable

Thiessen and Wilkins-Laflamme emphasize that the most dramatic religious shift in society is that it has become okay to say you don't go to church—and even more, to say that you don't believe. Until the early 1970s, telling someone you had no religious affiliation was to put yourself at some risk of being looked down upon by family, friends, co-workers, and society. Some researchers, particularly in the United States, have

35. Thiessen and Wilkins-Laflamme, *None of the Above*, 47.

36. Thiessen and Wilkins-Laflamme, *None of the Above*, 46–56.

37. Thiessen and Wilkins-Laflamme, *None of the Above*, 51.

likened "coming out" as a religious none to the experiences of those who have "come out" as gay, lesbian or transgender.[38]

While Canadians may have received the "evil eye" from some, such extremes have not typically been part of our experience. The softening of ethnic-religious ties (English-Protestant and French-Catholic) following the Second World War, the place of multiculturalism in Canadian society, and the relative lack of a religious "right" subculture have all made the path to religious disaffiliation in Canada somewhat easier than in the United States.[39] For example, Thiessen and Wilkins-Laflamme report that close to one-third of Americans (32%) assert that an atheist would be unfit for political office, compared to 18 percent of Canadians. If Canadians are likely to cast shade on anyone, it appears more likely to be directed at the overly-religious than it is the non-religious.[40]

Right Is Wrong

For a long time in the United States, religious conservatism and what is commonly referred to as the "Christian Right" served to delay the rise of its religious nones. Paradoxically, it seems, it is now also responsible for its rapid rise. Growing numbers of Americans are concerned about the marriage between religion and politics, especially between Evangelical Christianity and the Republican Party. In the 2016 United States presidential election, 81 percent of white Evangelicals voted for Donald Trump.[41] Many outside the US Evangelical world see this as a problem. They view US Evangelicals as having too much power in the political arena, allowing them to impose their beliefs, values, and behaviors onto others who think, believe, or act differently. They are concerned about the sweeping influence this could have over family, education, healthcare, women's rights, abortion, and foreign policy. The perception is that Evangelicals are "too political, judgmental, insincere, exclusive, homophobic,

38. Cragun, Kosmin, Keysar, Hammer, and Nielson. "On the Receiving End," 1052–57; Linneman and Clendenen, "Sexuality and the Sacred," 89–111; Niose, *Nonbeliever Nation*; Williamson and Yancey, *There Is No God*; Zimmerman, Smith, Simonson, and Myers, "Familial Relationship Outcomes," 11–13.

39. Adams, *Sex in the Snow;* Reimer, *Evangelicals and the Continental Divide.*

40. Haskell, *Through a Lens Darkly;* Thiessen, *The Meaning of Sunday.*

41. Smith and Martinez, "How the Faithful Voted."

hypocritical, and sheltered—traits unbecoming of a modern, democratic, liberal, and diverse society."[42]

While Canadians have not experienced this polemic between liberals and the Christian Right to the same degree, we are not immune. Many Canadians are just as inclined to watch CNN or MSNBC as CBC or CTV for their news. We are well aware of the role that religious conservatism plays in the United States, and any indication we may have of religion playing a central role in political decision-making, we view with suspicion.[43]

It is far more likely that our skepticism, and sometimes our fear, is reserved for religious extremism in Canada. For Canada's Muslim community, this has become an increasing concern in recent years. In the same week that the bodies of 215 children were discovered in the residential school in Kamloops, British Columbia, a twenty-year-old white male drove his vehicle through the path of a Muslim family of five. What began as a quiet evening walk in London, Ontario, ended with four dead and a nine-year-old boy orphaned and in hospital.[44]

Media response to the event predominantly expressed the country's outrage and grief. And yet, a recent report by the Noor Cultural Centre paints a tragically different picture. It includes recent survey findings that indicate:

- 46 percent of Canadians have an unfavorable view of Islam—more than any other tradition.[45]
- Fewer than half of Canadians would find it "acceptable" for one of their children to marry a Muslim—lower than any other religious group.[46]
- 56 percent of Canadians believe that Islam suppresses women's rights.[47]
- More than half of people living in Ontario feel mainstream Muslim doctrines promote violence.[48]

42. Thiessen and Wilkins-Laflamme, *None of the Above*, 34.

43. Bean, *Politics of Evangelical Identity*; Reimer, *Evangelicals and the Continental Divide*; Reimer and Wilkinson, *A Culture of Faith*.

44. Kanji, "Islamophobia in Canada."

45. Angus Reid, "Religious Trends."

46. Angus Reid, "Religious Trends."

47. Graveland, "Fear Is the Greatest Factor."

48. Keung, "Epidemic of Islamophobia."

- 52 percent of Canadians believe that Muslims can only be trusted "a little" or "not at all."[49]
- 42 percent of Canadians believe that discrimination against Muslims is "mainly their fault."[50]
- 47 percent of Canadians support banning headscarves in public (compared with 30 percent of Americans).[51]
- 51 percent support government surveillance of mosques (compared to 46 percent of Americans).[52]
- 31 percent of Canadians approved of former American President Donald Trump's restrictions on travelers from Muslim-majority countries.[53]

In Canada, it appears that we fear not only religious radicals but those who are *perceived* to be religious radicals—without cause or justification.

Shut the Door on Your Way Out

In both Canada and the United States, many religious nones grew up in what most would call religious homes.[54] In Canada, this was the case for 55 percent of religious nones (based on the 2015 Project Canada Survey).[55] In the U.S., the number was 56 percent. While there are obvious examples of individuals who leave non-Christian faith traditions,[56] it is primarily former Christians who appear to be leaving their faith at an accelerating rate.[57] Why do they leave? Some recent qualitative studies point to Christian exclusivity; scandals relating to the residential

49. Csillag, "Deep Mistrust for Muslims in Canada."

50. Csillag, "Deep Mistrust for Muslims in Canada."

51. Geddes, "Canadians Less Tolerant Than Americans."

52. Geddes, "Canadians Less Tolerant Than Americans."

53. Dale, "Under Trump."

54. This assumes that both parents were religious. In the case of single parent households, the only parent was considered to be religious.

55. Bibby, "Project Canada Survey."

56. Drescher, *Choosing Our Religion*, 161–67; Pew Research, "Canada's Changing Religious Landscape"; Sherkat, *Changing Faith*.

57. Bibby, *Beyond the Gods;* Clarke and Macdonald, *Leaving Christianity*; Sherkat, *Changing Faith*.

school system; sexual abuse of parishioners by clergy; hypocrisy, political and personal conflicts within the church body; and intellectual disagreements.[58] Regardless of the reasons, over the last half-century, the church has witnessed the exit of vast numbers of people who are quite happy to close the door behind them.

Throwing Babies Out with the Bathwater

In 1849, the Scottish essayist and historian Thomas Carlyle wrote an essay entitled: *Occasional Discourse on the Negro Question,* in which he argued for the abolition of slavery. Acknowledging that many would not accept this social transition readily, he proposed a model of indentured servanthood, lasting from four to seven years. Under this framework, the individual would enter into a work contract where they would be granted the freedom to manage their own affairs at the end of it. At the conclusion of these contracts, individuals were also sometimes awarded land and money. Carlyle writes:

> And if true, it is important for us, in reference to this Negro Question and some others. The Germans say, "you must empty out the bathing-tub, but not the baby along with it."[59] "Fling-out your dirty water with all zeal, and set it careening down the kennels, but try if you can keep the little child."[60]

As the number of religious nones in Canadian society grows, so does the number of children growing up without the influence of religious communities. In Canada, let us recall that 45 percent of religious nones grew up in homes where both parents were religious. Even when parents may have been only nominally religious themselves, many continued to provide their children with some exposure to religious beliefs and rituals by involving them in Sunday School, daily vacation Bible schools, and Christian camps. But today's religious nones, who may have little or no religious background themselves, are raising children without any formal

58. Drescher, *Choosing Our Religion;* Manning, "Unaffiliated Parents," 149–75; Thiessen, *The Meaning of Sunday*; Zuckerman, *Faith No More.*

59. "Don't throw the baby out with the bathwater" is an expression originating in German meaning "be careful not to throw out something good when trying to get rid of something bad."

60. Wilton, *World Myths,* 666–67.

exposure to religious teaching, history, beliefs, or behaviors.[61] All it takes in many cases is just one generation for the Canadian church to discover that its babies are figuratively being thrown out with the bathwater, resulting in an exponential rise in the country's religious nones.

Elephants in the Room

Of course, in our discussion of religious nones, at least one elephant in the room bears acknowledgment. Sociologists like Cragun and Hammer,[62] along with Thiessen and Wilkins-Laflamme, are careful to point out that terms like religious "none," "irreligion," and "non-religious" imply that religious belonging, belief, and behavior are the norm. Its use also does not adequately describe the personal or private religiosity of these individuals. Those we describe as religious nones may well be highly orthodox in their religious beliefs, but simply choose not to identify or be actively associated with a particular religious group. As an increasing number do, they may describe themselves as "spiritual, but not religious."[63]

In exploring this question further, Bibby et al. note that 67 percent of Canadians openly acknowledge spiritual needs. This figure includes 60 percent of millennials, 69 percent of Gen Xers, 68 percent of Baby Boomers, and 74 percent of pre-Boomers. While the term "spiritual" continues to be both subjective and varied, it points to a consensus among many Canadians that, somehow, we need a connection that transcends everyday life.

When Bibby and colleagues asked Canadians to flesh this out a bit further, they observed that 39 percent of Canadians describe themselves as spiritual but not religious; 24 percent describe themselves as religious *and* spiritual; 10 percent describe themselves as religious but not spiritual, and 27 percent describe themselves as neither religious nor spiritual (see Fig. 9).

Canadians across the board were least likely to identify themselves as religious but not spiritual. Interestingly, pre-Boomers, who were also the most likely to self-identify as religious *and* spiritual, had the highest percentage of individuals who identify as religious but not spiritual (15%).

61. Thiessen and Wilkins-Laflamme, *None of the Above*, 9.

62. Cragun and Hammer, "One Person's Apostate," 149–75.

63. Cragun and Hammer, "One Person's Apostate," 149–75.

Figure 9: Religious and Spiritual Self-Descriptions of Canadian Adults

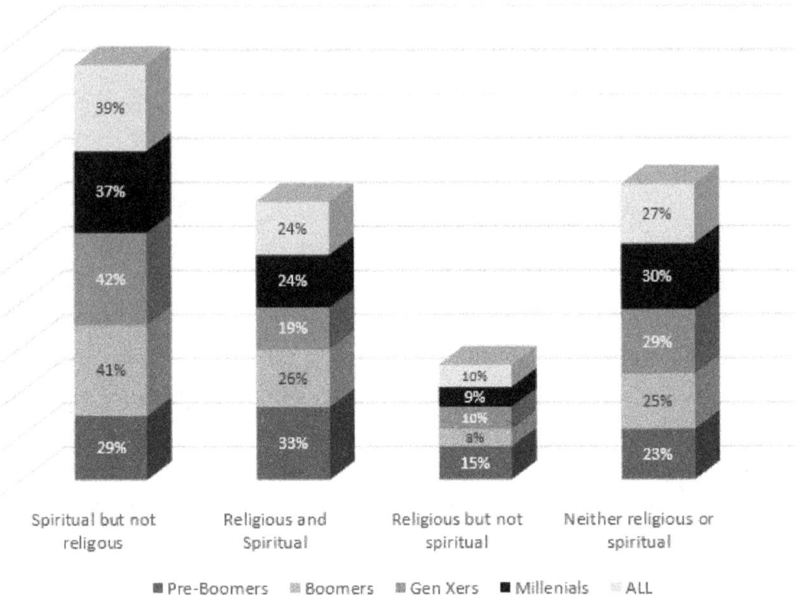

Source: Bibby et al., 2019

We see a similar trend in the United States. In a 2007 article, Richard Flory and Donald Miller reported on a qualitative study of 100 teens in five U.S. cities. They found that Millennials are clearly not "the spiritual consumers of their parent's generation, rather they are seeking both a deep spiritual experience and a community experience, each of which provides them with meaning in their lives and is meaningless without the other."[64] In other words, while they may not be looking to attach themselves to an institution that relies on a religious creed, they are still looking for something that combines spirituality and community, "and they can't lead a meaningful life without it."[65]

So, is the term "none" acceptable or not? Cragun and Hammer help us to find a degree of comfort with the term:

> "None" is widely used, but is also a value-laden term. None suggests that these individuals are without something and, in this context, they are: institutional religious identification. As the

64. Flory and Miller, "Spirituality of the Post-Boomer Generations," 217.
65. Thurston and ter Kuile, "How We Gather."

> lack of an association is part of their identity, this appears to be a situation where a seemingly pejorative term is, in fact, acceptable given the frame of reference. If the comparison between "nones" and "affiliates" or "identifiers" focused on something other than associating with a religious institution, like morals or values, the label "none" would be wholly inappropriate. But assuming the term "none" is limited strictly to the lack of an association with organized religion, it is accurate to say that people who have no religion are religious "nones."[66]

It is vital, however, for us to remember that this is all it is. Identifying someone as a religious "none" says nothing about the person's moral or ethical worldview. It says nothing about who they are as partners or parents. It says nothing about how they operate their businesses, how they relate to co-workers or neighbors, and it certainly does not say anything about whether they are "good" or "bad" people. All it says is that they do not belong to a group that chooses to meet regularly in a church, mosque, temple, synagogue, or other places of worship. Like any one of the rest of us, they are like a brick—just not one that has been used to piece together a particular religious tradition. They are, so to speak, just another "brick in the wall"—just not one of "our" walls.

66. Cragun and Hammer, "One Person's Apostate is Another Person's Convert," 160.

7

House for Sale

A Market Update

"Torture numbers and they'll confess to anything."

—GREGG EASTERBROOK

THE NATIONAL TRUST FOR Canada estimates that 9,000, or one-third of Canada's religious buildings, will disappear over the next decade. Speaking to the CBC in 2019, National Trust project manager Rob Pajot described the situation: "Neighborhoods are going to have multiple churches closing," he said. "Some people qualify this as a crisis, and I kind of agree. It is going to hit everybody. . . . [T]hese places are more than just places of worship, they are landmarks in their communities."[1] Imagine what Canadians would say if a third of the Canadian housing market were to disappear over the next decade. Market analysts would shudder. The figure is startling, and the estimate has Canada's church leaders worried about the state of God's house.

There is also an old saying that says, "Numbers don't lie." Perhaps they don't. But their meaning is often hidden, and they do not always communicate the whole story. Vaclav Smil is distinguished professor

1. Allen, "From Sacred to Secular."

emeritus at the University of Manitoba. He is also Bill Gates's "go-to" person when it comes to an understanding of our world and how its various systems interact.[2] In his book, *Numbers Don't Lie,* Smit takes his readers on a statistical adventure meant to challenge lazy thinking. Let's join him for a moment and think about what the potential loss of 9,000 churches means. Based on everything we have shared in the preceding chapters, it is hard not to imagine a scenario in which Pajot's estimate *could* be true. Church attendance and religious affiliation in Canada are on the decline. Maintenance costs have skyrocketed. In rural areas, congregations are shrinking as members age or move away. Increasing secularization, the proliferation of modern spiritual practices, and the church's very public mistreatment of Indigenous Canadians, LGBTQ2S individuals, women, and other marginalized groups has caused the church to be suspect in the eyes of many. Based on these challenges, the estimate *could* be true. However, let us take a closer look at what *has* been happening in recent years.

By the Numbers

Let's begin with how many churches are currently active. In chapter one, we explored the tension between the church as people and as place. In theological terms, both are true. Churches can be churches with or without buildings. Traditionally, Canadian lawmakers have also taken this understanding into account. According to the Canadian Charities Directorate, the advancement of religion and associated legal designation as a place of worship means, "to promote the spiritual teachings of a religious body and to maintain doctrines and spiritual observances on which those teachings are based. There must be an element of theistic worship which means the worship of a deity or deities in the spiritual sense."[3]

This definition is rooted in a longstanding belief that religion benefits society whether the whole of society participates in religious activities or not. The earliest examples of "charitable" recognition for religious communities date back as early as 2600 BCE in Egypt. During what is known as the Old Kingdom (c. 2613—2181 BCE), the Egyptian rulers built their now-famous mortuaries at Giza and other places throughout Egypt. These sites required priests to perform the same rituals they did at the temples to ensure the continuance of souls in the

2. Voosen, "Meet Vaclav Smil."

3. Government of Canada, "Advancement of Religion."

afterlife. The monarchs rewarded the priests by making their land and its harvest tax-exempt.[4] Similar examples are found in ancient Israel[5] and the early Christian world with Constantine, emperor of Rome from 306–337, who granted Christian churches a complete exemption from all forms of taxation.[6]

In Canada, religious tax exemption traces back to the English Statute of Charitable Uses, adopted in 1601.[7] This law granted churches and other charitable institutions an exemption from taxes based on the understanding that these organizations relieved the state of some governmental functions, and therefore deserved a benefit in return. In Canada, these benefits include:

1. Permission to issue official receipts for the gifts it receives, enabling donors to reduce their taxable income.
2. Exemption from paying income tax under Part 1 of the Income Tax Act.
3. Permission to receive gifts from other charities, such as foundations.
4. Increased credibility in the community through following certain rules and guidelines in order to maintain their registration.
5. Many goods and services provided by registered charities are exempt from Canada's goods and services tax / harmonized sales tax. In many situations, registered charities can also claim a partial rebate on the GST/HST they pay.[8]

While it is possible, then, to operate a worshipping community without being a charity, most churches register in order to take advantage of the benefits associated with this designation. The number of churches that do not register is believed to be small, and as a result, the "churches" discussed here refer to those that are currently, or were at one time, formally registered as charities.

4. Allen, "Agriculture, Origins, State in Ancien Egypt."
5. Selvén, "In or Out."
6. Lenski, *Constantine and the Cities.*
7. United Kingdom. "Charities Bill 83."
8. Government of Canada, "Advantages of Registration."

Table 5: Canadian Church Closures—Mainline Denominational Affiliation

Canadian Church Closures 20092–018	Roman Catholic	Anglican	Baptist	Lutheran	Mennonite	Presbyterian	United	Other	TOTAL
Number of Churches Closed	728	325	209	85	54	138	431	2319	4289
Percentage of Churches Closed	17%	8%	5%	2%	1%	3%	10%	54%	100%
% Of Christian population	58%	7%	3%	2%	1%	2%	9%	18%	100%
Total Assets	$471,252,854	$52,673,921	$24,513,576	$18,944,914	$11,453,919	$25,866,261	$67,014,948	$181,316,069	$853,036,462
Receipted Donations	$28,341,773	$5,698,336	$2,928,653	$1,046,162	$3,055,231	$2,497,503	$6,009,564	$37,363,173	$86,940,395
Government Grants	$152,381	$35,754	$6,762	$7,697	$8,604	$9,810	$57,939	$164,244	$443,191
Fundraising	$2,935,896	$527,280	$15,917	$27,003	$9,795	$64,899	$515,610	$2,142,643	$6,239,043
Sales	$7,074,675	$948,356	$1,831,555	$1,311,211	$155,360	$588,031	$4,181,106	$2,974,670	$19,064,964
Total Revenue'	$58,677,344	$11,677,805	$7,717,116	$4,937,961	$4,674,686	$6,849,186	$27,761,527	$72,123,567	$194,419,192
Total Expenses	$66,215,175	$12,899,130	$12,634,265	$11,843,327	$4,668,484	$5,974,745	$39,118,609	$115,621,996	$268,975,731
Revenue as % of Expenditures	89%	91%	61%	42%	100%	115%	71%	62%	72%
Halo Loss*	$279,428,039	$54,434,329	$53,316,598	$49,978,840	$19,701,002	$25,213,424	$165,080,530	$487,924,823	$1,135,077,585
Percent of Halo Loss	25%	5%	5%	4%	2%	2%	15%	43%	100%

Source: Canada Revenue Agency and Charities Directorate, 2009 to 2018

Table 6: Canadian Church Closures—Other Faith Traditions

Other Traditions	Other Christian	Salvation Army	Adventist	Jehovah's Witness	Pentecostal	Total Other Christian
Number of Churches Closed	1894	19	23	258	125	2319
Percentage of Churches Closed	44%	0%	1%	6%	3%	54%
Total Assets	$94,873,173	$1,034,973	$194,213	$67,078,067	$18,135,643	$181,316,069
Receipted Donations	$31,944,112	$407,315	$450,054	$2,437,263	$2,124,429	$37,363,173
Government Grants	$168,430	$42,790	$5,099	$15,078	$18,427	$164,244
Fundraising	$2,092,244	$42,419	$0	$0	$7,980	$2,142,643
Sales	$2,137,452	$50,838	$7,444	$699,198	$79,738	$2,974,670
Total Revenue	$60,282,411	$1,578,009	$507,958	$6,817,300	$2,937,889	$72,123,567
Total Expenses	$100,824,136	$2,217,542	$652,496	$7,564,950	$4,362,872	$115,621,996
Revenue as % of Expense	60%	71%	78%	90%	67%	62%
Halo Loss	$425,477,854	$9,358,027	$2,753,533	$31,924,089	$18,411,320	$487,924,823
Percent of Halo Loss	87%	2%	1%	7%	4%	100%

Source: Canada Revenue Agency and Charities Directorate, 2009 to 2018]

In 2009, a Natural Resources Canada energy audit listed 27,601 faith-owned buildings in Canada. That same year, referencing worshipping communities rather than buildings, Canada Revenue identified just under 25,000 Christian congregations. By 2018, the number of active churches had fallen to less than 21,000. There were 4,289 church closures during that ten-year period, a closure rate of 17 percent (see Table 5). In their final year of operation, these congregations listed more than $850 million in assets, with expenditures of close to $269 million, exceeding revenues by 38 percent. And while 4,300 closures over ten years is less than half of the ten-year prediction put forward by the National Trust, clearly, these are not the kind of numbers churches are looking to celebrate.

Denominational Differences

Canada's 2011 National Household Survey, still the most recent and complete analysis of religious affiliation in Canada, identified roughly two-thirds of Canadians (67%) as Christian. Of those who identified as Christian, 58 percent identified as Roman Catholic. Seven percent were Anglican, 3 percent were Baptist, 2 percent were Lutheran, 1 percent were Mennonite, 2 percent were Presbyterian, 9 percent were United, while the remaining 18 percent was made up of a diverse group of Adventists, Orthodox, Independents, Pentecostals, Salvation Army, and Jehovah's Witnesses (see Table 6).[9]

Amongst mainline traditions, the Roman Catholics closed the highest percentage of churches with 728, or 17 percent of the total closures. The United Church followed with 10 percent of the total churches closed, Anglicans (8%), Baptists (5%), Presbyterians (3%), Lutherans (2%), and Mennonites (1%). And, while much of the mainstream and Christian media has focused on Catholic and mainline Protestant closures in recent years, it is important to note that more than half (54%) of the church closures between 2009 and 2018 were by churches designated as "other." Notable amongst this group were Jehovah's Witnesses with 6 percent, the Pentecostals with 3 percent, and Adventists with 1 percent of the total churches closed.

Earlier, we recognized the spending challenges that many congregations face. Nationally, spending in churches that closed exceeded income by 38%. Only in Presbyterian and Mennonite congregations did we

9. Statistics Canada, "NHS Profile 2011."

observe revenues exceeding spending at the time of closure. Lutherans and Baptists appeared to be in the worst financial position when closing. Baptist spending exceeded revenues by 63%, while Lutheran spending was 140% higher than annual income. At that rate, it is not hard to see why they closed.

Closure Designations

There are many reasons why churches close. Finances, maintenance needs, failure of leadership, organizational breakdown, lack of motivation, and changes in congregational and community demographics can be significant factors. According to Table 7, more than half (54%) of the church closures between 2009 and 2018 were considered to be voluntary. Seventeen percent were due to delinquency (failure to file). Another 25 percent of congregations actively closed their charitable registration to merge with another congregation. Two percent lost their charitable status due to an audit, and another twelve congregations lost their charitable status for some other reason.

Table 7: Canadian Church Closures—Reason Codes

Canadian Church Closures Reason Codes 2009—2018	Voluntary Revocation	Delinquent Failure to File	Annulled	Terminated For Merger	Revoked with Cause (audit)	Revoked with Cause (other)	TOTAL
Number of closures	2388	729	0	1090	70	12	4289
Percentage of total closures	56%	17%	0%	25%	2%	0%	100%
Total Assets	$350,009,862	$65,666,167	$0	$420,623,080	$14,863,694	$1,873,659	$853,036,462
Receipted Donations	$43,003,031	$11,910,427	$0	$23,769,375	$7,897,974	$359,588	$86,940,395
Government Grants	$242,914	$104,087	$0	$82,563	$13,201	$426	$443,191
Fundraising	$2,360,082	$555,521	$0	$1,630,924	$1,585,246	$107,270	$6,239,043
Sales	$13,909,556	$875,763	$0	$4,187,442	$75,228	$16,975	$19,064,964
Total Revenue	$111,743,095	$18,347,237	$0	$52,504,898	$11,069,108	$754,854	$194,419,192
Total Expenditures	$177,540,443	$17,958,874	$0	$53,769,832	$18,731,533	$975,049	$268,975,731
Revenue as % of Expenditure	63%	102%	0%	98%	59%	77%	72%
Loss of Halo Impact *	$749,220,669	$75,786,448	$0	$226,908,691	$79,047,069	$4,114,707	$1,135,077,585
Percent of Total Halo Impact	66%	7%	0%	20%	7%	0%	100%

* Halo (socio-economic) Impact loss is based on Halo Canada Research that suggests that religious congregations contribute an average of $4.22 worth of social benefit for every dollar spent.

Source: Canada Revenue Agency and Charities Directorate, 2009 to 2018

The 25 percent of churches that closed their charitable registration in order to merge with another congregation raise an important consideration. When a church closes, its members do not just disappear. In the case of mergers, the vast majority of those members will continue to attend church—just not in the same location. Even when a congregation closes and does not formally merge with another one, its members are still likely to find another church to attend. Perhaps not right away, or perhaps not with the same denomination, but closing a church does not necessarily mean its members will be any less spiritual or see their desire to attend worship diminish.

Table 8 below illustrates how these closure types are experienced differently across faith traditions. Adventists (91%), Mennonites (85%), and Baptists (80%) had the highest rate of voluntary revocations. Pentecostals (25%) and "other" Christian traditions (24%) had the highest rates of cancellation because they failed to file their charitable returns. The Salvation Army also registered as being high in this category, although the percentage in their case represents revocations in only eight congregations. While the differences are slight, we also see higher cancellation rates due to audits amongst Pentecostal churches and "other" Christian traditions. In total, 19 percent of churches that closed either failed to file their financial reports or had them revoked for other reasons such as failed audits. When many Canadians are skeptical of institutional religion and the merits of maintaining charitable status for faith communities, this does not bode well for the relationship between church and society. Faith groups that want to remain credible need to include fiscal responsibility and integrity as part of that intention.

Table 8: Canadian Church Closures—Reason Codes with Denominational Affiliation

Faith Tradition	Voluntary Revocation	Failure to File	Terminated (Merged)	Revoked with Cause (Audit)	Revoked with Cause (Other)	TOTAL
Anglican	61%	19%	20%	0%	0%	100%
Baptist	80%	16%	3%	1%	0%	100%
Lutheran	79%	14%	6%	1%	0%	100%
Mennonite	85%	15%	0%	0%	0%	100%
Pentecostal	69%	25%	2%	4%	0%	100%
Presbyterian	75%	17%	9%	0%	0%	100%
Roman Catholic	57%	8%	35%	0%	0%	100%
Other	46%	24%	26%	3%	0%	100%
Salvation Army	61%	35%	4%	0%	0%	100%
Adventist	91%	9%	0%	0%	0%	100%
United	62%	11%	27%	0%	0%	100%
Jehovah's Witness	50%	1%	49%	0%	0%	100%
TOTAL	56%	17%	25%	2%	0%	100%

Source: Canada Revenue Agency and Charities Directorate, 2009 to 2018

This type of intentionality is also exhibited when congregations facing closure plan beforehand to unite with another congregation. For example, almost half (49%) of Jehovah's Witness closures led to unions with other congregations. With their highly developed ecclesial structure, Roman Catholics also saw more than one-third (35%) of their congregational closures lead to mergers with another. Among the remaining mainline denominations, the United Church at 27 percent and Anglican Church (20%) lead the way. In contrast, faith traditions with more autonomous, less hierarchical organizational structures such as Baptists (3%), Mennonites (0%), and the Adventists (0%) show little evidence of working towards intentional mergers.

Socioeconomic Impacts

When a church closes, the results can be devastating for church members and the denominational leaders working to support them. However, they are not the only ones who lose out when a church closes. Between 2009 and 2018, church closures cost the Canadian economy close to $270 million in expenditures alone. And the negative impacts reach even deeper than that.

In 2010, U.S.-based Partners for Sacred Places teamed up with the University of Pennsylvania's School of Social Policy and Practice to complete a study of the economic impact of twelve congregations in the city of Philadelphia. Headed by Ram Cnaan, the research group explored almost fifty factors in testing a new quantitative approach to how congregations influence and benefit local economies. The study examined seven broad areas, including 1) open space, 2) direct spending, 3) educational programs, 4) magnet effect, 5) individual impact, 6) community development, and 7) social capital and care. Relying on a variety of different valuation methods, researchers estimated an annual economic contribution of almost USD 52 million, leading them to conclude that congregations can "now be viewed as critical economic catalysts."[10]

In 2016, with support from Cnaan and colleagues at Cardus and Ryerson University, we replicated the Halo study with ten congregations in Toronto. Using modified values that reflect the Canadian economic landscape more accurately,[11] this study revealed a cumulative socio-economic benefit or "Halo Effect" of $45.4 million. This value means that for every dollar these congregations spent, their respective communities received an average of $4.77 in social-economic benefit.[12]

Since June of 2016, the Halo Canada Project has increased the number of participating study congregations to close to 100. In 2020, this expanded data set led to a revised estimate of $3.87 worth of impact for every dollar that churches spend. When applied to the 2018 spending of Canada's religious congregations, this factor revealed a contribution of close to $15.5 billion by Canada's churches and other worshipping communities towards Canada's social economy.[13] Current research suggests that the average contribution to Canadian society is now about $4.22 for every dollar spent (median = $3.39).

Similarly, when applied to the final-year expenditures, these factors suggest that between 2009 and 2018, Canadians lost more than $1.1 billion in community economic impact due to church closures (see Table 5). Church closings represent losses not just for church-goers; they represent a loss for all Canadians. When churches close, Canadians lose space for dance recitals, community concerts, seniors' lunches, and children's

10. Partners for Sacred Places, "Halo Effect."

11. For a detailed discussion of the seven impact areas and assigned values, visit www.haloproject.ca.

12. Wood Daly, "Valuing Toronto's Faith Congregations."

13. Wood Daly, "Dollars and $ense."

programs. They lose the benefit of Bonzai classes, badminton, bridge, and basketball. These programs provided by and housed in churches offer communal and emotional value. But they also offer health benefits, reduce demand on municipalities for programs and services, stimulate volunteer participation and reduce demands on the criminal justice system—all of which have real dollar benefits for Canadians.

Although church buildings close, not all of the congregation's social impact is necessarily lost. A large percentage of that social impact is often transferred to the new churches that these individuals begin to attend. There are two qualifiers to that assumption. When moving to a new congregation, it usually takes time before individuals return to their previous level of donor activity and volunteer involvement. They are likely to "test the waters" with their new congregation before re-engaging wholeheartedly. So, while the social contributions they generate through their congregational involvement may come close to returning to previous levels, it may take some time before that happens. And while society as a whole may recoup the benefits that were attached to specific congregations, often the communities that lose these churches do not. This dynamic is particularly true in rural communities where the closure of church landmarks limits the options for worship and community gathering and the socioeconomic benefits that accompany them.

In most cases, the number of church closures reflects denominational affiliation. For example, 7 percent of Canadians identify as Anglican. Anglicans were responsible for 8 percent of church closures. Baptists, Lutherans, Mennonites, Presbyterians, and United Church members saw their percentage of church closures fall within a percent or two of their affiliation numbers (affiliation includes people who say they belong to a church, regardless of how often they attend). There are, however, two important exceptions. Roman Catholics represent the single largest group of Christians in Canada, comprising 58 percent of the Christian population. Yet, they were responsible for only 17 percent of church closures. At the opposite end of the spectrum, "other" Christian traditions represent 18 percent of the Christian population, while they were responsible for more than half (54%) of the closures. These variations highlight the occasional need to examine additional factors such as congregational size, denominational polity, and geographic factors. For example, Roman Catholic parishes often benefit from the support of a centralized, hierarchical leadership that can channel resources towards struggling congregations. On the other hand, churches that identify as "other" often act independently or more autonomously within their denominational framework and sometimes lack external support.

Regional Differences

Between 2009 and 2018, Canada lost 17 percent of its churches. One-third of these occurred in Ontario, where approximately 40 percent of Canada's churches are located. In contrast, while Ontario was losing less than its share, Quebec was losing more. In 2018, Quebec held only 11 percent of the country's churches but had witnessed 20 percent of the country's closures in the ten years prior, representing 28 percent rate of loss. In each of the other provinces and territories, closure rates reflected the province's share of churches nationally (see Table 9).

Table 9: Canadian Church Closures—By Province

Description	2018 Total Churches	Total Closed	2009 Total Churches	Percentage of Churches Closed	Percentage of Total Churches	Rate of Loss
AB	2498	311	2809	7%	12%	-11%
BC	2551	443	2994	10%	12%	-15%
MB	1234	151	1385	4%	6%	-11%
NB	891	163	1054	4%	4%	-15%
NL	509	42	551	1%	2%	-8%
NS	997	156	1153	4%	5%	-14%
ON	8014	1401	9415	33%	39%	-15%
PE	183	18	201	0%	1%	-9%
QC	2223	844	3067	20%	11%	-28%
SK	1496	221	1717	5%	7%	-13%
NT/NU/YT	65	8	73	0%	0%	-11%
Other *	0	531	531	12%	0%	-100%
Total	20661	4289	24950	100%	100%	-17%

* Other denotes congregations whose T3010 was filed by an organization outside the country or where the congregations' address is listed under that of the parent denomination.

Source: Canada Revenue Agency and Charities Directorate, 2009 to 2018

Table 10, below, shows the reasons for closure by percentage in each province. In most cases, voluntary revocation served as the primary reason for the closure (56%). Prince Edward Island led the way with 83 percent of its closures in this category. Prince Edward Island was followed by Saskatchewan with 76 percent and British Columbia with 72 percent. The highest rates of filing delinquency were observed in the Yukon and Northwest Territories, although this represents a limited number of congregations. Amongst the larger provinces, Newfoundland and Manitoba led the way with 26 percent. With respect to congregations that intended to merge, Alberta's 60 percent rate is skewed by a significant number of Latter-Day Saints congregations that filed under a single Alberta address. Of the remaining provinces, Quebec (41%), Nova Scotia (25%), and Newfoundland (21%) all showed a significant number of congregations in this category.

Table 10: Canadian Church Closures—By Province and Reason Code

Province	Voluntary Revocation	Delinquent / Failure to File	Terminated for Merger	Revoked with Cause (audit)	Revoked with cause (other)	TOTAL
AB	31%	9%	60%	0%	0%	100%
BC	72%	23%	4%	1%	1%	100%
MB	70%	26%	5%	0%	0%	100%
NB	66%	19%	14%	1%	0%	100%
NL	50%	26%	21%	2%	0%	100%
NS	63%	12%	25%	0%	0%	100%
NT	57%	8%	35%	0%	0%	100%
ON	63%	22%	11%	4%	0%	100%
PE	83%	11%	6%	0%	0%	100%
QC	48%	11%	41%	0%	0%	100%
SK	72%	22%	2%	0%	0%	100%
YT	33%	67%	0%	0%	0%	100%
Other	55%	36%	0%	9%	0%	100%
TOTAL	56%	17%	25%	2%	0%	100%

Source: Canada Revenue Agency and Charities Directorate, 2009 to 2018

Urban and Rural Distinctions

In Canada, 90 percent of Canadians live within 160 km of the United States border, while 82 percent reside in Canada's urban regions. These dynamics emphasize the need also to consider the urban and rural distinctions associated with church closures.[14] The two widely used distinctions tend to be ones that people understand intuitively. Urban communities are ones with large populations and high density. Rural areas have small populations and low density. Statistics Canada further describes urban areas as communities with populations of at least 1,000 people and a density of four hundred people or more per square kilometer. All regions that do not fit this description are considered rural. While this description works well at both ends of the spectrum, it still lacks clarity in transitional areas where urban meets rural.

To avoid this ambiguity, our study applied Canada's postal code designations to the T3010 filings of closed congregations. In Canada, postal codes comprise six alphanumeric characters in the form A1A 1A1. The first three characters represent the Forward Sortation Area (FSA), while the remaining three characters represent the Local Delivery Unit (LDU). The first character of the FSA represents either a province, territory, or region. The second character identifies urban and rural regions. Rural regions are identified by a zero "0" and urban regions by the numbers 1 through 9.

One notable exception includes the Province of New Brunswick, which has no rural designated postal codes (even though Statistics Canada does classify much of New Brunswick as rural). To avoid confusion with Statistics Canada's definitions, we can say that postal codes with a zero "0" in the second character position describe addresses located on rural delivery routes. In contrast, all other postal codes describe addresses located on urban delivery routes.

Following this method, 26 percent of the Canadian churches that closed between 2009 and 2018 were located on rural delivery routes (see Table 11). Sixty-one percent were located on urban delivery routes. Prince Edward Island and Saskatchewan had the largest percentage of rural closures relative to urban closures (61% rural to 39% urban in both cases.) In contrast, 84 percent of British Columbia's closures took place in urban communities, followed by 68 percent in Alberta and 60 percent in Ontario.

When comparing provincial closings to national totals, the greatest percentage of rural closings took place in Quebec with 30 percent, followed by Ontario with 28 percent. Ontario also led the way with the greatest percentage of urban closings at 41 percent, followed by Quebec at 19 percent and British Columbia with 14 percent.

14. Statistics Canada. "Population and Dwelling Count, 2016."

Table 11: Canadian Church Closures—Urban and Rural Distinctions

Province Territory	Rural	Urban	Other	Rural as % of Rural Total	Urban as % of Urban Total	Rural as % of Provincial Total	Urban as % of Urban Total	Rural as % of National Total	Urban as % of National Total	TOTAL
NL	20	22		2%	1%	48%	52%	0%	1%	42
NS	72	84		6%	3%	46%	54%	2%	2%	156
PE	11	7		1%	0%	61%	39%	0%	0%	18
NB		163		0%	6%	0%	100%	0%	4%	163
QC	339	505		30%	19%	40%	60%	8%	12%	844
ON	319	1082		28%	41%	23%	77%	7%	25%	1401
MB	67	84		6%	3%	44%	56%	2%	2%	151
SK	135	86		12%	3%	61%	39%	3%	2%	221
AB	100	211	520	9%	8%	32%	68%	2%	5%	311
BC	69	374		6%	14%	16%	84%	2%	9%	443
NT/NU/YT	3	5		0%	0%	38%	63%	0%	0%	8
Other			11							531
TOTAL	1135	2623	531	100%	100%	26%	61%	26%	61%	4289

Source: Canada Revenue Agency and Charities Directorate, 2009 to 2018

Streams in the Wasteland

Our examination of church closures offers helpful insights into the past *and* future of the church in Canada. The evidence is clear: attendance is declining, congregations are aging out, finances are stretched, and churches are closing. But that is only one side of the coin. There are usually two sides to every story—both of which can sometimes be true. The prediction that Canada is about to lose one-third of its churches may well be true. However, the numbers we have presented have so far failed to recognize a critical factor. While churches have been closing in droves, they have also been *opening* at a surprising rate. The data suggests that churches have also been opening at roughly three-quarters of the rate that Canada's faith groups are closing them. The National Trust for Canada's prediction may not yet be the death knell that many Canadians have imagined.

Table 12: Canadian Church Closures—Rate of Loss and Decline

DESCRIPTION	R.C.	Anglican	Baptist	Luth	Menn	Presb	United	OTHER	Total
2018 TOTAL	3311	1574	1769	839	545	860	2194	9569	20661
20092–18 Closed	728	325	209	85	54	138	431	2319	4289
20092–18 Opened	108	60	121	12	32	47	39	2868	3287
2009 TOTAL	3931	1839	1857	912	567	951	2586	9020	21663
Net Loss	620	265	88	73	22	91	392	-549	1002
Rate of Loss	-18%	-17%	-11%	-9%	-9%	-14%	-16%	-20%	-17%
Rate of Decline	-16%	-14%	-5%	-8%	-4%	-10%	-15%	6%	-5%

Source: Canada Revenue Agency and Charities Directorate, 2009 to 2018

Table 12 reveals that between 2009 and 2018, 3,287 new congregations registered as charities. With 4,289 closings, this represents a net loss of only 1,002 congregations during those years. So, while the ten-year closure rate is about 17 percent, the net rate of decline is only about 5 percent. Of the mainline traditions, Catholics showed the most significant rate of loss at 18 percent and a decline at 16 percent. The Anglican and United Churches followed only a percentage point or two behind in both categories. A striking anomaly involves churches described as "other." While churches in this group led the way with a 20 percent rate of loss, they actually opened 549 more churches than they closed. Their numbers *increased* by about 6 percent. While churches are dying, it is not taking place in a vacuum. Churches are also being birthed.

Jesse Wente is chairperson of the Canadian Council for the Arts. He is also a writer and broadcaster of Anishinaabe descent. In a November 2020 lecture entitled "A Story of Joy: Reducing the Harm So We Can Heal," Wente suggests that the stories we tell *and* how we tell them matters. He argues that the stories that settler Canadians hear about Indigenous people have too often been framed by pain and hurt. "The trauma, the pain, all of that is very real. It's in our bones," Wente says. "And yet we also live with joy."[15] This joy has not always been front and center, especially in the media accounts of recent months. And yet, it is not hard to find, says Wente. "One of my favorite sounds in the world is when our aunties laugh. I've been fortunate enough to travel the world and visit with a lot of Indigenous aunties. And they all laugh." When asked what their laughter sounds like, Wente himself responded with laughter, saying, "It sounds like home. It sounds like comfort, . . . sounds like a hug if that makes sense."

Hugs. Laughter. Comfort. Joy. All of these sound like home. Even to Indigenous people, whose culture is so deeply rooted in the value of land and place, home is more than that. It is rooted in relationships, belonging, and bonds between people, societies, and the environments in which they live. As difficult as our own experience has been, the church in Canada also has its stories of joy. New churches are just one of them. These "streams in the wasteland,"[16] to borrow a phrase from Isaiah, stand out as glimpses of hope for what our new home in Canadian society can and might be. In their book, *Turning Ourselves Inside Out,*[17] Russ Daye, of Bloor Street United Church in Toronto, and Rob Fennell, professor of theology at the Atlantic School of Theology, describe some of these wasteland streams that are bubbling up and bringing life to the wilderness. In interviews with thirty-five faith communities as part of the Thriving Christian Communities Project, the authors heard that amid considerable dis-ease, hope, humility, love, courage, and integrity still exist as signs of life and vitality in the Canadian church. In some churches, like Northside Memorial (a pseudonym used to protect the identity of

15. Wente, "Reframing Indigenous Stories."

16. Isaiah 43:18.

17. Daye and Fennell, *Turning Ourselves Inside Out.*

church members), even the willingness to accept the possibility of death stands out as a sign of life and resurrection.

John Bowen, professor emeritus of evangelism at Wycliffe College in Toronto, agrees. One of the most significant challenges facing the church in Canada, shares Bowen, is, "[t]o face death—the death of much of what we have known and treasured as 'church'—and to believe there will be resurrection." It is also our greatest opportunity, he says, offering us the chance to "reinvent ourselves . . . and recover our authentic DNA."[18]

Whenever I see a for-sale sign go up in my neighborhood, I wonder what is behind the family's move. Perhaps the occupants are now empty-nesters and are feeling a need to downsize. Maybe they are dealing with health issues that make the house too demanding to maintain. Maybe their growing family needs more space. Their move might be job-related, or perhaps they are just looking to move to a different neighborhood, a different city, a different province. There is always a story, memories, and history attached to the sale of someone's house. But there is also opportunity. Putting up a for-sale sign creates opportunity for someone else to move in, for new stories to be told, for new life to begin. While the church in Canada is not what it once was, the for-sale signs dotting Canada's religious landscape have also prompted many to rethink how we "do church" in Canada.

Rev. Alexa Gilmour, a United Church minister and founder of the Stone Soup Network, describes how some Canadians are beginning to re-imagine church:

> The idol of Christendom blinds many of us to the resurrected Spirit of Christ who calls us from our fortress-turned-tomb churches into the community. One church I served, followed that resurrected Christ and the week filled up with ministry outside the walls. They saw their membership, staff hours, giving, and engagement with the community rise between 50–90%. The one statistic that never grew was Sunday morning attendance. If we say we are the body of Christ, it's a 24/7 life of integrating spirituality into every day, rather than relegating it to one hour on Sunday.

Linda Nicholls, primate of the Anglican Church of Canada, adds how the COVID-19 pandemic has been informing this conversation.

18. Private email correspondence with John Bowen.

> The greatest opportunity has been given to us through the challenges of the pandemic. We have been released from our buildings to discover God present among us online, offline, in our homes, in our gardens and in our relationships. Many people were able to dip their toes into worship online without the fear of entering a foreign "sacred space." We have discovered new resilience and creativity that we had not imagined before. We have had to look at our traditions in new ways. Now the opportunity is to reflect on our learning and let it guide us into the future. How will we continue to engage with those who have met us online? How will we build community that is not so dependent on a building? What part will technology play in our future? Exciting, scary possibilities lie before us. The only question will be will we have the courage to embrace change?[19]

Another vital contribution to this re-imagining of the church has emerged with the folks at Sacred Design Lab in the United States. Inspired by the Ministry Innovation program at Harvard University, this group describes itself as a "soul-centered research and development lab . . . devoted to understanding and designing for twenty-first-century well-being. We translate ancient wisdom and practices to help our partners develop products, programs, and experiences that ground people's social and spiritual lives."[20]

Their work is rooted in the premise that increasingly our time in history is being shaped by unmet soul needs and that "the more we go hungry for meaning, connection and purpose, the more we act from isolation and despair."[21] This dynamic plays out, they suggest, in how we live, love, work, and lead, and finds expression in the ways Millennial communities gather to fulfill the functions that religious congregations have traditionally performed.

Church or not, today's soul-nurturing organizations, they write, offer six essential elements:

1. **Community**: valuing and fostering deep relationships that center on service to others.
2. **Personal transformation**: making a conscious and dedicated effort to develop one's own body, mind, and spirit.

19. Private email correspondence with Linda Nicholls, Primate of the Anglican Church of Canada.

20. Sacred Design Lab, "How We Work."

21. Sacred Design Lab, "Insights."

3. **Social transformation**: pursuing justice and beauty in the world through the creation of networks for good.
4. **Purpose-finding**: clarifying, articulating, and acting on one's personal mission in life.
5. **Creativity**: allowing time and space to activate the imagination and engage in play.
6. **Accountability**: holding oneself and others responsible for working towards defined goals.

They offer examples of ten different organizations, none of which are "church" in the traditional sense, but all of which provide the prescribed elements in one way or another. This, they say, poses a challenge for traditional religious institutions. Are churches truly providing a culture of connection and meaning? Who are they serving? Are they ensuring that transformation is open to all? Are they willing to promote diversity at institutional levels with shared power to undo systems of oppression and genuinely contribute to the common good?

How are churches leading? In an environment where young people are less likely to have a religious home, are religious leaders willing to be vulnerable, hold space for sacred listening, and acknowledge spiritual growth outside of their long-established religious traditions?

And finally, what about God? On the one hand, Christians and church leaders have grown up with a very prescribed view of who God is. At the same time, we acknowledge that God is ultimately mystery. From a tradition that has spent decades, even centuries, trying to tell people who God is, can the church imagine a world where it seeks to rediscover or even co-discover a God who is revealing Godself beyond the institutions we have long known?

In Canada, Joel Thiessen and others at Ambrose University's Flourishing Congregations Institute have been asking similar questions of congregations, trying to better understand how dynamics like organizational ethos, outward focus, and inward attention contribute to congregational and community well-being. Congregations that are thriving, they say, are clear on where they have come from, realistic about their place and role in society, and intentional about their futures. They take leadership seriously. They are open to new ideas, trying them, and not being afraid to fail at them. They engage people, are hospitable, and work at celebrating diversity. They look outwards, find value in partnerships, and work hard to establish a collective story.[22]

We see further examples of this in denominational organizations such as the United Church's Network for Ministry Development, EDGE. This institutional arm helps churches think *un-institutionally* by curating imagination related to property, programs, and partnerships. The Halo Canada Project has been a grateful recipient of their collaboration and support. Another important partner is the Trinity Centres Foundation (TCF). Inspired and led by Graham Singh, an Anglican priest based in Montreal, the Trinity Centres Foundation "transforms church properties for community impact."[23]

Foundational to TCF's work is the acknowledgment that churches dot the main streets of our communities mainly due to colonial privilege. In an article co-authored with Barbara Myers, the two write:

> A 150 plus year old social contract provided colonial land for early Canadians to build churches without any tax obligation. Many of Canada's finest church buildings were given free land and encouraged to gather second nations of French, English, Scottish, Irish and later other European migrants. The practice of gifting land stopped for new Canadians arriving after the Second World War, but generally land used by a religious organization as a place of worship is exempt from property tax.[24]

As church steeples crumble and worship attendance reaches its lowest point in Canadian history, the social benefit of many of these properties is increasingly being called into question. "If the social contract around public support for church buildings is to continue,"[25] argues Singh, "then it's time to hand churches back to the communities that need them[;] . . . we need a totally new model for co-owning these spaces, as equals across race, religion and community perspective."[26]

Singh laments the fact that Canada's mainline denominations hold a legacy of more than $30 billion in land and savings.[27] The 4,300 churches that closed between 2009 and 2018 carried more than $874 million

22. Flourishing Congregations Institute, "Flourishing Congregations Construct."
23. Trinity Centres Foundation, "Homepage."
24. Singh and Myers, "Memos from Main Street."
25. Singh and Myers, "Memos from Main Street."
26. Singh, "Hand Churches Back."
27. Singh, "Hand Churches Back."

combined assets, with much of this value lost to a "poorly coordinated pathway to private development at pennies on the dollar."[28] To address this concern, the Trinity Centres Foundation has assembled a team of social innovators and urban planners along with professionals from the property, finance, management, legal, government, and faith sectors to demonstrate new ways to assemble, fund, and operate churches. With transformational projects underway in Montreal, Toronto, Kitchener, Cambridge, Windsor, Calgary, and Edmonton, TCF generates new ways for shrinking congregations in old "Main Street" churches to create community identity and remain solvent as community hubs. Instead of just being a "House of God," they are and can become homes to engaging hubs of cultural and community activity. Maybe that is just what a "House of God" was meant to be.

Regeneration Works, a partnership of Faith and the Common Good and the National Trust for Canada, offers further examples of how worship spaces can be reimagined. They cite Kingsbridge Cathedral near Goderich, Ontario. In 2012, the 300-person congregation was faced with closure. The landmark building had become too expensive to operate on its own. Partnering with the local community, they formed a not-for-profit corporation known as the St. Joseph's Kingsbridge Community (SJKC) to establish a multi-use facility that would serve as a community hub, incorporating faith, arts, and community gatherings. In 2014, they were successful in purchasing the property from the Diocese of London for a dollar per acre, due in large part to the support and advocacy of the community and significant coverage from local media outlets. Renovations began in 2015, and while the project is not yet complete, the new community partnership has succeeded in increasing the community's use of renovated space through concerts, meetings, choir space, and yoga classes, generating new and stable sources of revenue for their operations.[29]

In order to support community renewal, many faith properties are being redeveloped to support housing needs. In British Columbia, the United Church has proposed a partnership with the provincial government to build 400 new affordable rental homes for individuals, families, and seniors at four church-owned properties in Coquitlam, Nanaimo, Richmond, and Vancouver. The homes target people with average incomes of between $50,000 and $100,000. Terry Harrison, of the

28. Singh, "Hand Churches Back."

29. Slater, "Making a Historic Community Hub."

denomination's property resource team, describes their involvement this way: "The United Church in BC has more property than we need. . . . [W]e must use these valuable assets wisely, in ways that will help congregations develop new and sustainable models of ministry while . . . providing a practical benefit to the wider community."[30]

Faith communities are not the only groups looking to make more effective use of congregational space. In 2020, a joint study by the Ontario Non-Profit Network, Faith and the Common Good, the National Trust for Canada, and various other partners recognized how significantly community non-profits rely on congregational space to deliver community programs and services.[31] Similarly, Brotsky, Vinokur-Kaplan, and Eisinger have published a workbook to assist non-profit organizations in finding space in faith buildings, where rents are usually more affordable, and the atmosphere is conducive to community engagement.[32]

We began this chapter by talking about numbers—the stories they tell and the stories they do not tell. At the very least, they describe a church that finds itself at the tipping point between one paradigm and the next, of coming to understand the challenge not only of being the church in new ways but of being human. Like never before, we need to unravel and remodel the elements that help us make meaning of our lives. Fifty or a hundred years ago, most people in Canada relied on a single religious community to participate in spiritual practices, celebrate and memorialize life moments, find healing, connect to tradition, mark holidays, find transcendence, serve others, and work for justice. The church no longer owns that story. It is time to write a new chapter—or perhaps permit it to be written for us.

"Two roads diverged in a yellow wood,
And sorry I could not travel both
And be one traveler, long I stood
And looked down as far as I could
To where it bent in the undergrowth."

—ROBERT FROST

30. Zimmer, "BC Partners with United Church."

31. Fry and Friesen, "No Space for Community."

32. Brotsky, Vinokur-Kaplan and Eisinger, *Shared Space*.

8

No Place Like Home

Finding a Way Forward

"Where is the horse? Where is the rider? Where is the treasure-giver? Where are the seats at the feast? Where are the revels in the hall? Alas for the bright cup. Alas for the armoured warrior. Alas for the splendor of the prince. How that time has passed away, dark under the cover of night as if it had never been?"

—"THE WANDERER," AUTHOR UNKNOWN[1]

THIS PASSAGE FROM "THE Wanderer" represents one of English literature's earliest existing compositions. Preserved only in an anthology known as the *Exeter Book*, this tenth-century, 115-line poem provides a striking first-person lament of an Anglo-Saxon warrior wandering the world alone after becoming isolated from his community. At the outset, the Wanderer, who is also referred to in the poem as the *earth-stepper*, feels lost. He has recently buried his warlord and finds himself alone in the world; he is in exile. He cries out, lamenting not only his current circumstance but the once meaningful and secure life he appears to have lost. According to

1. CBC Radio, "Move Over Beowulf."

Manish Sharma, chair of the English Department at Concordia University in Montreal, the Wanderer's cry depicts a longing for community that can only be known by someone who has been separated from their friends and a sense of purpose and belonging for too long.

Canadians, and many others around the globe, know that feeling all too well. Emerging from the legislated lockdowns and isolation of COVID-19, we share the Wanderer's sense of loneliness and grief. Many of us have found ourselves separated from friends and family for too long. Some of us have lost friends and family members during this time, if not from COVID, from other causes. We have not been able to love, care, or say goodbye in the ways we are accustomed to. Like the Wanderer, we grieve that loss. We feel its sharp, aching pain. We have grown tired from the heaviness of COVID and the many directions in which it has pulled our energy and emotions. Many of us feel alone.

But as the American-Irish poet Greg Delanty suggests, the Wanderer's malady or dis-ease involves more than just loneliness. It is not just his friends and companions that he has lost, but his "habitat." It is as though his entire way of being in the world has been torn away and lost. With many of our pews empty, our church doors locked, and our steeples toppling, this is how many western Christians feel. It is not just our friends and church members that we have lost, but our "habitat." It is not just our significance and influence in society that seems to have disappeared, but our entire way of being in the world. For us, it is not just two roads that diverge ahead—but many. We long for the "Before Time." And we are afraid that things will never be the same again.

Fear like this can chase us in two different ways. When we find ourselves under threat, our brains trigger a physiological response that prepares our bodies to either stay and deal with the danger or run and seek safety. This "fight or flight" response was first described in the early 1900s by American physiologist Walter Cannon. Cannon observed that a rapid release of hormones inside the body leads to a cascading series of physiological changes that stimulate the body's ability to respond to threatening circumstances.[2]

While Cannon was writing about a biological response in individuals, we know from experience that this same fight or flight response also occurs in groups. When friends, neighbors, or people of different cultures, backgrounds, or belief systems feel threatened, they also find ways

2. Cannon, *Bodily Changes*.

to fight or ways to hide. For thousands of years, the church has been finding ways to fight for what it believed. From its days of Roman resistance to the Crusades, the Witch Hunts, and the conquest of the Americas, the church has fought hard. Or so it seemed. Because if the recent revelations of unmarked burial sites at Canada's former residential schools are any indication (and I believe they are), the church in Canada has been hiding more than it has been fighting. And it has been hiding for much longer than many of us are prepared to admit. The spiriting away of school records, the burials in unmarked graves, the defensiveness and complicity of church leaders with government officials, the presumption of explorers and colonizers, can hardly be used to describe an organization in control of itself—let alone anyone else. Power is not about controlling other people. Power is about controlling oneself. Trying to control other people is usually the first sign that someone is losing control. Controlling others is what weak people think power looks like.

Anglican priest Jason McKinney likens the church's current state to Ivan Illich's theory on the life cycle of institutions.[3] Illich, a twentieth-century Catholic priest turned philosopher and social critic, argued that all institutions have their limits and ultimately pose more threat than harm. Institutions, Illich suggests, have two major watersheds or thresholds. The first is when the institution demonstrates its effectiveness so widely that it surpasses or even wipes out its competition. The second is when the institution begins to enjoy unquestioned prominence and privilege. When this happens, he says, its failures are soon overlooked and its harms normalized. The harmful effects start to crowd out the good: the institution starts doing more harm than good. In *Medical Nemesis,* Illich offers the example of institutional medicine. Health, says Illich, is someone's capacity to cope with the human reality of pain, sickness, and death. Advances in drugs, surgical techniques, and technology can help, but institutional medicine, Illich says, has gone too far, "launching into a godlike battle to eradicate death, pain, and sickness. And in doing so, turns people into consumers or objects, destroying their capacity for health."[4] Thus, it seems in the church. The evidence is clear. What was created for good—now delivers harm.

While illuminating, Illich's thoughts are not new. In the late nineteenth century, Lord Acton, writing to the local Anglican bishop,

3. McKinney, "North American Church Decline."

4. Smith, "Limits to Medicine."

famously advised: "Power tends to corrupt, and absolute power corrupts absolutely. Great men are almost always bad men, even when they exercise influence and not authority."[5] Much of this book has highlighted the Canadian church's oppression of First Nations people and how these dynamics have undermined the church's own sense of home in Canadian society. While these stories may have dominated recent headlines, they are not the only situations where the church in Canada has abused its power, taken advantage of its social standing, and judged those who did not conform to its expectations. These are not the only examples of where the Canadian church has stepped into Illich's "second watershed."

In 1989, the Royal Newfoundland Constabulary re-opened an investigation into allegations of child abuse at the Mount Cashel Boys' Home in Newfoundland. Over the following months, the public learned that young boys had been subjected to acts of physical and sexual abuse for decades by the Christian brothers who operated the home. While many Christian denominations now have groups within their tradition who support LGBTQ2S individuals, historically Christianity has dealt harshly with people who identify as Queer. In May of 2021, the Toronto Catholic School Board voted for the first time to observe Gay Pride Month.[6] In 2003, the denomination I grew up in and was ordained in passed a resolution indicating that any minister affiliated with the denomination who conducted a marriage ceremony for a gay couple would have their registration to marry revoked. Women, too, have felt the oppressive hand of the Canadian church. While the Baptist denomination officially supported the ordination and employment of women in professional ministry, my wife, herself a trained minister, experienced the distance between policy and practice when we explored the option of ministering together.

At first glance, all of this looks like control. It looks to us like the exercise of power and authority. But these recent controversies cause me to ask, "Has the church ever really been in control?" Has it ever really been up for the fight? Or have the battles it fought to advance the church through the ages been more a sign of our fear than our faith? Some may hope, myself included, that the recent discoveries and the reminders of past atrocities are finally opening this settler society's eyes to the harms we have caused, stirring us from our places of hiding, and setting us on a different journey.

5. Dalberg-Acton, "Letter to Bishop Mandell Creighton."

6. Sheikh, "Toronto Catholic School Board Votes."

There is increasing evidence that this is so. There is also little doubt that some, if not many, will resist this path. There will be many people who say, "My ancestors came to Canada, but I'm not responsible." We may not be responsible for the slaughter of Muslims during the Crusades, the burning of witches during the Middle Ages, or the abduction of Indigenous children in Canada during the nineteenth and twentieth centuries in Canada. But by ignoring the systematic, left-over oppression that contributed to these events and allowing it to continue—for that, we are responsible. Settler Canadians might say, "I've never spoken to or treated an Indigenous person harshly." That does not matter. What matters is the residual effect of oppression that has been handed down for generations, and if we do not stop that ball from rolling, we are responsible for that. It is far too easy to say, "I didn't do it."

Imagine being in a park. A group of children is playing. One of the children gets pushed over, is hurt, but none of the children move to help the child up. Which offender is worse? The one who pushed the child over? Or the ones who refused to offer any help? Too many Canadians, for too long, have been saying, "I didn't do it." And too many Canadians, for too long, have been standing idly by, refusing to offer help.

Idle No More

In November 2012, an Indigenous-led social movement known as Idle No More began amongst Treaty People to protest the Canadian government's introduction and later adoption of Bill-C45 by Prime Minister Stephen Harper's government. Sparked by four Saskatchewan women, Jessica Gordon, Sylvia McAdam, Sheelah McLean, and Nina Wilson, the group expressed concern over the far-reaching impact this legislation would have on the rights and authority of Indigenous communities while making it easier for government and business to push through projects without strict environmental assessment or Indigenous consultation. Less than a year later, on January 28, 2013, fifty events were held worldwide to observe the Idle No More World Day of Action. Twenty-five of these were in Canada and twenty in the United States, along with rallies in London, Paris, and Greenland.[7]

Following the discovery of 751 bodies at the Marieval Indian Residential School in June of 2021, Father John Mock shared with CBC News

7. Idle No More, "Indigenous-Led Social Movement."

how hard the shame of idleness can be. Two and half years earlier, Mock had been serving as the parish priest in Grayson, Saskatchewan. The town of Grayson sits in a corner of Southeast Saskatchewan, where it is possible to drive for kilometer after kilometer, between vast fields of wheat and canola, without seeing another person. But on the morning of November 14, 2018, Mock drove the seventeen kilometers from his parish in Grayson to stand amidst the pile of ashes that had once been Sacred Heart Catholic Church, near the residential school on the grounds of the Cowessess First Nation. Although not formally connected to the school, Mock reflected on how global headlines about the recent discoveries had sparked debate in his own parish between neighbors about who knew what and when:

> I have a very simple faith, despite all the ritual and everything else. And I believe God is good, and that somehow, in becoming a priest, I was going to be helping people. But when you're confronted with your history? The history of Canada? The history of the church from the time the Europeans arrived here? And the role we played in genocide? I mean, dear God, did they really think they were doing this for the highest of motives?[8]

It may be hard for Christians to acknowledge that by participating in historical, systemic oppression, we have been both pushing people over *and* failing to lift them up. A quote popularly (mis)attributed to Plato says, "We can easily forgive a child who is afraid of the dark; the real tragedy of life is when men are afraid of the light." It is frightening to think that the light we thought we were sharing has been darkness to others, and where darkness has been present, we have failed to share true light.

Where Mistakes Are Made

Not far from where I live in Toronto is the city's oldest surviving building. Built in 1794, Scadding Cabin was first owned by John Scadding, an assistant to John Graves Simcoe, Upper Canada's first lieutenant governor. The name "Toronto" derives from the Mohawk *tkaronto*,[9] and was used broadly to describe an area where trees grow in shallow water. The name first appears in the historical record as "lac de Taranteau," used by French explorers to refer not to the current location of Toronto, but Lake Simcoe,

8. Boyd, "Priests Ran the Residential School."
9. Reproduced from Steckley, "Toronto . . . or Is That Taranteau."

about 100 km to the north. Later, it was used to describe the present-day Humber River, and finally, to the city that grew up around the mouth of the Humber River at Lake Ontario.

In public school, I was taught that "Toronto" meant "meeting place," an interpretation popularized by Scadding's son, Henry, who was himself a prominent nineteenth-century historian. However, like the "well-meaning" settlers before him, Scadding tackled native words without full knowledge and with little regard for the word's grammar or common use. As the City of Toronto website records:

> Scadding mistakenly connected "Toronto" (which he felt was a more accurate representation of the word than "Taronto") with "atonronton," a Huron verb meaning "to be plenty." A "meeting place" could be thought of as "plenty of people," but to have this meaning, the verb would need to be altered to "ondatonronton" or "ayontronronton" ("they are plenty.") This is a long way from "Taranteau." As they say in some parts, "You can't get there from here."[10]

Toronto—the city where mistakes are made. Branding experts will probably tell us this is not the best marketing slogan for what has become a world-class city. They even have a hard time getting their own name right! And yet, perhaps, there is a lesson here for Canadians and especially still-faithful, church-going Canadians. The church in Canada has made mistakes. Our enabling of the European monarchs' thirst for empire, our participation in capitalism's exploitation of natural resources, and our complicity with the Canadian government's quest to kill the "Indian" in Indigenous children has not only played a part in the human genocide of Canada's First Nations, but depleted and undermined the church itself.

Mistakes happen. They are part of life, and they are an essential part of learning. They are the raw material of growth. They are how we get to know more. Do better. Be better. Yet, as Paulo Coelho writes, "A mistake repeated more than once is a decision." Repeating our mistakes shows an unwillingness to grow or to change. It conveys stubbornness and ignorance. The church in Canada can no longer claim or pretend to be above or better than this country's Indigenous people or any other disenfranchised people group, for that matter. Three hundred years ago, we might have got away with calling it a mistake. Today, it is a crime.

10. Steckley, "Toronto . . . or Is That Taranteau."

Like the people of Canada's First Nations, the church in Canada now finds itself "without a home." Mocked by many as outdated, accused by just as many of abuse and oppression, we find ourselves with dwindling significance and influence. Like the Wanderer, we have lost our "habitat." We feel off course. We are grieving our loss. We are fearful of our future. We are people without a home.

Seven Sacred Teachings

For many Indigenous people, the Seven Sacred Teachings represent a collection of teachings on how to be at home on earth and with each other. Some nations referred to them as the Seven Grandfather Teachings or the Seven Grandmother Teachings. Different stories and different symbols are used across Turtle Island to impart these teachings. Still, the same guiding principles of responsibility to the world, others, and ourselves are embedded in them all.

For the Anishinaabe, the dominant Indigenous people group in the Great Lakes area of Canada and the United States where I live, that story of Turtle Island begins with The Creator, who gives the Seven Grandfathers responsibility to watch over the Anishinaabe people. The Grandfathers sent a Messenger to earth to find someone who could communicate the values of the Anishinaabe. After searching in all directions, the Messenger found a baby. The Seven Grandfathers instructed the Messenger to take the baby around the earth for seven years to learn their way of life. After their return, the grandfathers gave the now young boy seven teachings to share with his people. They were truth, humility, respect, love, honesty, courage, and wisdom.[11]

1. **Debwewin—Truth**
   Truth is a gift from the Turtle. Turtles are one of the oldest species on earth and are believed to carry the teachings of life on their backs. To speak the truth is only to share what we have lived or experienced.

2. **Dabasendiziwin—Humility**
   Humility is a gift from the Wolf. The wolf lives for its pack. It bows in deference to others, but not in fear. To live humbly is to respect

11. Seven Generations Education, "Seven Grandfather Teachings"; Bouchard and Martin, *Seven Sacred Teachings*.

the power of others while staying confident in our own power. Respect is knowing that we are always part of something bigger than ourselves.

3. **Manaaji'idiwn—Respect**
   Respect is a gift from the Buffalo. In Indigenous culture, the buffalo sacrificed themselves to provide warmth, food, and shelter to sustain human life. To live respectfully is to live in balance with the needs of others and of creation.

4. **Zaagi'idiwin—Love**
   Love is a gift from the Eagle. It is everyone's right to have and experience it. But to love others, one must first know how to love oneself. Like the eagle, love requires strength and offers the ability to rise above. Love for humans, non-humans, and all of creation, is meant to be unconditional.

5. **Gwayakwaadiziwin—Honesty**
   Honesty is a gift from the Raven. They understand who they are and their purpose in life. To live honestly is to live as one is intended to live. That is where one finds power.

6. **Zoongide'ewin—Courage**
   Bravery is a gift from the Bear. The mother bear has the courage and strength to face her fears, even when her young are threatened. To live courageously is to stand tall in the face of threat.

7. **Nibwaakaawin—Wisdom**
   Wisdom is a gift from the Beaver. The beaver uses its unique teeth and the created world around it to ensure its family's survival by building sustainable communities. To live wisely is to know how the resources available to us can benefit everyone.

Seven as Symbol

While the number seven factors prominently in these foundational Indigenous teachings, seven also serves as a powerful symbol in many other cultures. As early as the third millennium BCE, the Sumerians, who inhabited the southern part of modern Iraq, used the number seven extensively to indicate religious importance, referring especially to the seven gods of wisdom, or seven sages, who taught humanity all of the known professions.[12] In the historic Babylonian text *Gilgamesh,* the epic's hero crosses seven mountains before the "cedars are revealed to his heart." Babylonian texts also included references to the seven sages, the seven gates of the underworld, seven days and seven nights, a man whose sons are seven, seven years, seven wisdoms, seven winds, and the seventh house.[13]

The ancient Egyptians believed there were seven paths to heaven and seven holy cows.[14] Pythagorean interest in the mathematical patterns of music formed the basis for much of musical theory, with seven being the number of distinct notes in a musical scale. There are seven days of the week. The four phases of the moon last seven days. Four times seven is also the number of days in a woman's menstrual cycle.

Many early cultures recognized seven planets: the Sun, Moon, Mercury, Venus, Mars, Jupiter, and Saturn.[15] They did not consider the earth to be a planet. In Indian culture, *Agni,* the god of fire, has seven wives and can produce seven flames. There are seven parts to the world, seven seasons, and seven fortresses. The sun-god has seven horses to pull his heavenly chariot, and in the *Rigveda,* one of the most sacred pieces of Hindu literature, there are seven parts to the world, seven seasons, and seven fortresses.[16] Even Snow White, a story first published by the Brothers Grimm in 1812 and popularized by the Disney Corporation in 1937, had her seven Dwarfs to provide a circle of protection around her against the evil witch.[17] Gamblers have their "lucky number seven," while breaking a mirror is rumored to produce seven years of bad luck.

In the Judeo-Christian tradition, the number seven appears more than 700 times in scripture. As a symbol of perfection and completeness, the word "created" is used seven times in the book of Genesis (1:1, 21, 27 [x 3]; 2:3, 4). A week has seven days, and God's Sabbath occurs on the seventh day. And by the fifth century, Christian scholars had symbolically divided the cannon into seven sections; 1) the Law; 2) the Prophets; 3) the Psalms; 4) the Gospels 5) the Acts of the Apostles and

12. Rashid, "Symbolic Number of Seven," 275–86.
13. Muroi, "Origin of the Mystical Number Seven."
14. Alabijeh, "Representations of Cow."
15. Stieglitz, "Hebrew Names of the Seven Planets."
16. Paramahamsa, "Symbolism in Rigveda."
17. Gillan, "True Origins of Snow White."

their Epistles; 6) the Letters of Paul, and 7) Revelation. In Genesis 7, God instructs Noah to take seven of every kind of clean animal. In Genesis 8, Noah waits seven days before the dove he sent out discovers dry land. In Genesis 41, Pharaoh dreams of seven cows and seven ears of corn. In Exodus 29, it takes seven days to sanctify the altar. In 2 Samuel, David is king in Hebron for seven years before he becomes king in Jerusalem. In 1 Kings, it takes Solomon seven years to build the temple, and in Luke 8, Jesus casts out seven demons who had plagued Mary Magdalene.

Seven Churches

For our current study, perhaps the most significant biblical "seven" is found in the seven churches of Revelation. As with the Seven Teachings of Indigenous Culture, the author's identification of seven churches is no accident. It is as though he is saying, "Listen, take notice; something important is happening here."

The Book of Revelation, also known as the Revelation to John and the Apocalypse of John, is the final book of the New Testament. The author names himself as "John." But who this John was, we are not entirely sure. Such noted historians as Justin Martyr, Irenaeus, and Clement of Alexandria believed him to be the apostle John. Many modern scholars argue against this and refer to him simply as "John of Patmos."

The eschatological imagery of Revelation has also led to a wide variety of Christian interpretations. Some argue that the Book of Revelation describes a critical stage in Christian history where the church experienced extreme persecution. Others suggest that Revelation's prophecies have already come true. Still, another school of thought believes the apocalyptic age described by John is still to come. Regardless of the stance one adopts, it is clear that John intended his letters to address the conditions facing each of these seven churches in the first and second centuries CE and also serve as a unified message to the church universal.

1. **The Church in Ephesus: Do Not Lose Focus** (2:1–7)
   The first of John's letters is to the church in Ephesus. At the time, Ephesus was one of the most dominant cities in Asia Minor. Nevertheless, it was also a city in decline. John praises the congregation for its hard work and patience. They have borne some heavy burdens, but they have been up to the task. They have remained

moral, and they have resisted evil. It seems as though they have done everything right.

However, there is one thing they had not done; they had not kept their "first love." The church in Ephesus had gone off-track in their love for Christ. They had fallen into a routine of rules and convention and forgotten their reason for doing it in the first place. John's message to the church in Ephesus was not to lose focus and remember their reason for being.

2. **The Church in Smyrna: The Problem of Suffering** (2:8–11)
In the first century CE, Smyrna was a beautiful, prosperous port city. It was also a difficult place to be a Christian. Under the Roman Emperor Domitian's reign, Christians in Smyrna faced intense persecution. "I know your works, your tribulations, and your poverty," the passage begins.

The problem of suffering has always troubled people—especially those who believe in God. Our question is this: "How can a good and loving God permit a world where people suffer?" Or, as Rabbi Harold Kushner put it in his 1981 book on the subject, "Why do bad things happen to good people?"[18]

John's response is that while suffering is hard, it is still possible to find meaning in the midst of it. Through suffering, we can learn obedience, as in Hebrews 5:8. Sometimes suffering can get our attention, as in Romans 5:3–5. And sometimes it comes as a warning that we have not been as godly or as faithful as we thought ourselves to be (1 Cor 11:30–32). Suffering is hard. But it is not always a meaningless experience. Suffering can help us to reflect, learn, and grow. It can help us to identify with others who suffer. And it can motivate us to change and adopt new ways of being.

3. **The Church in Pergamos: Worshipping False Idols** (2:12–17)
Pliny the Elder referred to Pergamos as the most illustrious city in Asia. It was here that Homer, one of Greek culture's earliest poets, and Herodotus, sometimes referred to as "the father of history," studied and wrote. For 250 years, Pergamos served as the official capital of the province and was home to some of the largest temples ever dedicated to Zeus, Apollo, Athena, and Caesar. Its citizens were

18. Kushner, *When Bad Things Happen*.

sophisticated and literate. And their teachings appealed to many—including Christians.

This passage begins with words of commendation for those in Pergamos who refused to deny their faith amidst the city's lack of belief. But some also called themselves Christians while gradually coming to support and practice many of the pagan worship rituals. These are the Christians with whom John is concerned:

> There are some among you who hold to the teaching of Balaam, who taught Balak to entice the Israelites to sin so that they ate food sacrificed to idols and committed sexual immorality. Likewise, you also have those who hold to the teaching of the Nicolaitans. Repent, therefore! Otherwise, I will soon come to you and will fight against them with the sword of my mouth. Whoever has ears, let them hear what the Spirit says to the churches.

4. **The Church in Thyatira: A Church That Compromised** (2:18–29)
Thyatira was an inland city located about 60 km southeast of Pergamos. As a commercial center that relied on trades, participating in the local economy would often have required membership in one of the city's many trade guilds. This reality presented a challenge for Christians since each of these guilds was associated with a particular guardian or patron god. To make matters worse, each guild expected its members to participate in festivals and celebratory meals that often involved licentious and immoral behavior. The church in Thyatira stands as a warning to the danger of compromise. Being Christian involves choices. Sometimes these choices are difficult. Often, they will be unpopular, and sometimes they will even demand going against concessions or compromises that the church has adopted.

5. **The Church in Sardis: Dead not Alive** (3:1–6)
While each of the first four letters begins with a commendation, the author starts this letter with condemnation. That cannot be a good sign! "I know your works, that you have a name that you are alive, but you are dead." On the outside, this was a church that looked good. It appeared to be doing all the right things. It appeared vibrant and had a reputation throughout the city as a trusted spiritual community with an effective ministry. But on the inside, it was spiritually lifeless.

The spiritual decline of a church is a gradual development, much like the popular tale of the frog in a kettle. As the anecdote goes, frogs won't normally go into boiling water. They will jump out immediately to avoid harm. But if they are placed in a pot of water at room temperature and heated slowly, they won't react and will end up dying in the boiling water.

While Douglas Melton of Harvard University and George Zug of Washington's National Museum of Natural History,[19] along with countless YouTube videos,[20] have discredited this theory, this cautionary tale about life remains. Letting small and seemingly harmless things slip can be bad for us. They can even end up killing us. The church in Sardis had been letting things slip. The water was heating up, and it was killing them.

6. **The Church in Philadelphia: Small but Faithful** (3:7–13)
In contrast to the other cities referred to in Revelation, Philadelphia was not a wealthy, sophisticated, or influential city. Its church, too, was small. But it was faithful. John commends them for their persistence in fulfilling their mission and for holding onto the Truth. "I know your deeds," he says. "See, I have placed before you an open door that no one can shut."

John presents Christ as a key—and that key is Truth. We learn from the church in Philadelphia that holding onto the truth, telling the truth, opens doors. More importantly, it aligns us with the One who opens doors and makes all things possible.

7. **The Church in Laodicea: The Lukewarm Church** (3:14–22)
By all appearances, Laodicea was a proud and prosperous city. But history also tells us that Laodicea played only a minor role in the spread of Greek culture. Its imposing walls gave the impression of strength and security, but its valley location and exposed water supply made it exceedingly vulnerable. Laodicea and its church imagined themselves more important than they really were.

The challenge facing them is suggested perhaps by the city's name itself. Named after Laodice, wife of the Syrian King Antiochus II, Strong's Concordance suggests the word derives from two words: *laos*, which means "people," and *dikē*, which as a noun means justice, or when applied as a verb, means "to decide" or "to rule."[21] In other words, in Laodicea, the people decide, or the

19. Kruszelnicki, "Frog Fable Brought to Boil."

20. As illustrated in https://www.youtube.com/watch?v=u5Fhek_f6GY.

21. Strong's Online Concordance. "2993 Laodikeia." biblehub.com, 2021. Accessed on Aug. 12, 2021: https://biblehub.com/greek/2993.htm.

people rule. John's criticism of the church in Laodicea was that they had grown lukewarm. As the city's name suggests, they were no longer fully under God's guidance or rule. Their wealth and prosperity had fostered a sense of worldliness and complacency that had undermined the church's spiritual health. The people had decided what was best.

The Revelation of John begins with seven letters to seven churches. Even though John addressed these letters to specific congregations, his use of the number seven indicates that his advice was intended for all Christian communities. Like the Seven Teachings of Canada's Indigenous people, they stand as a guidepost for today's church. They are offered as lessons for a church that has made mistakes, wavered in its focus, been unaccustomed to suffering, compromised its practice and belief, been pre-occupied with numbers and image, and perhaps, as some would suggest, lost its way entirely.

In chapter 6, we began with the words of Pink Floyd's *The Wall*. In the first verse, we hear the words, "Daddy's flown across the ocean, leaving just a memory." We commented on how easily Christian listeners to that song might have wondered if, in addition to writing about his own childhood experience, Roger Waters had also been writing about the church and its relationship with God.

For the past several decades, and at several points down through the centuries, Christians have asked, "Doesn't God live here anymore?" Based on our present experience, it is a fair question. But on closer analysis, perhaps it is not God, but we Christians, who have left home. Perhaps we "believers" have abandoned the church and its mission, not the other way around. Maybe the question that needs to be asked is not "Where has God gone?" but "Where have *we* gone, and how can we find our way home?"

No Place Like Home

And what is the answer? I find myself siding with the American ethnobotanist Terrence McKenna on this. Our problem is not so much *finding* the answer as it is *facing* the answer.[22] The institution we have come to call the church is dying. The decline is not just a social or cultural phenomenon, but also a natural consequence of past action and present

22. Danut, "100 Quotes from Terence McKenna."

apathy. God is dismantling the church. God is naming the idols we have built. God is extinguishing the political, cultural, and economic power we have accumulated over the centuries. God is exposing our inability to see our faults and unwillingness to change. God is calling us out of our fear toward something new. But are we listening? Are we willing to answer that call?

Recently, I came across a blog by Rebecca Seghini[23] that explores the iconic phrase, "There's no place like home," uttered by Judy Garland as Dorothy in *The Wizard of Oz*. Seghini reminds us that in Kansas, Dorothy and her family "live on a farm in the middle of nowhere." Even though her friends and family are caring and loving, Dorothy is bored. She and her dog, Toto, are constantly getting into trouble. Seghini suggests that Dorothy's song "Somewhere Over the Rainbow" shows her desire to be somewhere else, to go somewhere better, to live somewhere that is not at all like the home she is used to.

Seghini draws attention to the use of color in the film, meant to keep the divide between Kansas and Oz very clear:

> Kansas . . . is shot in sepia tone to emphasize the dull lifeless landscape and to let the audience truly see why it is that Dorothy wants to get out so badly. Then when we see Oz, this bright vibrant world that is shot in technicolour which was still uncommon at the time, the audience gain the same impact that Dorothy does as she opens the door into this new world.[24]

Primary colors are used to emphasize that Oz is so very different from the kind of world Dorothy is familiar with. Even though Oz represents a brand-new world for Dorothy, she still encounters reminders of home. She meets characters like the scarecrow, the tin man, and the lion, all of whom resemble the people at home, but with whom she makes much stronger attachments in Oz, reinforcing the belief that maybe Oz *is* the better place to be. Even on a social level, Seghini suggests that Oz may be a better place for Dorothy. Here, women seem to be in a position of power. Even though the Wizard appears at first to be the most powerful character in the film, he turns out to be a fraud. And when it seems that it is the witches who hold all the power, even the younger Dorothy holds some sort of power over them. Dorothy would never have had this

23. Seghini, "No Place Like Home."
24. Seghini, "No Place Like Home."

power the way things used to be. She would never have had this power in Kansas. She would never have had this power back home.

Throughout the film, we long with Dorothy for her home in Kansas while we simultaneously feel drawn to this new, spectacular upside-down world she has found herself flung into by the whirlwind. She never seems to give up her dream of returning home, except when it comes time to go. It is only when Dorothy utters the words, "There's no place like home" that her "strength and determination seem to falter as we see the reluctance to leave what is essentially her new home and her new family."[25] Even when she wakes up back in Kansas, she refuses to believe it was all a dream. Now it is Oz she longs for, not Kansas. "There is no place like home. There is no place like home." The truth is that once we have left our childhood homes, the real secret of the ruby slippers, suggests Seghini, is that there is no place like home, except of course, for the home we make or that is made for us in Oz, which, as she writes, "is anywhere, and everywhere, except for the place from which we began." The real question facing us is whether we can accept that, act on that, and live our lives as though everything depends on it.

God does not live in houses made by human hands.[26] If we lose the institution of the church, we have not lost everything. As the German scholar Jeremias points out, the kingdom of God is never a territory or place in a spatial sense. But neither is it abstract or static. As Donald Kraybill writes in his book *The Upside-Down Kingdom*, "The kingdom does not stand still on a particular piece of ground—it is always in the process of being achieved."[27] The kingdom is not a place, but a relationship. God's dwelling place is not a territory but a state of being. God's home is constantly moving, perpetually growing, continually expanding. The kingdom is present when women and men permit God and God's love to be the driving force in their lives. The kingdom is a place where death does not bring an end to the story. In God's world, resurrection is always possible.

There is no place like home. But the home we seek is not, and cannot be, like one we have ever known or could ever imagine. There is no going back to the status quo because the status quo no longer exists! Remember what Plato said? "You cannot step twice into the same river." The only

25. Seghini, "No Place Like Home."

26. Acts 7:48.

27. Kraybill, *Upside Down Kingdom*, 25.

path for the church in Canada is the one forward. The only path is the one that embraces change. The only path is the one that accepts death and believes that resurrection is possible. The only path is the one that refuses to be afraid of the new thing God is doing.

We started this book with a day when the world had stopped. But perhaps the isolation of COVID and the revelations associated with Canada's Indigenous schools during that time are precisely what the church in Canada has needed to stop, reflect, acknowledge, and reimagine its place in Canadian society. Despite the disconnect and pain we have experienced as a result, maybe it is the incentive we need to start again and move towards God's new home for the church in Canada. God is doing away with the altars and tabernacles and steeples we have long known. God is challenging the idols we have bowed down to. God is offering a new home, not of make-believe or fantasy, but of opportunity and discovery. God is establishing a home where the truth, humility, respect, love, honesty, courage, and wisdom that were planted from the time of creation on Turtle Island are honored; where the doors of our worship spaces are open to truth-telling, contrition, humility, and right relations with all those that the church has wronged; where the lights in the windows give warmth and welcome to the people of every race, culture, and gender; and where the roof offers shelter to all.

God doesn't live here anymore because God does not and will not stand still. When the church relies on its past instead of its future, it is diminished. When it depends on the safety of its walls, it loses light in the shadow of its spire. When the church oppresses those who believe differently, it undermines itself. When it lives in the past instead of the present, it dies. God doesn't live here anymore because God is creating a new home for the church and for all humanity. There is no place like home. There is no place like home.

"When a tree grows be it ever so strong and large; it rots away gradually and down it goes at last. But through time another young tree shoots forth from there, and as it grows, it gathers beauty and strength."

—CHIEF PEGUIS, SAULTEAUX FIRST NATION[28]

28. Chief Peguis lived from 1774 to 1864. In 1817, he signed the first treaty with Lord Selkirk granting land along the Red River to the Selkirk settlers. In 1840, he was one of the early western First Nations converts to Christianity. He and his people were instrumental in helping to establish the Hudson's Bay Company in the west and in preserving the Selkirk settlers from starvation. In addition to his commercial and humanitarian support, Peguis was an outspoken critic of the illegal settlement of settler Europeans on Indigenous lands.

Afterword

SINCE THE COMPLETION OF these chapters, and prior to the publication of this book, two significant events on the road to reconciliation have taken place. On March 28, 2022, more than 30 First Nation, Inuit, and Métis leaders traveled to Rome for meetings with Pope Francis at the Vatican. Meeting in the same room where a series of fifteenth-century papal decrees had established the Doctrine of Discovery, representatives shared their stories of the abuses Indigenous Canadians had suffered at Canada's Catholic-run residential schools, and the multigenerational trauma arising from it.

In July of that same year, Pope Francis traveled to Canada making stops in Alberta, Iqaluit, and Quebec. On Sunday, July 24, Pope Francis delivered the following apology:

> I have been waiting to come here and be with you. Here, from this place associated with painful memories, I would like to begin what I consider a penitential pilgrimage. I have come to your native lands to tell you in person of my sorrow, to implore God's forgiveness, healing and reconciliation, to express my closeness and to pray with you and for you.
>
> I recall the meetings we had in Rome four months ago. At that time, I was given two pairs of moccasins as a sign of the suffering endured by Indigenous children, particularly those who, unfortunately, never came back from the residential schools. I was asked to return the moccasins when I came to Canada, and I will do so at the end of these few words, in which I would like to reflect on this symbol, which over the past few months has kept alive my sense of sorrow, indignation and shame.
>
> The memory of those children is indeed painful; it urges us to work to ensure that every child is treated with love, honour

and respect. At the same time, those moccasins also speak to us of a path to follow, a journey that we desire to make together. We want to walk together, to pray together and to work together, so that the sufferings of the past can lead to a future of justice, healing and reconciliation.

That is why the first part of my pilgrimage among you takes place in this region, which from time immemorial has seen the presence of Indigenous Peoples. These are lands that speak to us; they enable us to remember.

To remember, brothers and sisters, you have lived on these lands for thousands of years, following ways of life that respect the Earth, which you received as a legacy from past generations and are keeping for those yet to come. You have treated it as a gift of the Creator to be shared with others and to be cherished in harmony with all that exists, in profound fellowship with all living beings.

In this way, you learned to foster a sense of family and community, and to build solid bonds between generations, honouring your elders and caring for your little ones. A treasury of sound customs and teachings, centred on concern for others, truthfulness, courage and respect, humility, honesty and practical wisdom.

Yet if those were the first steps taken in these lands, the path of remembrance leads us, sadly, to those that followed. The place where we are gathered renews within me the deep sense of pain and remorse that I have felt in these past months.

I think back on the tragic situations that so many of you, your families and your communities have known; of what you shared with me about the suffering you endured in the residential schools.

These are traumas that are in some way reawakened whenever the subject comes up; I realize too that our meeting today can bring back old memories and hurts, and that many of you may feel uncomfortable even as I speak.

Yet, it is right to remember, because forgetfulness leads to indifference and, as has been said, "the opposite of love is not hatred, it's indifference and the opposite of life is not death, it's indifference." To remember the devastating experiences that took place in the residential schools hurts, angers, causes pain, and yet it is necessary.

It is necessary to remember how the policies of assimilation and enfranchisement, which also included the residential school system, were devastating for the people of these lands. When the European colonists first arrived here, there was a great opportunity to bring about a fruitful encounter between cultures, traditions and forms of spirituality.

Yet, for the most part that did not happen. Again, I think back on the stories you told: how the policies of assimilation ended up systematically marginalizing the Indigenous Peoples; how also through the system of residential schools your languages and cultures were denigrated and suppressed; how children suffered physical, verbal, psychological and spiritual abuse; how they were taken away from their homes at a young age, and how that indelibly affected relationships between parents and children, grandparents and grandchildren.

I thank you for making me appreciate this, for telling me about the heavy burdens that you still bear, for sharing with me these bitter memories.

Today I am here, in this land that, along with its ancient memories, preserves the scars of still open wounds.

I am here because the first step of my penitential pilgrimage among you is that of again asking forgiveness, of telling you once more that I am deeply sorry. Sorry for the ways in which, regrettably, many Christians supported the colonizing mentality of the powers that oppressed the Indigenous Peoples.

I am sorry. I ask forgiveness, in particular, for the ways in which many members of the church and of religious communities co-operated, not least through their indifference, in projects of cultural destruction and forced assimilation promoted by the governments of that time, which culminated in the system of residential schools.

Although Christian charity was not absent, and there were many outstanding instances of devotion and care for children, the overall effects of the policies linked to the residential schools were catastrophic. What our Christian faith tells us is that this was a disastrous error, incompatible with the Gospel of Jesus Christ.

It is painful to think of how the firm soil of values, language and culture that made up the authentic identity of your peoples was eroded, and that you have continued to pay the price of this. In the face of this deplorable evil, the church kneels before God and implores His forgiveness for the sins of her children I myself wish to reaffirm this, with shame and unambiguously, I humbly beg forgiveness for the evil committed by so many Christians against the Indigenous Peoples.

Dear brothers and sisters, many of you and your representatives have stated that begging pardon is not the end of the matter. I fully agree: that is only the first step, the starting point. I also recognize that, "looking to the past, no effort to beg pardon and to seek to repair the harm done will ever be sufficient," and that, "looking ahead to the future, no effort must be spared to create a culture able to prevent such situations from happening." An important part of this process will be to conduct a serious investigation into the facts of what took place in the past and to assist the survivors of the residential schools to experience healing from the traumas they suffered.

I trust and pray that Christians and civil society in this land may grow in the ability to accept and respect the identity and the experience of the Indigenous Peoples. It is my hope that concrete ways can be found to make those peoples better known and esteemed, so that all may learn to walk together.

For my part, I will continue to encourage the efforts of all Catholics to support the Indigenous Peoples. I have done so at various times and occasions, through meetings, appeals and also through the writing of an Apostolic Exhortation. I realize that all this will require time and patience. We are speaking of processes that must penetrate hearts. My presence here and the commitment of the Canadian Bishops are a testimony to our will to persevere on this path.

Dear friends, this pilgrimage is taking place over several days and in places far distant from one another; even so, it will not allow me to accept the many invitations I have received to visit centres like Kamloops, Winnipeg and various places in Saskatchewan, Yukon and the Northwest Territories. Nonetheless, please know that all of you are in my thoughts and in my prayer. Know that I am aware of the sufferings and traumas, the difficulties and challenges, experienced by the Indigenous Peoples in every region of this country. The words that I speak throughout this penitential journey are meant for every Native community and person. I embrace all of you with affection.

On this first step of my journey, I have wanted to make space for memory. Here, today, I am with you to recall the past, to grieve with you, to bow our heads together in silence and to pray before the graves. Let us allow these moments of silence to help us interiorize our pain. Silence. And prayer. In the face of evil, we pray to the Lord of goodness; in the face of death, we pray to the God of life. Our Lord Jesus Christ took a grave, which seemed the burial place of every hope and dream, leaving behind only sorrow, pain and resignation, and made it a place of rebirth and resurrection, the beginning of a history of new life and universal reconciliation.

> Our own efforts are not enough to achieve healing and reconciliation: we need God's grace. We need the quiet and powerful wisdom of the Spirit, the tender love of the Comforter. May He bring to fulfilment the deepest expectations of our hearts. May He guide our steps and enable us to advance together on our journey.[1]

Perhaps, not surprisingly, reactions to the Pope's long-awaited apology have been mixed. In an interview with TV Ontario, Deputy Grand Chief Anna Betty Achneepineskum, of the Nishnawbe Aski Nation said: "The feedback and the comments that we're getting [from residential-school survivors] are that the apology was meaningful in terms of the church acknowledging their role"[2] but that there were also things missing, including references to the sexual abuse that children endured while they were in these schools, the sterilization some women and girls experienced in these institutions, and the deaths.

Sol Mamakwa, a member of the Kingfisher First Lake Nation and an elected member of the Provincial Legislature for the Ontario riding of Kiiwetinoong, added that while the Pope apologized for the actions of "many Christians" associated with the Catholic Church, he did not apologize for the church itself.[3]

Perhaps the final word, or maybe it is the starting word, comes from Ontario Regional Chief, Glen Hare. While applauding the Pope on his visit to Canada and for his words of apology, he also offered these words of caution:

> Let's hope he follows up on the next steps, releasing the records and the documents and all that. The Vatican needs to build up from this visit. He can't just come here and say what he said and go back, and that's it. No, the real work begins now.[4]

1. Canadian Press. "'I am deeply sorry': Full text of residential school apology from Pope Francis."

2. Anderson, "The Real Work Begins Now."

3. Anderson, "The Real Work Begins Now."

4. Anderson, "The Real Work Begins Now."

Bibliography

Adams, Michael. *Sex in the Snow: The Surprising Revolution of Canadian Social Values*. Toronto: Penguin, 2006.

Alabijeh, Ali Zamani. "Representations of Cow in Different Social, Cultural, Religious and Literary Contexts in Persia and the World." *Asian Journal of Social Sciences and Humanities* 3.1 (2014) 215–18. http://ajssh.leena-luna.co.jp/AJSSHPDFs/Vol.3(1)/AJSSH2014(3.1-20).pdf.

Albertz, Rainer, and Rudiger Schmitt. *Family and Household Religion in Ancient Israel and the Levant*. Winona Lake, IN: Eisenbrauns, 2012.

Alcock, Pete, et al., eds. *The Student's Companion to Social Policy*. 5th ed. Oxford: Wiley and Sons, 2016.

Alikin, Valeriy A. *The Earliest History of the Christian Gathering: Origin, Development and Content of the Christian Gathering in the First to Third Centuries*. Supplements to Vigiliae Christianae, vol. 102. Leiden: Brill, 2010.

Allen, Bonnie. "From Sacred to Secular: Canada Set to Lose 9,000 Churches, Warns National Heritage Group." *CBC News*, March 10, 2019. https://www.cbc.ca/news/canada/losing-churches-canada-1.5046812.

Allen, R. C. "Agriculture and the Origins of the State in Ancient Egypt." *Explorations in Economic History* 34.2 (1997) 135–53. https://www.sciencedirect.com/science/article/abs/pii/S0014498397906732.

American Turf Register. "Steeplechase in Montreal." *American Turf Register*. Baltimore, 1840.

Anand, Aniel. "The Institutionalization and Suicide Crisis amongst Indigenous Youth." Frontier Centre for Public Policy. February 9, 2020: https://fcpp.org/2020/02/09/the-institutionalization-and-suicide-crisis-among-indigenous-youth/.

Anderson, Charnel. "'The Real Work Begins Now': Three Indigenous Leaders on the Pope's Apology." *TVO*. July 27, 2022. https://www.tvo.org/article/the-real-work-begins-now-three-indigenous-leaders-on-the-popes-apology?gclid=CjoKCQjwuuKXBhCRARIsAC-gMogDkYSo7GW8DkmeoZXqU4y56XoaV9aszaKlxrXbRBoMPuovI3UG7PgaAqd7EALw_wcB.

Andrews, Edward E. "Christian Missions and Colonial Empires Reconsidered: A Black Evangelist in West Africa, 1766–1816." *Journal of Church and State* 51.4 (2009) 663–91. https://doi.org/10.1093/jcs/csp090.

Andrews, Tamara. *Dictionary of Nature Myths: Legends of the Earth, Sea and Sky*. New York: Oxford University Press, 1998.

Anglican Church of Canada. "Response of the Churches to the Truth and Reconciliation Commission of Canada." July 2, 2015. https://www.anglican.ca/tr/response-of-the-churches-to-the-truth-and-reconciliation-commission-of-canada/.

Anglican Samizdat. "Latest Anglican Church of Canada Membership and Attendance Statistics." *Anglican Samizdat,* October 5, 2019. https://www.anglicansamizdat.net/wordpress/latest-anglican-church-of-canada-membership-and-attendance-statistics/.

Angus Reid. "Religion and Faith in Canada Today: Strong Belief, Ambivalence and Rejection Define our Views." Angus Reid Institute, 2017: http://angusreid.org/wp-content/uploads/2016/01/2015.03.25_Faith.pdf.

———. "Religious Trends: Led by Quebec, Number of Canadians Holding Favourable Views of Various Religions Increases." Angus Reid Institute, April 4, 2017: http://angusreid.org/religious-trends-2017/.

———. "What Makes Us Canadian? A Study of Values, Beliefs, Priorities and Identity." Angus Reid, 2016: http://angusreid.org/canada-values.

Assembly of First Nations. "Dismantling the Doctrine of Discovery." January 2018. https://www.afn.ca/wp-content/uploads/2018/02/18–11–22-Dismantling-the-Doctrine-of-Discovery-EN.pdf.

———. "First Nations Post-Secondary Fact Sheet." Assembly of First Nations, 2018: https://www.afn.ca/wp-content/uploads/2018/07/PSE_Fact_Sheet_ENG.pdf.

Baird, Joseph L., ed. "Letter #45." In *The Personal Correspondence of Hildegard of Bingen.* Oxford: Oxford University Press, 2006.

Bean, Lydia. *The Politics of Evangelical Identity: Local Churches and Partisan Divides in the United States and Canada.* Princeton, NJ: Princeton University Press, 2014.

Berton, Pierre. *The Comfortable Pew.* Toronto: McLelland and Stewart, 1965.

Bibby, Reginald. *Beyond the Gods and Back: Religion's Demise and Rise and Why It Matters.* Lethbridge, AB: 2011.

———. *Fragmented Gods: The Poverty and Potential of Religion in Canada.* Toronto: Stoddart, 1987.

———. *Project Canada Survey.* Data Collected by Reginald Bibby. Lethbridge, AB, 2015. http://www.reginaldbibby.com/codebooksdata.html.

Bibby, Reginald, Joel Thiessen, and Monetta Bailey. *The Millennial Mosaic.* Toronto: Dundurn, 2019.

Biden, Joe. "Joe Biden's Inaugural Address." CNN. January 20, 2021. https://www.cnn.com/2021/01/20/politics/joe-biden-speech-transcript/index.html.

Blackwell, Richard. "No Longer Fake." *The Globe and Mail,* July 4, 2008. https://www.theglobeandmail.com/report-on-business/no-longer-fake/article1057023/.

Blunden, Andy. *Hegel for Social Movements.* Leiden: Brill, 2018.

Bokma, Anne. "Adoptees Seeking Redress: Canada Confronts the Sixties Scoop." *Indian Country Today,* January 2, 2017. Updated September 13, 2018. https://indiancountrytoday.com/archive/adoptees-seeking-redress-canada-confronts-sixties-scoop.

Bouchard, David, and J. Martin. *The Seven Sacred Teachings of White Buffalo Calf Woman = Niizhwaaswi aanike'iniwendiwin: waabishiki mashkode bizhikiins ikwe.* Ojibwe translation by Jason and Nancy Jones. Vancouver: More Than Words, 2009: http://www.btgwinnipeg.ca/uploads/5/2/4/1/52412159/the_seven_sacred_teachings_.pdf.

Boyd, Alex. "Priests Ran the Residential School at Cowessess. Now the Pastor Next Door Wonders, What Now?" *The Toronto Star* June 26, 2021. https://www.thestar.com/news/canada/2021/06/26/priests-ran-the-residential-school-at-cowessess-now-the-pastor-next-door-wonders-what-now.html?fbclid=IwARoEUsdsNWYaDCKWaWgbmhcgRi6DFVcoFI37zApjsmllN4VDBN8f5nmzFfo.

Brecht, Martin. *Martin Luther: His Road to Reformation 1483–1521. Vol. 1.* Translated by James L, Schaaf. Philadelphia: Fortress, 1985.

Broedel, Hans Peter. *The Malleus Maleficarum and the Construction of Witchcraft: Theology and Popular Belief.* Manchester, UK: Manchester University Press, 2003: https://library.oapen.org/bitstream/handle/20.500.12657/35002/341393.pdf?sequence=1&isAllowed=y.

Brooks, Laken. "Women Used to Dominate the Beer Industry—Until the Witch Accusations Started Pouring in." *The Conversation* March 7, 2021: https://theconversation.com/women-used-to-dominate-the-beer-industry-until-the-witch-accusations-started-pouring-in-155940.

Brotsky, China, Diane Vinokur-Kaplan, and Sarah Eisinger. *Shared Space and the New Nonprofit Workplace.* Oxford: Oxford University Press, 2019.

Brown, Callum. *The Death of Christian Britain: Understanding Secularization 1800–2000.* London: Routledge, 2001.

Brown, Colin, ed. *The New International Dictionary of New Testament Theology*, vol. 2. Grand Rapids: Zondervan, 1986.

Brown, Desmond. "Discovery of 751 Unmarked Graves 'has to be a wake-up call,' Indigenous Women's Group Says." *CBC News*, June 25, 2021: https://www.cbc.ca/news/canada/toronto/canada-indigenous-751-unmarked-graves-1.6079485.

Brown, Pete. *Through the Eye of a Needle: Wealth, the Fall of Rome, and the Making of Christianity in the West.* Princeton, NJ: Princeton University Press, 2012.

Bruce, F. F. *The Spreading Flame: The Rise and Progress of Christianity from Its First Beginnings to the Conversion of the English.* Grand Rapids: Eerdmans, 1973.

Bryce, Peter H. *The Story of a National Crime: An Appeal for Justice to the Indians of Canada.* Ottawa: James Hope and Sons, 1922: https://openhistoryseminar.com/canadianhistory/chapter/document-2-bryce-the-story-of-a-national-crime-1921/.

Burckhardt, Jacob. *The Age of Constantine the Great.* New York: Taylor & Frances, 1949.

Burrage, H. S., ed. *Early English and French Voyages, Chiefly from Hakluyt, 1534–1608.* New York: Scribner's Sons, 1906.

Bytwerk, Randall L. "The Jew as World Parasite." German Propaganda Archive. Calvin University, 2008: https://research.calvin.edu/german-propaganda-archive/weltparasit.htm.

Campbell, Nathaniel M. "The Prophetess and the Pope: St. Hildegard of Bingen, Pope Benedict XVI, and the Prophetic Visions of Church Reform." *Postmedieval* 10 (2019) 22–35.

Canadian Press. "'I am deeply sorry': Full text of residential school apology from Pope Francis." *CBC News.* July 25, 2022. https://www.cbc.ca/news/canada/edmonton/pope-francis-maskwacis-apology-full-text-1.6531341#:~:text=I%20am%20here%20because%20the,I%20am%20sorry.

———. "Researchers say that TB at Residential Schools Was No Accident." *CTV News*, July 18, 2021. https://beta.ctvnews.ca/national/canada/2021/7/18/1_5513755.html?s=09.

Cannon, Walter B. *Bodily Changes in Pain, Hunger, Fear and Rage: An Account of Recent Researches into the Function of Emotional Excitement*. New York. Appleton, 1915.

Carrol, John. *Case and His Contemporaries*, vols 1–4. Toronto: Wesleyan Conference Office, 1867–74.

CBC News. "Windsor's Assumption Church Hits 'New Milestone' in Interior Renovations." *CBC News*, March 4, 2021: https://www.cbc.ca/news/canada/windsor/assumption-church-windsor-1.5937048.

CBC News. "Cowessess First Nation Chief on 'Heartbreaking' Discovery of Unmarked Graves." *The National*, June 27, 2021. https://www.cbc.ca/player/play/1914227267751.

CBC Radio. "Move over Beowulf: Why the First Good Poem in English May Be Something Else." *Ideas*, hosted by Tom Howell, 15 March 2021. https://www.cbc.ca/radio/ideas/move-over-beowulf-why-the-first-good-poem-in-english-may-be-something-else-1.5950692.

Chadwick, Owen. *The Reformation*. London: Penguin, 1972.

Chandler, Graham. "Selling the Prairie Good Life." Canada's History, September 7, 2016: https://www.canadashistory.ca/explore/settlement-immigration/selling-the-prairie-good-life.

Charlotte Steeplechase Foundation. "About Steeplechasing." https://www.queenscup.org/steeplechasing/.

Chaves, Mark, and David. E. Cann. "Religion, Pluralism and Religious Market Structure." *Annual Review of Sociology* 4.3 (1992) 272–90.

Chaves, Mark, Peter J. Schraeder, and Mario Sprindys. "State Regulation of Religion and Muslim Religious Vitality in the Industrialized West." *Journal of Politics* 56.4 (1994) 1087–97.

Clarke, Brian, and Stuart Macdonald. *Leaving Christianity: Changing Allegiances in Canada Since 1945*. Montreal, QC: McGill-Queen's University Press, 2017.

Clark, Victor. "Christian Symbols on Bronze Coins of Constantine the Great." constantinethegreatcoins.com.

Coblenz, Stanton A. *The Day the World Stopped*. New York: Double Dragon, 1969.

Colson, F. H. trans. In Eusebius *Praeparatio Evangelica*, 8.7.12–13. http://www.earlyjewishwritings.com/text/philo/book28.html.

Cook, Ramsay. *The Voyages of Jacques Cartier*. Toronto, University of Toronto Press, 1993.

Cooper, John Irwin. *The History of the Montreal Hunt 1826–1953*. Montreal: Montreal Hunt, 1953.

Copernicus, Nicolaus. "15 Nicolaus Copernicus Quotes (That Will Get Your Brain Working). https://wiseowlquotes.com/nicolaus-copernicus/.

Copernicus, Nicolaus. "The Text of: Nicolas Copernicus—*De Revolutionibus* (On the Revolutions), 1543 CE." In *Calendars through the Ages*, 1–41. Austin, TX: University of Texas. http://www.geo.utexas.edu/courses/302d/Fall_2011/Full%20text%20-%20Nicholas%20Copernicus,%20_De%20Revolutionibus%20(On%20the%20Revolutions),_%201.pdf.

Cornelissen, Louis. "Religiosity in Canada and Its Evolution from 1985 to 2019." Ottawa: Statistics Canada, 2021: https://www150.statcan.gc.ca/n1/pub/75-06-x/2021001/article/00010-eng.htm.

Coulton, George G. *Medieval Panorama: The English Scene from Conquest to Reformation*. New York: MacMillan, 1938.

———. *Medieval Village, Manor and Monastery*. New York: Harper and Row, 1960.

Cragun, Ryan T., and Joseph H. Hammer. "'One Person's Apostate is Another Person's Convert': What Terminology Tells Us about Pro-Religious Hegemony in the Sociology of Religion." *Humanity and Society* 35 (2011) 149–75.

Cragun, R. T., B. Kosmin, A. Keysar., J. Hammer, and M. Nielson. "On the Receiving End: Discrimination toward the Non-Religious in the United States." *Journal of Contemporary Religion* 27.1 (2012) 105–27.

Csillag, Ron. "Survey Finds Deep Mistrust for Muslims in Canada." *Washington Post*, March 26, 2012. A https://www.washingtonpost.com/national/on-faith/survey-finds-deep-mistrust-for-muslims-incanada/2012/03/26/gIQAjDCMcS_story.html?utm_term=.86d3e80b7e56.

Cull, Ian, et al., eds. "Myths That Impact Indigenous Student Experience." In *Pulling Together: A Guide for Front-Line Staff, Student Services, and Advisors*. Victoria, BC: BC Campus, 2018: https://opentextbc.ca/indigenizationfrontlineworkers/chapter/myths-that-impact-indigenous-student-experience/.

Dalberg-Acton, John. "Letter to Bishop Mandell Creighton, April 5, 1887." Excerpt from *Historical Essays and Studies*. https://history.hanover.edu/courses/excerpts/165acton.html.

Dale, Daniel. "Under Trump, a Majority of Canadians Dislike the US for the First Time in 35 Years, Likely Much Longer." *Toronto Star*, June 26, 2017: https://www.thestar.com/news/world/2017/06/26/amajority-of-canadians-dislike-the-us-for-the-first-time-in-35-years-likely-much-longer.html.

Daniélou, Alain. *Gods of Love and Ecstasy: The Traditions of Shiva and Dionysius*. New York: Inner Traditions, 1980.

Danut, Incrosnatu. "100 Quotes from Terence McKenna." *Awaken*, June 9, 2019: https://awaken.com/2019/06/100-quotes-from-terence-mckenna/.

Davies, G. "The Significance of Deuteronomy 1:2 for the Location of Mount Horeb." *Palestinian Exploration Quarterly* 111.2 (1979) 87–107.

Deacon, Richard. *Matthew Hopkins: Witch Finder General*. London: Muller, 1976.

Delaney, Janice, Mary Jane Lupton, and Emily Toth. *The Curse: A Cultural History of Menstruation*. Rev. ed. Urbana, IL: University of Illinois Press, 1988.

Dickason, O. *Canada's First Nations: A History of Founding Peoples from Earliest Times*. Toronto: McLelland and Stewart, 1992.

Dickson, Courtney, and Bridgette Watson. "Remains of 215 Children Found Buried at Former B.C. Residential School, First Nation Says." *CBC News*, May 27, 2021. https://www.cbc.ca/news/canada/british-columbia/tk-eml%C3%BAps-te-secw%C3%A9pemc-215-children-former-kamloops-indian-residential-school-1.6043778.

Dickson, Courtney. "Residential School Survivors Society Calls for Action Following Discovery of Children's Remains." *CBC News*, May 28, 2021. https://www.cbc.ca/news/canada/british-columbia/indian-residential-school-survivors-society-calls-for-action-1.6045448.

Diefenbaker Canada Centre. "The Enfranchisement of the Aboriginal Peoples of Canada: A Virtual Exhibition from the Diefenbaker Canada Centre." January 25, 2021. https://diefenbaker.usask.ca/the-enfranchisement-of-canadas-aboriginal-peoples/-10.php.

Diefenbaker, John D. Quoted in the *Toronto Star* October 8, 1960. http://diefenbaker.usask.ca/the-enfranchisement-of-canadas-aboriginal-peoples/-10.php.

Discover. "Henry's Big Mistake." https://www.discovermagazine.com/planet-earth/henrys-big-mistake.

Donkor, K. "New Testament House Churches: A Model for Today's Complex World." *Ministry: International Journal for Pastors* (2008). https://www.ministrymagazine.org/archive/2008/04/new-testament-house-churches.html.

Doward, Jamie. "Why Europe's Wars of Religion Put 40,000 'Witches' to a Terrible Death." *The Guardian*, January 7, 2018. Accessed on October 20, 2021. https://www.theguardian.com/society/2018/jan/07/witchcraft-economics-reformation-catholic-protestant-market-share.

Draaisma, Muriel, and Jessica Ng. "Sir John A. Macdonald Statue Toppled in Hamilton Park after Hundreds Attend Rally, March." *CBC News*, August 14, 2021. https://www.cbc.ca/news/canada/hamilton/rally-macdonald-statue-gore-park-hamilton-1.6141279.

Drescher, Elizabeth. *Choosing Our Religion: The Spiritual Lives of America's Nones*. New York: Oxford University Press, 2016.

Economist Intelligence Unit. *The Safe Cities Index 2015: Assessing Urban Security in the Digital Age." Economist Intelligence Unit—2015*. https://safecities.economist.com/wp-content/uploads/2019/08/eiu-safe-cities-index-2015-white-paper-1.pdf.

Einstein, Albert. "Inspiriting Quotes." https://www.inspiringquotes.us/quotes/hdUE_XdlV4bIh.

Epp, Roger. "Land Is the Heart of the Matter." *Canadian Mennonite* 21.10 (2017) 537–58. https://canadianmennonite.org/stories/land-heart-matter.

Eusebius. *Ecclesiastical History*. Book 8. http://www.historytimeline.org/docs/eusebius/church_history/book_08.php.

———. *The Life of Constantine*. Translated by Ernest Cushing Richardson. http://www.prenicea.net/doc4/40203-en-01.pdf.

Faris, Nick. "The Catholic Church Is Worried about What's Happening to Their Old Churches." *National Post*, November 30, 2018. https://nationalpost.com/news/canada/the-catholic-church-is-worried-about-whats-happening-to-their-old-churches.

Farrell, Jennifer. "How the Medieval Witch Image Has Evolved over the Centuries." *The Independent*, October 28, 2018: https://www.independent.co.uk/life-style/history/medieval-witch-origin-image-evolution-gender-stereotype-witchcraft-history-halloween-a8599521.html.

Faulkes, A. "Snorri Sturluson—Edda—Prologue and Gylfaginning." *Viking Society for Northern Research*. London: University College, 2005. http://www.vsnrweb-publications.org.uk/Edda-1.pdf.

Faust, Lena, and Courtney Heffernan. "Residential School Deaths from Tuberculosis Weren't Unavoidable—They Were Caused by Deliberate Neglect." *Globe and Mail*, July 12, 2021: https://www.theglobeandmail.com/opinion/article-residential-school-deaths-from-tuberculosis-werent-unavoidable-they/.

Ferrara, Peter. "The Great Depression Was Ended by the End of World War II, Not the Start of It." *Forbes Magazine*, November 30, 2013. https://www.forbes.com/sites/peterferrara/2013/11/30/the-great-depression-was-ended-by-the-end-of-world-war-ii-not-the-start-of-it/?sh=7e3ee6cf57d3.

Findlay, Heather, and Anna Sajecki. "Canada's First Peoples." Canadian Heritage, 2007: https://www.firstpeoplesofcanada.com/fp_creators.html.

Fletcher, Richard. *The Barbarian Conversion: From Paganism to Christianity*. New York: Holt, 1997.

Flint, Valerie. *The Rise of Magic in Early Medieval Europe*. Princeton: Princeton University Press, 1991.

Flourishing Congregations Institute. "Flourishing Congregations Construct." https://www.flourishingcongregations.org/about-us.

Flory, Richard W., and Donald E. Miller. "The Embodied Spirituality of the Post-Boomer Generations." In *A Sociology of Spirituality*, edited by Kieran Flanagan and Peter C. Jupp, 201–18. Farnham, UK: Ashgate, 2007.

Forest, A. C. "The Present." In *Religion in Canada*, edited by William Kilbourn, 63–96. Toronto: McLelland Stewart, 1968.

Fournier, Suzanne, and Ernie Crey. *Stolen from Our Embrace*. Vancouver: Douglas and McIntyre, 1997.

Fox, Jonathan. "Building Composite Measures of Religion and State." *Interdisciplinary Journal of Research on Religion* 7 (2011) 1–39. https://epdf.pub/a-world-survey-of-religion-and-the-state-cambridge-studies-in-social-theory-reli.html.

France, R. T. *The Gospel of Matthew*. Grand Rapids: Eerdman's, 2007.

Fry, Kendra, and Milton Friesen. "No Space for Community: The Value of Faith Buildings and the Effect of their Loss in Ontario." July 2020: https://d3n8a8pro7vhmx.cloudfront.net/faithcommongood/pages/838/attachments/original/1594847267/No_Space_for_Community-compressed.pdf?1594847267.

Geddes, John. "On One Issue, Canadians Are a Lot Less Tolerant Than Americans." *Maclean's*. February 9, 2017. http://www.macleans.ca/politics/ottawa/on-one-issue-canadians-are-a-lot-less-tolerant-thanamericans/.

Gee, Ellen M., and Jean E. Veevers. "Religiously Unaffiliated Canadians: Sex, Age, and Regional Variations." *Social Indicators Research* 21 (1989) 611–27. https://doi.org/10.1007/BF02217996.

Giddens, Sandra, and Owen Giddens. *Chinese Mythology*. New York: Rosen, 2006.

Gill, Anthony. "Government Regulation, Social Anomie and Religious Pluralism in Latin America: A Cross-national Analysis." *Rationality and Society* 11.3 (1999) 287–316.

Gillan, Joanna. "Exploring the True Origins of Snow White and the Seven Dwarfs." *Ancient Origins*. June 2, 2020. https://www.ancient-origins.net/myths-legends/exploring-true-origins-snow-white-and-seven-dwarfs-004150.

Gladwell, Malcolm. *The Tipping Point: How Little Things Can Make a Big Difference*. Boston: Little, Brown, 2000. https://binyaprak.com/images/blog_articles/123/the-tipping-point.pdf.

Government of Canada. "Advancement of Religion." https://www.canada.ca/en/revenue-agency/services/charities-giving/charities/registering-charitable-qualified-donee-status/applying-charitable-registration/charitable-purposes/advancement-religion.html.

———. "Advantages of Registration." https://www.canada.ca/en/revenue-agency/services/charities-giving/charities/applying-registration/registration-right-you/advantages-registration.html.

———. "Covid-19 Vaccination Canada." Health Infobase Canada, September 17, 2021. https://health-infobase.canada.ca/covid-19/vaccination-coverage/.

———. "First Nations in Canada." https://www.rcaanc-cirnac.gc.ca/eng/1307460755710/1536862806124#chp1.

———. "National Day of Truth and Reconciliation." Updated September 29, 2021. Accessed on October 1, 2021: https://www.canada.ca/en/canadian-heritage/campaigns/national-day-truth-reconciliation.html.

———. "Reducing the Number of Indigenous Children in Care." https://sac-isc.gc.ca/eng/1541187352297/1541187392851.

Grant, John Webster. *The Church in the Canadian Era*. Vancouver: Regent College, 1998.

———. "The Reaction of WASP Churches to Non-WASP Immigrants." In *The Canadian Society of Church History Papers—1968—Part 1*. 1–15. file:///C:/Users/hp/Downloads/39616–48342–41-SM.pdf.

Graveland, Bill. "'Fear is the Greatest Factor': Survey Finds Canadians Worry about Rise of Racism." *Toronto Star*, September 16, 2017. https://www.thestar.com/news/canada/2017/09/16/fear-is-the-greatestfactor-survey-finds-canadians-worry-about-rise-of-racism.html.

Griffin, Kevin. "Sixties Scoop Survivors to Get Interim $21,000 Payments for Their Plights." *Vancouver Sun*, June 2, 2020. https://vancouversun.com/news/local-news/sixties-scoop-survivors-to-get-interim-21000-payments-for-their-plights.

Harland, Philip A. *Dynamics of Identity in the World of the Early Christians*. New York: Continuum, 2009.

Harper, Douglas. *Online Etymology Dictionary*. www.etymonline.com.

Haskell, David M. *Through a Lens Darkly: How the News Media Perceive and Portray Evangelicals*. Toronto: Clements, 2010.

Hemson Consulting. "Greater Golden Horseshoe: Growth Forecasts to 2051." Technical Report prepared for the Province of Ontario's Ministry of Municipal Affairs. August 26, 2020: https://www.hemson.com/wp-content/uploads/2020/08/HEMSON-GGH-Growth-Outlook-Report-26Aug20.pdf.

Hiemstra, Rick. "Church and Faith Trends in Canada." Presidents Day 2014 presentation to the Evangelical Fellowship of Canada. EFC, 2014. https://www.sharethejourney.ca/uploads/6/1/8/9/6189625/efc_survey_report.pdf.

Hiemstra, Rick, and Karen Stiller. "Religious Affiliation and Attendance in Canada." *Trust*, New Year 2016. https://intrust.org/Magazine/Issues/New-Year-2016/Religious-affiliation-and-attendance-in-Canada.

Hill, Sharon. "Revival for 107-Year-Old Holy Rosary Church an Historic Gem." *Windsor Star*, April 24, 2015. https://windsorstar.com/uncategorized/revival-for-107-year-old-holy-rosary-church-and-historic-gem/.

History Channel. "Eight Reasons Why Rome Fell." *History Channel*, January 14, 2014. Updated January 29, 2019. https://www.history.com/news/8-reasons-why-rome-fell.

Holy Bible, New International Version. Grand Rapids: Zondervan, 1984.

Huxley, Aldous. *The Devils of Loudun*. London: Chatto & Windus, 1922: https://archive.org/details/in.ernet.dli.2015.462211.

Idle No More. "An Indigenous-Led Social Movement." https://idlenomore.ca/about-the-movement/.

IMDb.com "The Borgias (2011–2013)". https://www.imdb.com/title/tt1582457/.

Indigenous Corporate Training. "Christopher Columbus and the Doctrine of Discovery—5 Things to Know." https://www.ictinc.ca/blog/christopher-columbus-and-the-doctrine-of-discovery-5-things-to-know.

———. "Four Common Barriers to Reconciliation with Indigenous Peoples." https://www.ictinc.ca/blog/four-common-barriers-to-reconciliation-with-indigenous-peoples.

———. "Myth #3: Do First Nations Get Free Housing on Reserves?" https://www.ictinc.ca/myth-3-do-first-nations-get-free-housing-on-reserves.

Intuit Turbo Tax. "Do First Nations Residents Have to Pay Tax in Canada?" https://turbotax.intuit.ca/tax-resources/tax-compliance/do-natives-pay-tax-in-canada.jsp.

Jacobs, Andrew S. "Jews and Christians." In *The Oxford Handbook of Early Christian Studies*, edited by Susan Ashbrook Harvey and David G. Hunter, 169–86. New York: Oxford University Press, 2008.

James 1. *Daemonlogie, In form of a Diologie*. The King's Printer, 1597: https://archive.org/details/daemonologie25929gut.

Jehovah's Witnesses. "Why Don't Jehovah's Witnesses Call Their Meeting Place a Church? https://www.jw.org/en/jehovahs-witnesses/faq/jehovahs-witnesses-church-kingdom-hall/.

Johnston, Patrick. *Native Children and the Child Welfare System*. Toronto: Lorimer, 1983.

Jones, Evan T., and Margaret M. Condon. *Cabot and Bristol's Age of Discovery: The Bristol Discovery Voyages 1480–1508*. Bristol, UK: University of Bristol, 2016: https://archive.org/details/Cabotdigital/page/2/mode/2up.

Jorgenson, Allen G. "Embodying Truth in Ecclesial Practices." In *Truth-Telling and Other Ecclesial Practices of Resistance*, edited by Christine Helmer, 21–28. Lanham. MD: Lexington/Fortress, 2021.

Josephus. *The Antiquities of the Jews*. https://www.gutenberg.org/files/2848/2848-h/2848-h.htm.

Kanji, Azeezah, et al. "Islamophobia in Canada." http://www.noorculturalcentre.ca/wp-content/uploads/2018/01/Islamophobia-in-Canada-2017.pdf.

Kennedy, Maev. "Stonehenge may have been burial site for Stone age elite, say archaeologists." *The Guardian*, March 9, 2013: https://www.theguardian.com/science/2013/mar/09/archaeology-stonehenge-bones-burial-ground.

Keung, Nicholas. "Ontario Facing 'Epidemic of Islamophobia,' Survey Finds." *Toronto Star*, July 4, 2016. https://www.thestar.com/news/immigration/2016/07/04/ontario-facing-epidemic-of-islamophobia-survey-finds.html.

Kilbourn, William, ed. *The Restless Church: A Response to the Comfortable Pew*. Toronto: McLelland and Stewart, 1966.

King, Ruth, and Sandra Clarke. "Contesting Meaning: Newfie and the Politics of Ethnic Labelling." *Journal of Sociolinguistics* 6 (2002) 537–58.

Krasskova, Galina. "Nerthus, Mother of Vanahelm." http://northernpaganism.org/shrines/nerthus/about.html.

Kraybill, Donald B. *The Upside Down Kingdom*. Kitchener, ON: Herald, 1978.

Kruszelnicki, Karl. "Frog Fable Brought to Boil." *Australian Broadcasting Corporation (ABC News)*, December 7, 2010: https://www.abc.net.au/science/articles/2010/12/07/3085614.htm.

Kuhn, Thomas. *The Structure of Scientific Revolutions*. 2nd ed. Chicago: University of Chicago Press, 1970.

Kushner, Harold S. *When Bad Things Happen to Good People*. New York: Anchor, 2004.

Ladd, John. "The Issue of Relativism." *The Monist* 47.4 (1963) 585–609. https://www.jstor.org/stable/27901528.

Lambdin, Thomas, trans. "Gospel of Thomas." https://www.marquette.edu/maqom/Gospel%20of%20Thomas%20Lambdin.pdf.

Leeson, Peter, and Jacob Russ. "Witch Trials." *The Economic Journal* 128.613 (2018) 2066–2105. https://www.peterleeson.com/Witch_Trials.pdf.

Lenski, N. *Constantine and the Cities: Imperial Authority and Civic Politics (Empire and After)*. Philadelphia: University of Pennsylvania Press, 2016.

Leo X. "Exsurge Domine 1520 (Condemning the Errors of Martin Luther)." In *Papal Encyclicals Online*. https://www.papalencyclicals.net/Leo10/l10exdom.htm
Levack, Brian P. *The Witch Hunt in Early Modern Europe*. New York: Longman, 1987.
Levinson-King, Robin, "Toronto Lockdown—One of the World's Longest?" May 24, 2021. https://www.bbc.com/news/world-us-canada-57079577.
Lewis, Nicola Denzey. *Introduction to "Gnosticism": Ancient Voices, Christian Worlds*. Oxford: Oxford University Press, 2012.
———. "Lived Religion among Second-Century Gnostic Hieratic Specialists." In Beyond Priesthood: Religious Professionals in the Roman Empire, 79–102. Berlin: de Gruyter, 2017. https://www.degruyter.com/document/doi/10.1515/9783110448184-004/html.
Liddle Henry G., and Robert Scott. "A Greek—English Lexicon." http://www.perseus.tufts.edu/hopper/text?doc=Perseus%3Atext%3A1999.04.0057%3Aentry%3Dkri%2Fkos
Lindow, John. *Norse Mythology: A Guide to the Gods, Heroes, Rituals and Beliefs*. New York: Oxford University Press, 2001.
Linneman, Thomas, and Margaret Clendenen. "Sexuality and the Sacred." In *Atheism and Secularity*, vol. 1, edited by Phil Zuckerman, 89–111. Santa Barbara, CA: Praeger, 2010.
Loveland, Ann. C., and Otis B. Wheeler. *From Meetinghouse to Megachurch: A Material and Cultural History*. Columbia: University of Missouri Press, 2003.
Mackinnon, Ian F. *Canada and the Minority Churches of Eastern Europe, 1945–1950*. Halifax: The Book Room, 1959.
Mair, Victor H. "Danger + Opportunity ≠ Opportunity: How a Misunderstanding about Chinese Characters Has Led Many Astray." Pinyin.info (a guide to the writing of Mandarin Chinese in romanization). http://www.pinyin.info/chinese/crisis.html.
Manchester, William. *A World Lit Only by Fire: The Medieval Mind and the Renaissance*. New York: Little Brown, 1993.
Mango, Cyril. "Constantinople." In *The Oxford Dictionary of Byzantium*, edited by Alexander Kazhadan, 508–12. Oxford: Oxford University Press, 1991.
Manning, Christel J. "Unaffiliated Parents and the Religious Training of Their Children." *Sociology of Religion* 74.2 (2013) 149–75.
Mark, Joshua J. "Religion in the Ancient World." *Ancient History Encyclopedia*. March 23, 2018. https://www.ancient.eu/religion/.
———. "Religion in the Middle Ages." *Brewminate*, September 29, 2019. https://brewminate.com/religion-in-medieval-europe/.
Marks, Lynne. "Exploring Regional Diversity in Patterns of Religious Participation; Canada in 1901." *Historical Methods: A Journal of Quantitative and Interdisciplinary History* 33.4 (2000) 247–54.
Marshall, H. "Church and Temple in the New Testament." *Tyndale Bulletin* 40.2 (1989) 203–22.
Mathers, Donald M. *The Word and the Way*. Toronto: United Church Publishing House, 1962.
McKinney, Jason. "North American Church Decline as a Divine Phenomenon." September 5, 2021: https://www.facebook.com/744821997/posts/10159013979551998/?sfnsn=mo.
Medlen Hutchings, William. "When Mothers of Salem, Their Children Brought to Jesus." https://hymnary.org/text/when_mothers_of_salem_their_children_bro.
Merriam-Webster Dictionary (online version). https://www.merriam-webster.com/.

Meisel, A. C., and M. L. del Mastro, eds. *The Rule of St. Benedict.* Garden City, NY: Image, 1975.

Meslet, Francis. *Abandoned Churches: Unclaimed Places of Worship.* Germany: Jonglez, 2020.

Metso, Sarianna. *The Community Rule: A Critical Edition with Translation.* Atlanta: Society of Biblical Literature, 2019.

Miller, J. R. *Skyscrapers Hide the Heavens: A History of Indian/White Relations in Canada.* Toronto: University of Toronto Press, 1989.

Milloy, John S. "The Early Indian Acts: Developmental Strategy and Constitutional Change." In *As Long as the Sun Shines and Water Flows,* edited by Ian Getty and Anttoinne Lussier, 56–64. Vancouver: University of British Columbia Press, 1983.

———. *A National Crime: The Canadian Government and the Residential School System, 1879—1986.* (e-book) Winnipeg: University of Manitoba Press, 1999.

Mislin, David. "The Complex History of 'In God We Trust.'" *The Conversation,* February 8, 2018. https://theconversation.com/the-complex-history-of-in-god-we-trust-91117.

Monkman, Lenard. "Debunking the Myth That All First Nations People Receive Free Post-Secondary Education." *CBC News,* January 29, 2016. https://www.cbc.ca/news/indigenous/debunking-the-myth-that-all-first-nations-people-receive-free-post-secondary-education-1.3414183.

Muroi, Kazuo. "The Origin of the Mystical Number Seven in Mesopotamian Culture; Division by Seven in the Sexagesimal Number System." In *arXiv1407.6246v1 (math).* Cornell University, 2014. https://arxiv.org/ftp/arxiv/papers/1407/1407.6246.pdf.

Murray, Alexander E. "Piety and Impiety in the Thirteenth-Century Italy." *Studies in Church History* 8 (1993) 83–106.

Naas, A. R. "Etymology of the Word 'Church.'" Carolina Bible Group, 1–11. https://carolinabiblegroup.com/wp-content/uploads/2019/03/CHURCH-ETYMOLOGY.pdf.

National Enquiry into Missing and Murdered Indigenous Women and Girls. *Interim Report: Our Women and Girls are Sacred.* https://www.mmiwg-ffada.ca/wp-content/uploads/2018/03/ni-mmiwg-interim-report.pdf.

Niose, David. *Nonbeliever Nation: The Rise of Secular Americans.* New York: Palgrave Macmillan, 2012.

Norris, Pippa, and Ronald Inglehart. *Sacred and Secular: Religion and Politics Worldwide.* Cambridge: Cambridge University Press, 2004.

O'Connor, Freddy. *A Pub On Every Corner.* Liverpool, UK: Bluecoat, 1995.

O'Donoghue, Heather. *From Asgard to Valhalla: The Remarkable History of the Norse Myths.* New York: I. B. Tauris, 2007.

O'Neill, Jessica. June 28, 2021: https://www.facebook.com/oneill.jes/posts/10157701850167827.

Olson, David T. *The American Church in Crisis: Groundbreaking Research Based on a National Database of Over 200,000 Churches.* Zondervan: Grand Rapids, 2008.

Otto, Rudolf. *The Idea of the Holy.* Translated by H. Milford. London: Oxford University Press, 1923.

Papandrea, J. L. *Reading the Early Church Fathers: From Didache to Nicaea.* Mahwah, NJ: Paulist, 1993.

Paramahamsa, K. R. *The Symbolism in Rigveda.* Total Recall, 2008: http://www.vedamu.org/Veda/KRP-Sir/The%20Symbolism%20in%20Rigeda.pdf.

Parliament of the United Kingdom. *House of Commons Charities Bill [Bill 83] 9th of November 2005*. https://publications.parliament.uk/pa/cm200506/cmbills/083/en/06083x—.htm.

Partners for Sacred Places. "The Halo Effect." http://www.sacredplaces.org/tools-research/the-halo-effect.

Pearson, Craig. "Sign of the Times? United Church Becomes a Mosque." *Windsor Star*, August 21, 2015. Accessed on March 8, 2021: https://windsorstar.com/news/sign-of-the-times-united-church-becomes-a-mosque/.

Pelletier, Francois-Nicolas. "Faux comme diamants du Canada." https://www.afis.org/Faux-comme-diamants-du-Canada.

Pelz, Lotte, and Werner Pelz. "The Uncomfortable Few: A Prophecy." In *The Uncomfortable Pew*, edited by William Kilbourn, 103–11. Toronto: McLelland and Stewart, 1966.

Pew Research Center. "Canada's Changing Religious Landscape." https://www.pewforum.org/2013/06/27/canadas-changing-religious-landscape/.

Phelan, Matthew. "The History of 'History Is Written by the Victors.'" *Browbeat*, November 26, 2019: https://slate.com/culture/2019/11/history-is-written-by-the-victors-quote-origin.html.

Picot, Garnett. "Immigrant Economic and Social Outcomes in Canada: Research Data Development at Statistics Canada." Ottawa: Statistics Canada, 2008. https://www150.statcan.gc.ca/n1/pub/11f0019m/11f0019m2008319-eng.pdf.

Pihlajamaki, Heiki. "Swimming the Witch, Pricking for the Devil's Mark: Ordeals in the Early Modern Witchcraft Trials." *The Journal of Legal History* 21.2 (2007) 35–58. https://www.tandfonline.com/doi/abs/10.1080/01440362108539608.

Pope Francis. "Message of the Holy Father Francis to Participants at the Conference: Doesn't God Dwell Here Anymore? Decommissioning Places of Worship and Integrated Management of Ecclesiastical Cultural Heritage." http://www.vatican.va/content/francesco/en/messages/pont-messages/2018/documents/papa-francesco_20181129_messaggio-convegno-beniculturali.html.

Post Media News. "It's Still Going to be Used as a House of God: Century-Old Windsor Protestant Church Will Become a Mosque." *National Post*, August 21, 2015. https://nationalpost.com/news/canada/its-still-going-to-be-used-as-a-house-of-god-windsor-protestant-church-built-a-century-ago-will-become-a-mosque.

Power, Eileen. *Medieval Women*. Cambridge: Cambridge University Press, 2019.

Rashid, Adel Faeq. "Symbolic Number of Seven." *Midad Al-Adab Refereed Journal* 1.10 (2015) 275–86. https://www.iasj.net/iasj/article/99928.

Read, Donna. *The Burning Times*. Ottawa: National Film Board, 1990. http://www.nfb.ca/film/burning_times/.

Reaves, W. "The Vanir Gods Njord and Nerthus." In "Odin's Wife: Mother Earth in Germanic Mythology." https://norroena.org/the-vanir-gods-njord-and-nerthus/.

Reimer, Sam. *Evangelicals and the Continental Divide: The Evangelical Subculture in Canada and the United States*. Montreal, QC: McGill-Queen's University Press, 2003.

Reimer, Sam., and Michael Wilkinson. *A Culture of Faith: Evangelical Congregations in Canada*. Montreal, QC: McGill-Queen's University Press, 2015.

Riley, Gregory J. *One Jesus, Many Christs*. Minneapolis: Fortress, 2001.

Roberts, Callum. *The Unnatural History of the Sea*. Washington, DC: Island, 2007.

Rosen, Frederick. "Piety and Justice: Plato's 'Euthyphro.'" *Philosophy* 43.164 (1968) 105–16. https://www.jstor.org/stable/3748839?seq=1.

Royal Canadian Mounted Police. "Missing and Murdered Aboriginal Women: A National Operational Overview." https://www.grc-rcmp.gc.ca/en/missing-and-murdered-aboriginal-women-national-operational-overview.

Roza, Greg. *Incan Mythology and Other Myths of the Andes*. New York: Rosen, 2008.

Sacred Design Lab. "How We Work." https://sacred.design/how-we-work.

———. "Insights." https://sacred.design/insights.

Sainte-Marie, Buffy. "The Genocide Basic to This Country's Birth Is Ongoing." Buffy Sainte-Marie Land Acknowledgement 2021 Juno Awards. *CBC Music*, June 6, 2021: https://www.cbc.ca/player/play/1905719363600.

Sangster, Joan. *100 Years of Struggle: The History of Women and the Vote in Canada*. Vancouver, BC: University of British Columbia Press, 2015.

Schaff, Philip. *History of the Christian Church, Volume II: Anti-Nicene Christianity. A.D. 100–325*. Oak Harbour, WA: Logos Research Systems, 1997.

Schindler, D.C. "The community of the one and the many: Heraclitus on reason." *Inquiry* 46.4 (2003) 413–48.

Seghini, Rebecca. "There's No Place Like Home: Dorothy Proclaims 'There's no place like home,' but Is That the Message of the Wizard of Oz." Blog post Drapes and Squares, June 2, 2012: https://drapesandsquares.wordpress.com/2012/06/02/dorothy-proclaims-that-theres-no-place-like-home-but-is-that-the-message-of-the-wizard-of-oz-please-incorporate-detailed-reference-to-the-film-in-your-answer/.

Selvén, Sebastian. "In or Out—The Privilege of Taxation: The Half-Shekel and the Temple Tax in the Talmud Yerushalmi." Uppsala universitet, Gamla testamentets exegetic. https://www.diva-portal.org/smash/get/diva2:724005/FULLTEXT01.pdf

Seven Generations Education Institute. "Seven Grandfather Teachings." http://www.7generations.org/seven-grandfather-teachings/.

Sewell, John. "Don Mills: E. P. Taylor and Canada's First Corporate Suburb." In *The Second City Book: Studies of Urban and Suburban Canada*, edited by James Lorimer and Evelyn Ross, 26–40. Charlottetown, Canada: CharlottetownGroup, 2017. https://books.google.ca/books?id=dCM59VdSylwC&printsec=frontcover&source=gbs_ge_summary_r&cad=0#v=onepage&q&f=false.

Sheikh, Maleeha. "Toronto Catholic School Board Votes to Recognize Pride Month." *City News*, May 7, 2021. https://toronto.citynews.ca/2021/05/07/toronto-catholic-school-board-pride-month/.

Sherkat, Daren E. *Changing Faith: The Dynamics and Consequences of Americans' Shifting Identities*. New York: New York University Press, 2014.

Sinclair, Raven. "Identity Lost and Found: Lessons from the Sixties Scoop." *First Peoples Child and Family Review* 3.1 (2007) 65–82. https://fncaringsociety.com/sites/default/files/online-journal/vol3num1/Sinclair_pp65.pdf.

Singh, Graham. "Opinion: It's Time to Hand Churches Back to the Communities That Need Them." *Montreal Gazette*, September 10, 2020: https://montrealgazette.com/opinion/opinion-its-time-to-hand-churches-back-to-communities-that-need-them.

Singh, Graham, and Barbara Myers. "Memos from Main Street—Memo #13: Main Street Faith Buildings: Evolving through Covid-19 and Beyond." https://bringbackmainstreet.ca/memos-from-main-street/memo-13-main-street-churches?mc_cid=c1865ed7c6&mc_eid=%5BUNIQID%5D.

Slater, Gabriel. "The Making of a Historic Community Hub." https://www.faithcommongood.org/st_josephs_kingsbridge_community.

Smith, Gregory, and Jessica Martinez. "How the Faithful Voted: A Preliminary 2016 Analysis": https://www.pewresearch.org/fact-tank/2016/11/09/how-the-faithful-voted-a-preliminary-2016-analysis/.

Smith, Richard. "Limits to Medicine. Medical Nemesis: The Expropriation of Health." *Journal of Epidemiology and Community Health* 57.12 (2003) 928. file:///C:/Users/hp/Downloads/Limits_to_medicine_Medical_nemesis_the_e.pdf.

Snyder, Graydon F. *Ante Pacem: Archaeological Evidence of Church Life Before Constantine.* Atlanta: Mercer University Press, 2003.

Special Commissioners appointed to Investigate Indian Affairs in Canada. "Report of the Special Commissioners Appointed to Investigate Indian Affairs in Canada." *Journals of the Legislative Assembly of the Province of Canada from 25th February to 1st June, 1858*, appendix no. 21, part 3, session 1853. The Head Commission Report.

Stanley, Arthur P. "Lecture vi." In *Lectures on the History of the Eastern Church*, edited by Ernest Ryhs. New York: Dutton, 1918: https://archive.org/details/lecturesonhistoroostanrich.

Stark, Rodney. *The Rise of Christianity: How the Obscure, Marginal Jesus Movement Became the Dominant Religious Force in the Western World in a Few Centuries.* San Francisco: Harper Row, 1997.

———. *The Triumph of Christianity: How the Jesus Movement Became the World's Largest Religion.* (ebook) San Francisco: Harper-Collins, 2011.

Statistics Canada. "Canada's Population Estimates: Age and Sex, July 1, 2019." *The Daily*. September 30, 2019. https://www150.statcan.gc.ca/n1/daily-quotidien/190930/dq190930a-eng.htm.

———. "Census Profile, 2016 Census." https://www12.statcan.gc.ca/census-recensement/2016/dp-pd/prof/details/page.cfm?Lang=E&Geo1=PR&Code1=01&Geo2=PR&Code2=01&SearchText=canada&SearchType=Begins&SearchPR=01&B1=Immigration%20and%20citizenship&TABID=1&type=1.

———. "From Urban Areas to Population Centres." https://www.statcan.gc.ca/eng/subjects/standard/sgc/notice/sgc-06.

———. "NHS Profile, Canada, 2011." https://www12.statcan.gc.ca/nhs-enm/2011/dp-pd/prof/details/page.cfm?Lang=E&Geo1=PR&Code1=01&Data=Count&SearchText=canada&SearchType=Begins&SearchPR=01&A1=Religion&B1=All&Custom=&TABID=1.

———. "Population Centre and Rural Area Classification." https://www.statcan.gc.ca/eng/subjects/standard/pcrac/2016/introduction.

———. "Population and Dwelling Count Tables, 2016 Census." https://www12.statcan.gc.ca/census-recensement/2016/dp-pd/hlt-fst/pd-pl/index-eng.cfm.

———. "Projections of Aboriginal Population and Households in Canada, 2011 to 2036." *The Daily*, September 17, 2015: https://www150.statcan.gc.ca/n1/daily-quotidien/150917/dq150917b-eng.htm.

———. "Rural and Small Town Canada." *Analysis Bulletin* 3.3 (2001) https://www150.statcan.gc.ca/n1/en/pub/21-06-x/21-06-x2001003-eng.pdf?st=D-Wk95os.

Steckley, John. "Toronto . . . or Is That Taranteau." Reproduced from *Explore Historic Toronto*. Toronto: Toronto Historical Board, 1992. https://www.toronto.ca/311/knowledgebase/kb/docs/articles/311-toronto/information-and-business-development/origin-of-the-name-of-toronto.html.

Stein, Elissa, and Susan Kim. *Flow: The Cultural Story of Menstruation*. New York: St. Martin's Griffin, 2005.

Stephenson, Barry, and Nicholas Lynch. "After Church Atlas." Open source online resource of Memorial University, 2019. https://www.afterchurchatlas.org/.

Stern, David. "Heraclitus' and Wittgenstein's River Images: Stepping Twice into the Same River." *The Monists* 74.4 (1991) 579–604.

Stern, Robert, David Fishman, and Jacob Tilove. *Paradise Planned: The Garden Suburb and the Modern City*. New York: Monacelli, 2013.

Stewart, Jane. "Statement of Reconciliation." In "Address by the Honourable Jane Stewart . . . on the Occasion of the Unveiling of Gathering Strength—Canada's Aboriginal Action Plan." http://sisis.nativeweb.org/clark/jan0798can.html.

Stieglitz, Robert. R. "The Hebrew Names of the Seven Planets." *Journal of Near Eastern Studies* 40.2 (1981) 135–37. https://www.journals.uchicago.edu/doi/10.1086/372867.

Strauss, Gerald. "Success and Failure in the German Reformation." *Past and Present* 67 (1975) 30–63.

———. "The Reformation and Its Public in an Age of Orthodoxy." In *The German People and the Reformation*, edited by R. Po-Chia Hsia, 194–214. Ithica, NY: Cornell University Press, 1988.

Strong's Online Concordance. "2993 Laodikeia." https://biblehub.com/greek/2993.htm.

Stumph, Chad. "The Development of the Church in Medieval Christianity." *Brewminate*. https://brewminate.com/the-development-of-the-church-in-medieval-christianity/.

Swiggum, S., and M. Kohli. "Extracts from the 1901 Immigration Report for Canada." Citing Sessional Papers of the Government of Canada 1–2 Edward VII (25) 1902, Report of the Department of the Interior (Immigration)." http://www.theshipslist.com/Forms/Canreport1901.shtml.

Taylor, Brooke, and Brooklyn Neustaeter. "Cowessess First Nation Says 751 Unmarked Graves Found Near Former Saskatchewan Residential School." *CTV News*, June 24, 2021: https://www.ctvnews.ca/canada/cowessess-first-nation-says-751-unmarked-graves-found-near-former-sask-residential-school-1.5483858.

Tecumseh. Tecumseh Quotes. https://www.allgreatquotes.com/authors/tecumseh-quotes/.

"The Temple." In *The Oxford Dictionary of the Christian Church*, 3rd ed., edited by F. L. Cross and E. A. Livingstone. New York: Oxford University Press, 2005.

Tenant, Zoe. "Pushed Out and Silenced: How One Doctor Was Punished for Speaking Out about Residential Schools." *Unreserved. CBC Radio*. April 17, 2020: https://www.cbc.ca/radio/unreserved/exploring-the-past-finding-connections-in-little-known-indigenous-history-1.5531914/pushed-out-and-silenced-how-one-doctor-was-punished-for-speaking-out-about-residential-schools-1.5534953?fbclid=IwAR17QWFFf-rKpQyYEgKMrqhLNkSTI47-YbEB1fUnqUwIR1Zi5kMLGTQeDvaY.

Tenney, Jonathan S. "The Elevation of Marduk Revisited: Festivals and Sacrifices at Nippur during the High Kassite Period." *Journal of Cuneiform Studies* 68 (2016) 153–80.

Thacker, P. "Headmaster's Notes: History Is Written by the Victors" https://www.princesmeadschool.org.uk/5871-72/.

Thevet, André, and Jean Dorat. *Les singularitez de la France antarctique, autrement nommée Amérique: & de plusieurs terres & isles découvertes de nostre temps.* Edited by Paul Gaffarel. Paris, Maisonneuve, 1878. https://archive.org/stream/lessingularitezoothevgoog/lessingularitezoothevgoog_djvu.txt.

Thiessen, Joel. *The Meaning of Sunday: The Practice of Belief in a Secular Age.* Montreal, QC: McGill-Queen's University Press, 2015.

Thiessen, Joel, and Sarah Wilkins-Laflamme. *None of the Above: Nonreligious Identity in the US and Canada.* New York: New York University Press, 2020. https://doi.org/10.18574/nyu/9781479817399.001.0001.

Thomson Reuters. "'Astonishing' Giant Circle of Pits Found near Stonehenge." *CBC News,* June 22, 2020. https://www.cbc.ca/news/world/stonehenge-pits-archeologists-1.5621840.

Thornton, A. *People and Themes in Homer's Odyssey.* London: Methuen, 1970.

Thoroughbred Heritage. "Steeplechasing Notes." *Historic Sires.* https://www.tbheritage.com/TurfHallmarks/Jumphiststeeple.html.

Thurston, Angie, and Casper ter Kuile. "How We Gather." Sacred Design Lab, 2020: https://sacred.design/insights.

Tindall, Chris. "Donnacona." *Acres of Snow,* February 28, 2018. https://acresofsnow.ca/donnacona/.

Tobias, J. L. "Protection, Civilization, Assimilation: An Outline History of Canada's Indian Policy." In *As Long as the Sun Shines and Water Flows,* edited by Ian Getty and Antoinne Lussier, 39–55. Vancouver: University of British Columbia Press, 1983.

Trinity Centres Foundation. https://trinitycentres.org/.

Trudel, Marcel. "Donnacona." In *Dictionary of Canadian Biography. I (1000–1700),* edited by George Williams Brown. Toronto: University of Toronto Press, 1966. http://www.biographi.ca/en/bio/donnacona_1E.html.

Truth and Reconciliation Commission of Canada. "Calls to Action." https://ehprnh2mwo3.exactdn.com/wp-content/uploads/2021/01/Calls_to_Action_English2.pdf.

———. "Honouring the Truth, Reconciling for the Future: Summary of the Final Report of the Truth and Reconciliation Commission of Canada." https://publications.gc.ca/collections/collection_2015/trc/IR4-7-2015-eng.pdf.

———. "The Survivors Speak: A Report of the Truth and Reconciliation Commission of Canada." Survivors_Speak_English_Web.pdf (nctr.ca).

———. "They Came for the Children." ResSchoolHistory_2012_02_24.pdf (publications.gc.ca).

Turner, Ralph H., and Lewis M. Killian. *Collective Behaviour.* 3rd ed. Englewood-Cliffs, NJ: Prentice-Hall, 1987.

Tutu, Desmond. *No Future without Forgiveness.* New York: Doubleday, 1999.

United Church Observer. "National Survey Points to Looming Surge in Vacant United Church Buildings." *Newswire,* September 10, 2013. https://www.newswire.ca/news-releases/national-survey-points-to-looming-surge-in-vacant-united-church-buildings-512907931.html.

United States Holocaust Memorial Museum. "Indoctrinating Youth." *Holocaust Encyclopedia*: https://encyclopedia.ushmm.org/content/en/article/indoctrinating-youth.

Van Dam, Raymond. *Remembering Constantine at the Milvian Bridge.* New York: Cambridge University Press, 2011.

Vanderspoel, J. "Lactantius: Of the Manner in which the Persecutors Died." University of Calgary, Ch. 34. http://people.ucalgary.ca/~vandersp/Courses/texts/lactant/lactpers.html.

Vatican. "Indulgences." In *The Catechism of the Catholic Church*. Vatican City: Libreria Editrice Vatican City, 2003. Ch. 2. Article 4. X. https://www.vatican.va/archive/ENG0015/_INDEX.HTM.

Vermes, Jason. "Amid Calls to Cancel Canada Day, Historian Says Opposition to the Holiday Has a Long History." *Toronto Star*, June 27, 2021. https://www.cbc.ca/radio/checkup/how-are-you-marking-canada-day-what-does-canada-mean-to-you-1.6081664/amid-calls-to-cancel-canada-day-historian-says-opposition-to-the-holiday-has-a-long-history-1.6081921.

Vikander, Tessa. "'Quit burning down churches': Indigenous Minister Pleads for an End to the Church Fires." *CTV News*, July 5, 2021. https://bc.ctvnews.ca/quit-burning-down-churches-indigenous-minister-pleads-for-an-end-to-the-church-fires-1.5497404.

Voosen, Paul. "Meet Vaclav Smil, the Man Who Has Quietly Shaped How the World Thinks about Energy." *Science Magazine*, March 21, 2018: https://archive.fo/kemFn.

Wallimann, Isidor, Nicholas C. Tatsis, and George Zito. "On Max Weber's Definition of Power." *The Australian and New Zealand Journal of Sociology* 13.3 (1977) 231–35. https://journals.sagepub.com/doi/10.1177/144078337701300308.

Warick, Jason. "Catholic Church Dedicated Nearly $300M for Buildings Since Promising Residential School Survivors $25M in 2005." *CBC News*, July 6, 2021. https://www.cbc.ca/news/canada/saskatoon/catholic-buildings-fundraising-residential-school-survivors-1.6090650.

Wente, Jesse. "Reframing Indigenous Stories in Joy: Jesse Wente." *CBC Radio*, January 5, 2021. Updated September 1, 2021: https://www.cbc.ca/radio/ideas/reframing-indigenous-stories-in-joy-jesse-wente-1.5861848.

Wilkins-Laflamme, Sarah. "Religious-Secular Polarization Compared: The Cases of Quebec and British Columbia." *Studies in Religion* 46.32 (2017) 166–85.

Williamson, David, and George Yancey. *There Is No God: Atheists in America*. Lanham, MD: Rowman & Littlefield, 2013.

Wilson, Bryan R. *Religion in Sociological Perspective*. Oxford: Oxford University Press, 1991.

———. *Religious Sects: A Sociological Study*. London: McGraw-Hill, 1970.

Wilton, David. *World Myths: Debunking Linguistic Urban Legends*. New York: Oxford University Press, 2004.

Wood Daly, Jan. "Canada Is the 'Home and Native Land' Only for Indigenous Communities." *Toronto Star*, September 30, 2021. https://www.thestar.com/opinion/contributors/2021/09/30/canada-is-the-home-and-native-land-only-for-indigenous-communities.html.

Wood Daly, Mike. "Dollars and $ense: Uncovering the Socio-Economic Benefit of Religious Congregations in Canada." *Studies in Religion* 49.4 (2020) 587–610. https://journals.sagepub.com/doi/10.1177/0008429820921498.

———. "Valuing Toronto's Faith Congregations." https://www.haloproject.ca/toronto-report/.

Woods, Thomas E. "What We Owe the Monks." Catholic Education Resource Centre, 2005. https://www.catholiceducation.org/en/education/catholic-contributions/what-we-owe-the-monks.html.

Worldometer. "Coronavirus: Canada." https://www.worldometers.info/coronavirus/country/canada/.

Woroniak, Monique, and David Camfield. "Choosing Not to Look Away: Confronting Colonialism in Canada." *The Bullet*, January 31, 2013: https://socialistproject.ca/2013/01/b768/.

Zimmer, Eric. "BC partners with United Church to Build 400 Rental Homes across the Province." *Vancouver Urbanized*, April 13, 2018: https://dailyhive.com/vancouver/affordable-housing-coquitlam-united-church.

Zimmerman, K. J., J. M. Smith, K. Simonson, and B. W. Myers. "Familial Relationship Outcomes of Coming Out as an Atheist." *Secularism and Nonreligion* 4.4 (2015) 1–13.

Zuckerman, Phil. *Faith No More: Why People Reject Religion*. New York: Oxford University Press, 2012.

Index

CPSIA information can be obtained
at www.ICGtesting.com
Printed in the USA
LVHW101923190223
739892LV00003B/500